DIRTBAG QUEEN

A MEMOIR OF MY MOTHER

ANDY CORREN

GRAND
CENTRAL

New York   Boston

Grand Central Publishing
Hachette Book Group
1290 Avenue of the Americas, New York, NY 10104
grandcentralpublishing.com
@grandcentralpub

First Edition: January 2025

Grand Central Publishing is a division of Hachette Book Group, Inc. The Grand Central Publishing name and logo is a registered trademark of Hachette Book Group, Inc.

The publisher is not responsible for websites (or their content) that are not owned by the publisher.

The Hachette Speakers Bureau provides a wide range of authors for speaking events. To find out more, go to hachettespeakersbureau.com or email HachetteSpeakers@hbgusa.com.

Grand Central Publishing books may be purchased in bulk for business, educational, or promotional use. For information, please contact your local bookseller or the Hachette Book Group Special Markets Department at special.markets@hbgusa.com.

LCCN: 2024025664

ISBNs: 9781538742228 (hardcover), 9781538742242 (ebook)

Printed in Canada

MRQ

Printing 1, 2024

For Renay Mandel Corren
1937–2021

She broke me.
Then she bought it.

Thanks, Mom.

"All of it is true, but none of it happened."
                                        —Tina Howe

"And the past, being past…does not exist. Its presence in us is an illusion only. So the thing that makes us human does not exist!"
                              —Kim Stanley Robinson, *The Martians*

"Incidentally, which one of you bitches is my mother?"
                                        —Shirley Conran, *Lace*

THE DEATH OF LICORICE KATZ

1.

My mother's *nuts*.

Walnuts, chestnuts, Brazil nuts, cashews—Renay left bowls of shells and nut dust just about everywhere during the Summer of Divorce '78. But not pecans, though. The relentless Carolina summer had climaxed over late August in a grimy, dirty-hot, wet squeeze of a week. Temperatures hovered over 100 degrees, so the pecans fell early, and they fell *green*, blanketing our scrubby yard in an ocean of unripened nuts.

There would be no pecans this season for the ravenous and ravishing redheaded Renay.

Our harvest, and this house, and her marriage, was near its fetid end.

Still, I would be left to wonder, only a few weeks from now: *Was it an unripened pecan that killed Licorice Katz in the end?*

Renay loved pecans.

We loved picking them! She had assembled an enterprising tribe of tireless, nut-picking sons around her. There was me, of course, the youngest, who a lot of folks back then affectionately called "Jewboy." Try not to get too bent out of shape about it. My brothers called me Jewboy, every friend I made in twenty-two long North Carolina years called me Jewboy, several state bowling and drama teams knew me as Jewboy, even a few teachers up until my freshman year of college. Next in line was my brother Twin. Fifteen months older than me, Twin was, thus, not my biological twin at all. He was just a very large, standard-issue, simple country-fried jock who got held back a year, so the two of us were often confused for mismatched twins in our various school homerooms—even though we could not have looked, sounded, or operated in any more dissimilar a fashion. Then there was Asshole, two hot years and change older than me, a year older than Twin, a bit of a ringleader of our triopoly of Renay's youngest sons. Asshole seemed to have skittered directly from the hellmouth with a sneer and a whip in hand, peering so malevolently out at you from behind thick Coke-bottle glasses; his gaze, if fixed upon you, turned you to stone. Asshole had a way of fogging up any room he entered, sort of like a bug bomb; his righteous fury, his certain judgment silencing all. Finally, and certainly least, our weakest link, the next oldest of Renay's four very large, idiot sons, my darling brother Rabbi, who I have always looked up to, both for his ability to cheat death in at least three states (and counting) and for his genial optimism that he will, eventually, strike it rich, or get it right. He won't do much of either, but he will endure. Rabbi was the only one of us who had ever managed to sneak in a Fayetteville bar mitzvah, hence his unimaginative nickname. There you have it: a Jewboy; an extra-large dimwit called Twin; a wrath-of-God temperamental nightmare who is still, to this day, fearfully referred to as Asshole; and the only good Jew between four rebel dirtbags, a collegial doofus called Rabbi. Got it?

She never did.

Despite giving birth to and indifferently raising all of us, Renay never could quite get our names straight, frequently spewing a fire-hose of invective in our general vicinity, nonsense words flying at us when things went wrong, "Rab-GOD-Ass-DAMN-Jewbo-IT-I mean Ass-MOTHERSHITFUCK!-I mean Andy! *One of you!*" It never mattered which one of us it was meant for: we were all, always, in trouble, and always in the line of fire. Anytime something went wrong, Renay shot first, asked questions later. And something was always going wrong with at least one of Renay's sons.

There was one more son, but he's not here.

The "away-son," we'll call him.

We'll get to that soon enough.

Whatever Renay called us, we always knew who had fucked up when the hollers and the books came flying out of the bathroom. In these early years, we all spoke the same language: trouble. We were Renay's little tribe of nose-picking, to-the-quick-nail-biting, change-stealing, dirty-minded, no-good fuckup sons, but we kept close to home, so she could clean up after us after we fucked up good, once again. We were her tribe.

"My little fuckups," she would say, affectionately. "Now clean up this shithole."

Renay loved nearly all of us, it is true, and we loved her back something *fierce.*

And we loved nuts, too.

The harder the nut, the more enterprising my brothers and I were about the getting. Harvest it, buy it, or steal it from a produce stand, we'd smash, grind, and stab our way through heaps of them. We'd polish off acres of Tidewater pecans or Georgia peanuts with our mother, whether picked from a can or fresh from the trees we had just climbed, with their pecan-heavy swollen limbs that waved listlessly above us on Pamalee Drive.

But there would be no pecans this year. Just when we needed them most, too.

During the summer of Divorce '78, Renay *tore through* nuts. She was a nervous eater already, and Renay had *a lot* to be nervous about. Any week now, the end of her marriage would be officially thumped from a bench in far-off Arkansas, where our dad, Shithead, currently resided, patiently teaching ROTC to farmer sons and slinging cocktails at night to all the farmer wives at a plantation-themed steakhouse bar. On the one hand, this long-overdue marital terminus might spell a new beginning for us all. Alimony and child support would finally flow like water, and our pre-divorce desiccation would disappear. On the other hand, we lived in Fayetteville. It was probably too late for us.

2.

I was nine that fall, and so you might rightly ask: what does a bookish, sissy nine-year-old know about nuts, endings, even his own mother, for that matter?

I knew a lot.

So did my brothers, and so, too, did Cathy Sue, our sole and beloved sister, the oldest of us, now living far away in that wretched remove called Virginia Beach, being a proper teenager with a proper teen pregnancy, a wife playing house with the first in a rotating cast of husbands.

We were terrible students, all of Renay's children, most of us dropouts, but we were clever in the ways of the streets, raised by our streetwise mother to raise ourselves, to ask wrong questions only, to always be braced for impact. We were a gruesome foursome, destroying, dismantling, and taking Fayetteville for ourselves. We did it all together back then, we were *real* brothers, inseparable and united. Except, that is, when the three youngest of us would be annually exiled, each July and August, down to torrid Miami Beach, to be shuffled between two sets of babysitters who happened to be our skeptical elderly Jewish grandparents—Renay's parents, and Renay's in-laws, the Katzes. The Katzes enjoyed their daughter-in-law so much they thought of her as their own daughter, and their son as a kind of intruder. The Katzes and the Mandels annually allowed Renay's children to invade their homes, steal from them, wet their beds, publicly embarrass and exasperate them in any number of Jewish delis along Collins Avenue. Me and Asshole and Twin pickpocketed anything from any Publix in Miami that looked like food, coins, or candy. We didn't think twice about criming our own grandparents, too; it's what we learned early, and often: *take it if you can make it away.* What were we supposed to do? Those old Jews of ours always left piles of silver change just sitting out in ashtrays and pickle jars, and my mother's father, Fat Sam, left racks of his old suits hanging unattended, their pockets stuffed with shiny silver dollars. Were we supposed to *not* steal those?

I would spend most of these exile months sulking alone under an umbrella by the community pool, stretched out alongside acres of hairy Jewish men still glowing onion-purple from the tiny pool house sauna, surreptitiously reading trashy books about twincest and horny, broad-chested adventurers, books that I stole from bored grandmothers while waiting for my brothers to return to Lake Park after they had committed sufficient petty crime up and down Northeast 199th Street to be escorted back, inevitably, by the police. We'd horrify our grandparents daily, until, defeated once again, Marian the Hungarian and her beloved Fat Sam heaved us onto a northbound Trailways bus, which shuttled us back to our proper place, back to the low-down Sandhills of North Carolina, where dirty little fuckups like Jewboy, Asshole, and Twin were not just welcome: they were kings.

Back to Pamalee Drive, our soon-to-be-lost family home.

There we would unite with our mother and our extravagantly brain-damaged brother Rabbi, nearly eighteen and already so dumb that a box of rocks could sue him for libel. Rabbi had been kicked out of at least three Fayetteville schools by this summer. Dodging a track record of sundry criminal enterprises that stretched from the Carolinas to Florida to Arkansas, Rabbi's long and tortured teenaged years were coming in for a landing at last after a recently completed, mandatory Arkansas residency, where he spent an entire year living in a camper van parked in our father's driveway in Pine Bluff. Rabbi spent his time there diddling the daughters of our father's many girlfriends, boosting frozen shrimp and steaks from a steakhouse owned by Goober from *The Andy Griffith Show*, and smoking all the Arkansas weed he could lay his hands on.

My brothers protected me, their youngest and their runtiest brother, they kept me alive in the ways that older brothers always do— whether intentionally or not—by throwing a hairy, big-brotherly, protective arm around their runt. They tossed down food scraps, put up shelter or shade when it rained, and an occasional Slurpee even came my way when we attacked a store together.

We loved Mid-Atlantic Championship Wrestling. We loved fishing anywhere, in any lake. And we loved our mother. We loved her laugh, her cigarettes, her big purses, her bigger personality.

We were a tight band of nefarious, nut-scavenging idiots, and we were reunited that late Summer of Divorce '78 on Pamalee Drive, melted back together like four slices of government cheese on a Spring Lake sidewalk, taking the gooey, elastic shape we would seize and hold for the next, fugitive decade: *survivors*.

Upon our return to Fayetteville this blistering August, my brothers and I took in the sight of our depleted mother, wilted damp and decalescent in her plaid chair, buried in a chaotic rubble of sweltry nut debris, and we four knew instantly: luck had slipped through Renay Mandel Corren's shapely hands.

A word about my mother's hands.

They. Were. *Beautiful!*

Ravishing. *Movie star hands.*

I mean, always *magnificent*. Show ponies! World-class *trophy hands*.

This was a hardworking, hard-partying, hard-bowling Lady of Fayetteville—those hands *worked*. Yet they were never less than immaculately detailed. In Renay's pre-divorce heyday, her hands were the product of weekly pampering trips across town to the Tallywood Mall for hair, nails, feet, and brow plump sessions. Me and the Twin routinely accompanied Renay on her beauty rounds, hanging out in the Tallywood courtyard, stealing from the A&P, running after each other through the metal shadows of the soaring Tallywood Tower, almost as tall as the eighty-foot Eiffel Tower replica across town at the Bordeaux Mall. Renay would emerge after hours of pampering, a celebrity ship, sails full mast, gliding past her sons in the setting sun, nearly three hundred regal pounds of bright and restored woman, her hair a flaming, rose-gold crown haloed and radiant, her face composed, layers of thick, sparkling paint lacquered upon her kabuki nails, the smell bitter, the sight sweet, each one polished to an incandescent, weaponized sheen. Buffed, shined, powdered, and painted, Renay Corren could once again face Fayetteville, a town that seemed ever intent on ending her. *Fuck with this woman*, those nails said. *I dare you.*

But Renay could no longer afford those weekly trips to Tallywood (frankly, she couldn't afford them in the first place). Three years into the smoldering waste of this long, nuclear divorce, the cash for nails had long since run dry.

So Renay took to home manicures, doing all that she could à la maison, filing and varnishing and approximating that Tallywood shine, enlisting me to bootblack and shellack her hard, calloused toes, fussing at bunions with scrapers and hammers and awls, all while she lay upon her side, plucking lazily at her brow with a gleaming tweezers in one hand, an eyelash press in the other. Renay's supple, pretty hands, while not as supple or nearly as pretty in these hard days of Divorce '78, were upheld with my gallant assistance. Appearances meant everything to my mother, and so they meant everything to me.

There was no need for Renay's hands to advertise all the bitter, hard truths that were tumbling down all around our Cumberland town.

Like that she couldn't keep the lights on.

Or the mortgage paid.

The car was knocking on death's door, and her bills and her sons were hungry.

Renay couldn't stop that car from being towed, hauled to or from another garage she couldn't afford. She couldn't stop begging Old Man Ferrell for another free oil change, or brake pads, or something, anything, to stop that loud, persistent knock in the guts of the Chevy Nova's radiator.

She couldn't stop any of it.

Money was a poisonous lake to Renay, one she drowned in many times over, but her hands sailed coolly on, like vain summer swans gliding away from smoking, burning shores. Renay's beautiful hands were perpetually fussing over piles of bills, bowls of divorce snacks, endlessly rooting in her bottomless pleather purse for a Virginia Slims 100, or the roach of a discarded joint, twisting and flicking at her raspy, gold-plated lighter during long, sweaty calls to Wagstaff, her Yellow Pages attorney in Arkansas. They fluttered before she dialed to borrow more money, clicked as she dialed to stop another check, clacked as she dialed to keep the power going or sweet-talk those Southern Bell ladies into keeping the phone turned on.

She needed that phone for agonizingly expensive long-distance calls with the attorney, her parents, Shithead's parents, her legion of bowling alley comrades at B&B Bowling Lanes, or Cathy Sue, my sister and her only daughter. They all called to advise and prop up the dissolution of this twenty-two-year-long grudge match that she and Shithead had called a marriage, a union that had lasted, in most people's estimation—especially theirs—twenty-one years too long.

Renay had six children, just the one daughter followed by five sons, spread out over twelve years of making babies. A devastating miscarriage, and two discreet abortions, plus six live births meant that Renay Corren had been a knocked-up, fed-up, broodmare since 1956. Twenty years of mostly unblemished fertility. I was her youngest, the final one, and she had desperately prayed day and night throughout my blessed germination that I would be a girl—and sort of got her wish, if we're being honest. There's that away-son that I mentioned, but he's still far away, far, at least, from the center of these events.

Four sons at home with Renay on Pamalee Drive.

It was a lot of hungry rednecks.

It took a long, expensive divorce, and two and a half shitty jobs, for Renay to fall this far behind in keeping all those rednecks fed. She went to the B&B Lanes most nights, where she ran leagues, ruled as a champion bowler, and dealt 'em in as after-hours in-house casino manager. During the days, she manned a Sunoco gas kiosk at the Eutaw Village Shopping Center, where she was situated perfectly to siphon gas, steal cigarettes, and swipe petty cash for us and for some minor gambling debts. She topped it all off by dealing a little weed and some glass bongs out of the trunk of the Nova.

Sometimes she had a Sunday off, maybe for fishing, for laundry, always for the Dolphins.

Renay didn't have all the time in the world for conventional mothering, not when her house of cards was being held up by one, single, shiny fingernail. If she was at home, she was catching a wink between shifts. But I really do believe Renay had the *exact* right amount of time and love to divide among us, the 2.5 jobs, the nails, the bills. We saw it all, down to the stitches, because our mother had nothing to be ashamed of, and no time to be ashamed, anyway, and thus nothing was ever held back.

Renay sought pleasure when her doom was near, and believe me when I say that in the Summer of Divorce '78 doom was breathing heavy up Renay Corren's skirt. Except Renay never wore a skirt, not one time. Renay wore pants. Renay wore fuck-it pants *only*.

When we got back from Miami that summer, Renay was looking for the divorce exit, or the divorce punchline. She chewed through bags of nuts the way Arkansas Wagstaff, Esquire, chewed through his billable hours, calling at all hours with the latest setbacks. Spent nut shells lay forgotten on every surface like bullet casings, grouped with piles of crumpled bills, smashed joints, ripped envelopes scrawled with frantic notes—important divorce details quickly forgotten. The calls from Wagstaff produced stacks of such notes, nervously shredded by her fiery, fuming, Tallywood-deprived talons. The shiny laminate walls of Renay's living room grew a layer of grime and smoke and began closing in on her.

She wanted off those calls. She wanted off the divorce train. It all cost too damned much, it took up too much time. It wasn't *fun*. It took everything from her. It took *war*.

Renay was no good at war.

Renay was good at peace.

Good at sex. Good at jokes. Good at eating. Good at leaving things for another day, at ditching checks and finishing off men before they hardly even noticed. Renay harried, cajoled, and flattered Wagstaff off those calls fast, just like one of her break time parking-lot handjobs at the B&B: lightning quick, full of fury. *Master class.*

Wagstaff's calls concluded, Renay would retreat behind closed doors to her bathtub, where she would float, nursing those long-distance Arkansas wounds with long, hot drafts of sympathetic water, billows of weed left unsold from the trunk of the Nova, waves of chemical-green sour apple bubble bath from the Kmart discount bin, a boxy white radio whispering Larry King into the dawn. She spent epic, mysterious nights cloistered in that tub, floating on the surface of sour apple water, while her troubles tried to pull her down below.

Renay floated through it all.

3.

From her tub, Renay whisper-shouted to me through the cracked door, using my private girl name, "Ann, bring me my macadamia!" Then: "And practice doing it like Mae West. Make 'em laugh, Ann!"

"I ain't got no nuts, lady, but why don't ya come up and see me *some time,*" I automatically replied, making Renay laugh real good. I had a solid Mae West up my sleeve, as well as a whole artillery of other celebrity impersonations at the ready to entertain my grandparents when they arrived.

This is what she made me for.

Renay had made me into her perfect little man, her best companion, her Mini-She, something badly divorced ladies are wont to do, I suppose, but I didn't mind. I was nine, and though I shared the same DNA as all her sons, I was aware, too, at an early age, that I was special, like a hothouse plant that needed a little extra attention, so it was nice to have Renay as my manager, mentor, and porcine Pygmalion. We spoke the same language: *hers*. My mother was a big lady with no big plans, and she already knew a good deal about the way of things in this world. She knew more about it than me, certainly, and more about *me*, even, than I knew about myself. Renay did the thinking for both of us, which is what a mother is supposed to do, right?

"Ann, get me another Pepsi," she called. Then she added as an afterthought, "De-grockerate my room!"

It was an *enormous* honor to be asked to de-grockerate Renay's chambers, which meant picking up all her bedroom litter—her tissues, papers, magazines, crumbs, stray pretzels, empty Pepsi cans, and nut shells. I was always bussing Renay's bedroom, dusting her trays of costume jewelry, putting fake pearls on and sliding fake silver bracelets off, rehanging all her gaily festooned rose-and-cabbage blouses, folding her discarded fuck-it pants and enormous bloomers, wrangling all the rubber mastectomy boob inserts that bounced to every corner the moment her bra slid off. I'd linger over Renay's racks of cosmetics, the shiny, lime-green bottles of Clinique, the Revlon polishes in every rainbow shade, the brow combs, all the creamy lip pens, her eye pencils, and tubes upon tubes of lipsticks—a *real* warrior's chest of paint for a *real* warrior painted Fayetteville red.

I slipped Renay a fresh Pepsi through the door and pushed a bowl of black walnuts in behind, a consolation prize for the lack of macadamia, the nuts already lightly cracked to make them easier for Renay to pick at, followed by a bowl of sliced cantaloupe—a favorite pairing—sliced on the rind into chunks she could spear with a glossy fingernail, like kebabs.

Renay routinely added a squirt of Joy for an extra, rich blast of lemony-jazz and foam, and the sour apple Jawbreaker smell lightly cut with a zest of lemon detergent mingled with the scent of her wet cigarettes and tangy marijuana into a skunky-fruity combo that was hers and hers alone. Renay loved her long, hot, post-Wagstaff, post-bowling, stoned soaks of redemption.

"Lemony-fresh." She sighed.

"We're out of nuts," I drawled, again as Mae West. This bowl of walnuts would be the last.

"Yes, and we have-a no macadamia," she said sadly, tilting her head back in the foam, affecting a tragedienne's resignation. *No macadamia.* A terrible blow for Renay.

Macadamia was rarely in the house. Macadamia was *expensive.* Rich people nuts. Unless they came our way as a thank-you gift from one of Renay's bowling alley lovers or, far more likely, got boosted from the base PX at Fort Bragg into Renay's bottomless bag of shopping thievery, we did not have macadamia flowing freely. Nuts from the PX rarely made it all the way home, anyway. Because of Shithead's military service we got to shop at the base once a month and Renay excelled at pinching, slicing open, and consuming entire bags of purloined macadamia before we ever so much as reached the commissary cashier, her four noisy, starving kids riding alongside four carts' worth of groceries, our rations on her one month's support check. Renay would eat whole meals while shopping at the PX. I once saw my mother steal and eat an entire pound of "shopping ham" before she hit the exit. Now *that's* talent.

"You are dismissed," she said airily from her bath—and she meant no harm. She added a jokingly faux-royal wave, her ringed, pruning hands foamy with Joy, her wedding band finger still white where her ring was so recently removed. She wiggled her perfectly pedicured, dainty fat toes off the side of the tub, as if to say, *It's all a joke, Ann! Life is a grand joke! But I have invited* you *along for the ride!* She remembered a last command: "Tell your brothers to get this shithole straight before Nana Minna and Papa Joe get here! I don't need the embarrassment!"

This was a woman who literally could not be embarrassed, and she slapped at her piles of Joy foam, giggling and making us both laugh as I quietly shut the door behind me, leaving Renay to her divorce soak and whatever comforts that green apple water could provide.

I strolled through the late-afternoon, orange-sun-dusted, nut-littered interior of our house, which came with rarely vacuumed wall-to-wall shag carpet in every room in two shades of algae green and dog diarrhea brown. Even the bathrooms had deep, plush shag. Fake-wood paneling floor to ceiling. If you had asked me then, I'd have said it was *a palace*. I'd have said *we had a lot*.

It was the most we would ever have.

We had a fish tank, sometimes even containing living fish, and a "nice furniture" room, too, filled with artifacts from Japan and a paisley yellow sofa I never sat on except for when I required complete darkness for my late-summertime migraines, or solace for the sudden and mysterious, angsty confusion of lusts that rushed to my downstairs place after watching *Donny & Marie*. We even had an enviable stereo in a polished wood console, the pride of our home, a grand Sansui 700 series with a receiver and a reel-to-reel. *Fancy people stereophonics*, I would think, passing it on my way to overfeed a doomed and desperately obese pair of guppies we called Frick and Frack.

Best of all, our house on Pamalee had *two* bathrooms, a championship, middle-class luxury, the ultimate sign of stability to our inbound, class-conscious grandparents, who had all risen high above their Carpathian ancestors, but not so high as to flush extravagantly in two rooms!

Just outside the kitchen door was a patchy yard with a picnic table, a half-ton circle of cement plunked on sandy, sooted ground that was always littered with pine needles and pollen, surrounded as we were by long, piney woods on all three sides. These were thick Carolina woods, teeming with loblolly and longleaf, with wasps lurking in the fallen pine below. There were thorny black huckleberries, too, and colonies of red cardinals. We had flowering bunches of tart wild grapes, fist-sized, "a redneck cocktail" my sister Cathy Sue always said. Our woods, which seemed infinite to me, were penned in by Cumberland County's ninth-most deadly intersection, and so our Pamalee Drive house was frequently buffeted by the ghostly echoes of ambulances, school bus accidents from E. E. Smith, and high-speed police chases inevitably leading to, or from, Rick's Topless down on Hay.

Ours was a single-story brick ranch, clean-looking on the outside with an up-jumped, white-people portico that faced Pamalee, and a roof low enough to access with an old, rusted ladder. We lived on our roof, Twin, Asshole, and I, as down below the calls from Wagstaff came, or did not come, or came too often to bear.

Our driveway plunged vertiginously down the long, deadly hill to Cain Road itself, on the other side of which was a whole other kingdom of woods. Those woods are now paved over—home to three different hair salons, and a graveyard parking lot—but back then it was a dark and inviting kingdom filled with pecan trees, and danger as far as the eye could see. If you were suicidal enough to attempt the crossing of the Cain, you could harvest sweet, tempting berries from low, spiny bushes, and brave the camouflaged minefield of pine-veiled yellowjackets' nests that lurked just beneath every step you took.

We had a sitting room. We had nuts. We had wild berries, and we had each other.

We had her.

Licorice Katz was alive and well in Miami that late September of Divorce '78, this I can confidently report, as my brothers and I had left him only weeks before, after our annual crime spree across North Miami. On a Thursday morning, long before dawn, Licorice was strapped into a shiny brown Cutlass Supreme and driven directly up the 95, onto the 401 bypass, then right up Pamalee Drive hill, to our house, accompanied by his persons, my grandparents Minna and Joseph Katz, for their biannual Jewish High Holy Days food delivery service.

Tucked away down deep in the remote and splendid isolation of North Carolina's aromatic butt crack, we didn't know that we were the poor sons of that poor fat lady down the road, the one about to lose her house. We didn't know what fat, or poor, or foreclosure was. We probably *looked* poor, especially when compared to folks up in Haymount, which was three miles and three hundred thousand light-years to the east. We probably looked *rich* to the folks down at Cobra, or to the unfortunates of Forest Hills Drive. We were Jewish, everybody knew that, but we were the poor Jews of Pamalee, the *only* poor Jews in all of Fayetteville, too poor, even, for shul. Still, whenever Renay had an extra five dollars for the can deposit, a sixteen-ounce tub of Charles Chips would be summoned by phone, and from whatever feral treetops we swung, my brothers and I would pause midair and watch, mouths wet with slobber as that podgy, yellow-and-beige Charles Chips van made its puttering way up the dark incline of our drive. In the shadow of that van, loaded down with all those expensive beige canisters of premium snacks, for just a moment our mother would glow in the damp, Fayetteville sun. Quality chips and fine nuts, polished nails and dirt-covered little servant boys, deferential deliverymen scattered about her like rose petals. A queen. A dirtbag queen, with a crown of rose gold, and we, her sons, her royal court.

In the Summer of Divorce '78, when Licorice Katz was still alive, this all seemed like enough to me.

More than that.

It seemed like *enormous riches*.

4.

"Hide the bacon." Asshole sneered from behind his Coke-bottle glasses, his permanent grimace smothered in the iron grip of the one, the only, Minna Klatskin Cohen Katz.

Materfamilias had arrived.

Since sometime before dawn, the Katzes' Supreme had been hauling up the I-95 from Miami, blowing through state lines and blazing past farm stands in one long, epic, blur, Joe at the wheel, Minna at his side, schmatta-wrapped head tilted to the sun, her Pall Mall Gold 100 out the window, Licorice Katz, their black standard poodle, wedged into the fully loaded creamy bucket seats.

Minna and Joe drove to Fayetteville because Minna was a survivor of the crash of National Airlines Flight 101. The plane, which was headed from Newark to Miami after midnight on February 11, 1952, had gone down shortly after takeoff, and fiery, fearless Minna Katz, my father's mother, had been ejected, careening through the midnight sky, burning and still strapped into her airplane seat, the most famous Jewish comet in all of New Jersey history. Minna survived, just barely. Years of recovery and skin grafts had left her with a small settlement, a fur coat, a diamond ring, some very impressive scars, and a lingering taste for long, languid drives accompanied by her first faithful husband, who was for the record her *second* husband, that short, randy socialist stud from the Bronx, Joseph Katz. Her first husband, small-time New York and Miami gangster Abraham "Al" Cohen, my cheating father's cheating father, had been shown the door in 1946, long, long before I was born.

"Joseph, you know what to do," Minna said, barreling into the house, hardly drawing a breath before tossing her beige cardigan onto Renay's tattered, upholstered woolly-plaid cube chair, setting down her enormous knitting bag in a puff of smoke, and pulling out a very large pair of cutting shears and a smock. Minna smiled tightly as she wound the smock around her tiny waist, a menacing smile that did not brook argument or debate from the dirty Jewish sheep arrayed before her.

"Let's not have any theatrics," she announced, exhaling a cloud of Pall Mall.

We were getting backyard haircuts, and we were getting them *now*.

Before the engine of the Cutlass went cold, mere seconds after we were revealed to be in our usual shabby, unsupervised state, we were paraded, brother by brother, to the concrete shearing table. Retired Miami Beach society cosmetologist Minna Katz *despised* an unkempt head of Jewish hair.

Haircuts dispensed with methodically, Minna pivoted to transferring an Army base commissary's worth of food from the Cutlass to the bare cupboards of our shag-carpeted kitchen, then set to cleaning and dusting our entire house, removing layers of ignored summer grease, chiseling grime from every surface as she scoured and prepped for the baking and stuffing and proofing of many Jewish foods, an intense, focused operation that would go long into the night.

Minna did it all, and she did it all at once, as she had done her entire magnificent, wildly topsy-turvy life. Brooklyn ingenue, wife, mother. Miami divorcée. Wife again. Stylist. Hostess. Traveler. Grandmother. *General.* Minna Katz was an unstoppable Hebrew comet, and we were all sucked into the gravitational pull of her kibbitzing, cleaning, cooking, canning, shearing, and schmaltzing. She and Joe were here for Renay, yes, but for all us meshuga grandkids, too, to wrap us up in love and loyalty as the final act of this great battle between Minna's son Shithead and her beloved chosen daughter Renay.

Let the record show it was Minna Katz who first called her son Shithead.

His mother. Not us.

Minna was tiny and she was fierce, her strong arms and gaunt cheeks mottled with burn scars. She was a tireless schlepper, always prepared, hilariously funny. She was deeply religious, but always outrageously mindful of others. She was loud, salty, and as funny as Buddy Hackett killing on the Vegas Strip, yet Minna kept a meticulous, ahead-of-its-time organic garden back at home like it was her full-time job, and she had more than two hundred fired-up Hadassah mah-jongg ladies in her diary who would die for her. Minna put up with a lot of shit from Renay's summertime kids, yet she always came back to us, this forgiving, combative, fearless, redheaded fireball.

The Katzes were stepping into a clearly broken home overseen, if at all, by a clearly broken woman, and a pack of braying, half-feral boys running wild. The only real home I ever knew, and the last that Renay would ever own, it was falling down around us, and it was obvious for all to see.

This was where Licorice Katz came to die.

"Licorice!" we screamed in unison, dumping bags of oranges and bagels on the counter and leaving them to drop to the shag for some premium poodle lickage. *Licorice was here! Licorice!*

Licorice Katz bounded inside, all thirty-plus pounds of him slobbering and tackling us in an unbridled love fury, his furry black tail a docked, mini pom-pom of unleashed excitement after finally being set free from his Cutlass cage. Smiling and whining, jumping directly into our arms, then running about the shag in wide, happy circles, Licorice barked his suitcase-sized poodle bark of love at the sight of his Carolina cousins. He loved us, a pure contentment, a blast of light and sweetness that parted the clouds above the Summer of Divorce '78. Licorice Katz was certainly the center of Minna and Joe's galaxy, their only child at home, but Licorice was part-time ours, too; we had put in hours by his side down in Miami. We could not *wait* to spend our days eating bagels and chasing after Licorice, already planning the adventures ahead, me and Twin and Asshole and Licorice exploring the sewers of Fayetteville, which ran right beneath our house, taking him up to Mintz Lake, befriending Maverick, the scary Doberman leashed up next door. We looked forward to the weeks ahead, running berserk those final days of summer, chasing into the fireball of fall alongside our favorite Miami cousin.

None of that would happen, because Licorice Katz would be dead before ten o'clock that night.

The Cutlass disgorged a conveyor belt of endless bags, crates, and boxes of foodstuffs direct from Miami. The car was a one-woman Jewish grocery that Minna Katz never hit the road without, its seats sparkling with the oil of orange rind, spicy smells escaping from tucked jars of hand-ground paprika, and clanging with meat grinders, stock pots, and other exotic kitchen tools. It was a complex intestinal surgery on wheels, a whole deli carted into our kitchen, sacks of front-yard Valencia oranges and backyard Pehoski purple garlic from Minna's organic garden, bundles of dried spices and herbs she grew and dried herself. She would grind and chop and sizzle and stew, all this day and into the Rosh Hashanah dawn. A labor union picket line's worth of fresh and chewy bagels, all the seeds and flavors from that neon-lit haven on Collins Avenue, the world-famous Rascal House, because even though it was far from the Katzes' home in Central Miami, they knew Rascal House was the Corren Brothers' favorite place, and they went the extra bagel mile for their grandkids.

Renay swooned over icy coolers as pounds of tightly wrapped, fatty fishes appeared as if by Talmudic witchcraft, tendrils of frost licking at their oily butcher-wrapped shrouds: jaunty, swaddled herrings with cold, staring eyes; smoked and cured kippers; salty lox; silkily seductive sables—all the reeking, scaly whitefishes and novas a big Jewish broad could ever dream of and never get, because there was no real Jewish deli in North Carolina. Not one.

The Cutlass reeked of dark, delicious pumpernickels from Wolfie's, where, as Papa Joe loudly declaimed, "I saw Meyer Lansky again, walking that adorable dog, Bruiser!" using every inch of his deli patois to slather each deliciously elongated slice of vowel with the seedy, mustardy, starstruck ardor of a Miami boy from the Bronx made good. Made *real good*.

These people. These beautiful, loud, leathery, Jewish people. *My people.*

They arrived as if from a time machine, from a long-vanquished Jewish civilization, Miami Beach, from when it was exclusively a place by, and for, the Jews. Nana Minna Katz was determined to make our house, if only for a week, a *Miami Jewish home*. Clean. Ordered. Delicious. *Righteous on the Sabbath*. Minna Klatskin Cohen Katz was the single most gifted, courageous, creative, and completely terrifying Jew I knew.

Minna was wearing hand-sewn floral culottes the night Licorice Katz died.

Hand-sewn.

She would fix us with her bubbling pots of stock, her stuffed cabbages, her fried latkes, and she would strengthen and nourish Renay, too, this vivacious chosen daughter of hers. Minna would give her a style and a cut and some clean kids on the side. She bucked Renay up, laughing and cajoling, cooking and cleaning, all between overflowing jelly jars of cheap white wine, while the unyielding hot early-autumn sun struggled between verdant sappy pines and low, listless clouds. If she had done her job—and to Minna it *was* a job—Minna Katz would banish the memory of Shithead from this house, once and for all.

There would be a delicious Sabbath dinner later, the first unfrozen dinner in weeks. Then we'd gather around the television, bellies swollen with Minna's fine cuisine, and the final piece of the restored family puzzle would slide into place: the fall TV season of 1978.

We would be a family at last.

A *real* family.

And then Licorice Katz up and died.

5.

Licorice Katz died just a few minutes after eight thirty p.m. on Friday, September 22, 1978, or 20 Elul 5738 on the Jewish calendar.

Elul is the month of repentance, the clean slate month, the final month of the year before the High Holy Days of Rosh Hashanah and Yom Kippur. It's the Get Your Shit Together Month for Jews, before it's too late for the awakening of spirit. It's a time for cleansing of souls and dusting of homes and releasing the mistakes of the year just past.

Licorice died during the typically skit-heavy first half of *Donny & Marie*. That season was lamentably its fourth and last, meaning *Donny & Marie* has now been off the air for decades, and so you may never have seen, or may barely recall, its celestial wonders. If so, let me underline the important points: it was a Mormon variety hour led by a Mormon brother and a Mormon sister, Donald and Marie Osmond, who still, somehow, managed to have sexual tension. The siblings were ages twenty and eighteen, and they sported matching primitive butch lesbian haircuts, and both had exquisite, blinding orthodonture. The premise of the show was that Marie was "a little bit country," i.e., lesbian, while Donny was "a little bit rock and roll," ergo quietly bisexual. After the skits, the show would segue into its higher-energy, song-and-dance, guest-star-heavy second half, which I noted with passionate interest this season premiere featured an elaborately and daringly multihued disco stage. The seventies were simply incredible. You had to be there.

My brothers and I were scattered before the TV in a pile, joining in with the live studio audience from Osmond Entertainment Center in Orem, Utah, as it sparkled to life with hard-core Mormon rock and luminous, sequin-clad, closeted Mormon backup dancers shimmying to a wholesome cover of Heatwave's smash hit "The Groove Line," when Licorice Katz inhaled a weird and raspy, darkly-congested, shaky breath, and then, with a long, obstructed, snoring exhale that not one of us bothered to investigate, expired quietly beneath the reclining chair that cradled his beloved master, our Papa Joe.

Right there in the last Fayetteville home of Renay and Shithead Corren, during the very last week of their marriage, a final sacrifice was taken: thirty pounds of beloved, furry flesh, removed in the glittering shadow of the Osmonds' celestial kingdom.

The smell of schmaltz and endings was in the air.

I was much too young to fully process all the consequential endings and beginnings afoot, so I merely attended to my ordinary Friday night duties, paying my customary microscopic attention to each tiny detail of the tautly tailored pantsuits of the most-obviously gay Mormon backup dancers, and, when I felt nobody was observing me too closely, zeroing in on Donny's exceptionally fitted, nearly sheer white tuxedo pants, which he wore with an insouciant, hipless twenty-year-old's abandon, dancing with shameless Mormon joie de vivre. Donny was accessorized this night with a long, flowing Liberace-esque tie-scarf, which even I knew was gay, while Marie was wrapped in enough gold lamé to upholster an entire extra-special episode of *The Love Boat*, like one of those two-parters when they get stuck in the Panama Canal. Donny and Marie were the sexiest, most glamorous, and most celibate celebrity couple on Mormon God the Father's sweet earth. They made me *feel things*. They made me feel like I was their brother *and* their boyfriend. There was nothing Donny couldn't do that didn't turn me on, even though I didn't really understand what was *being* turned on.

There was just something about him.

Try as I might, I could not explain it, and yet I wanted to rush out into the green pecan-covered yard that hot September night and scream *something* to the leaden skies. I wanted to tell the world about Donny and me! Something was happening in my downstairs place, and I didn't even fully understand what my downstairs place did!

And then came the Big Gay Bang.

Watching Donny take his sweet, shallow sips of breath after his epic opening number, I was seized by my usual, insistent urge to explode with hot pee, a familiar rush of warmth that greeted every song of his, an urgent, bestial need to urinate whenever I was possessed by the animal magnetism of Donald Clark Osmond. With the exception of Oscar Goldman from *The Six Million Dollar Man*, who was obviously the most attractive Jew to ever wear a vest, no other man made me feel the way Donny did. I discreetly excused myself, anxious to relieve this confused, downstairs pressure, and I hobble-stepped down the shag runway and walked right into my baptism. *By gay fire.*

His name was Bernie Alphabet.

And Bernie Alphabet was *N-A-K-E-D.*

Bernie was naked, but he wasn't getting naked for my mother. It was Friday, and if he was in town, Bernie was always over at our house on Pamalee Drive on Fridays, usually taking a hot shower after one of his HALO night drops over Fort Bragg, where he shoved hundreds of hot, terrified Army Airborne recruits out of airplanes on their first live parachute jumps. Bernie was Renay's best friend. Of course, Renay had more than two hundred best friends, but Bernie was always at or near the top. Bernie and Renay were outrageous together, the best kind of best friends, the extra-loud low-life ones making a public ruckus, the ones you're jealous of, the ones who *got* each other *from the first jump out of the plane*, and never, ever let go, all the way to the bottom. Rude, funny, sacrilegious, stoned, loyal. Bernie came over Friday nights dirty and hungry, ready to get clean and fed and *laugh*. He was one of us, the closest thing to a father figure that my brothers and I ever had in Fayetteville.

Bernie was twenty-nine, Renay was forty-one, and they'd been thick as bandits since they first met five years before at B&B Lanes when Bernie, a pool-hustling stud straight outta Hartford, showed up in ripped pants and a purple Dodge Super Bee. He started jumping out of planes and landing on every horny and neglected Army wife. Nobody fucked shit up like Bernie, and nobody fucked it up louder, or with more primal, animalistic joy.

They were made for each other.

Renay didn't just love a bad boy. She didn't just *fuck* the bad boys.

Renay *was* a bad boy.

Whenever bad boy number one Bernie Alphabet came roaring back to Fayetteville from wherever the Army sent him, our family was *his* family. He loved blowing some hash on a glass lantern with Renay, hanging out with Rabbi and spinning records on the Sansui, taking Twin to all his baseball games, and gobbling up all our Florida bagels when they were in the house. When the Katzes came to town, Bernie was there, too. Minna loved feeding this tall, handsome, agreeable goy-ishe commando who was *nothing* like her own twisted shithead son. Joe Katz, a Seabee and World War II hero himself, saw in Bernie what he never saw in his wife's son: he saw humility. To be sure, my father's service in the United States Army was long and illustrious, highly decorated, but from where I sat in the cheap seats, it did not come without reputational baggage. Shithead was known far and wide, particularly at Fort Bragg, as Sergeant Major Prick, and Sergeant Major Prick was a supreme example of the kiss-up/kick-down ambition that got you ahead in the Green Berets. In my opinion, my father, the Notorious Shithead, was a pure-T Army dickhead, and my father figure, Bernie Alphabet, was pure-T Army class.

Of course we all loved Bernie.

God help us both, I walked in on my father figure dripping stark naked wet.

Uncomfortable, desperate to relieve this Donny-induced swelling in my downstairs, I had run to the guest bath and swung open the door without looking first. I walked into some kind of foggy, homosexual Oedipus complex, and my life has never been the same. A cloud parted, an actual cloud made of commando steam, revealing Bernie Alphabet standing starkers on the shag, posted up before the fogged-up mirror slick and wet, wearing nothing but the suggestion of vapor on his pink, muscled, commando buns. His hard, broad back to me, I could see Bernie's bemused face in the mirror.

"Ehhh! Sorry, occupied, grab the other latrine!" he Hartford-barked, gripping a soaking white towel in one fist, his back outrageously rippled, his shiny ass pale and firm.

"Thought it was locked. Try your ma's crapper, kid." He chuckled, turning to yank the door shut.

And then I saw the rest of it.

I saw it.

One minute, I was a bookish little kid with confused feelings for Oscar Goldman and Donny Osmond, and a strange but persistent need to pee *hard* whenever I interrogated those feelings.

The next minute I was gay. *I was so gay, y'all.*

I could see.

Tendrils of lustful, steamy soap smell escaped into the September night, teasing vapors mixed with *his* smell, the manly odor of detonation cord, bowling shoe resin, and sweet weed. I stepped back, *lurched back*, with Bernie's masterful crack still x-rayed onto my eyeballs, his chiseled form, beads of water taking a journey to places powerful and alluring.

He was showering right down the hall from Donny Osmond.
And I had seen it.

With this Sabbath gift from Bernie, I inhaled my first full breath of desire.

I had never considered a man fully in the nude before. I had never seen a pair of buttocks or a downstairs other than my own. Not even professional wrestlers, which in the 1970s was not particularly about physique, anyway. I had never seen a naked body in real life, unless you counted old man Jewish balls blasted purple by a cedar sauna in Miami. And I do not. *I do not.*

Now I had seen this tall, broad, chiseled, Catholic commando in the flesh. *A real man.* A pool hustler. A legend in his own time who adventured the world, spiked volleyballs, fell out of the night sky with muscular regularity. Here was a full-grown man with a monstrously sexy back, dripping on a shag carpet, forcing me to confront desire, attraction, and the physics and fuckability of the 82nd Airborne 6th Special Forces. I was confronting *all of this* during the season 4 premiere of *Donny & Marie.*

Talk about your inciting events.

I *loved* how it made me feel to see Bernie naked, as much as I was *horrified* how it made me feel to see Bernie naked.

I bid you welcome, sirs and gentlehumans, to homosexuality.

I stumbled backward, instantly forgetting my body's own needs, and meekly surrendered the bath to Bernie. I returned to my mother and my family in the living room, neon with desire, slick with steam and shame. My brothers sat in piles on the floor, transfixed by Bob Hope and Olivia Newton-John cavorting with all those Mormons as though nothing out of the ordinary had just happened.

Yet I was different. *Changed.*

Could they see it?

"I approve of these Osmonds. Goyishe as hell, but a very nice hell," Minna said, raising her jelly jar of Paul Masson white wine and exhaling her benediction in a cloud of Pall Mall. She turned to me and fixed me with her trademark stare. I thought—*I knew*—I was busted.

"Tell me, shaifeleh, how old are you now? Tell your Nana, quick."

"I'm nine," I said, crossing my legs daintily and sitting on the arm of our brownish sofa.

"Nine going on ninety," Twin quipped, and though I couldn't tell if it was an insult or a compliment, I glared at Twin and gave him the finger, anyway. Well, three fingers, with the middle in the middle. We still had *some* polite company rules in this house.

"Sit on it!" I said to Twin, trying and failing to model my manly hero, the Fonz from *Happy Days.*

"He's a Klatskin, this one," Minna said, nodding to Renay. "And tell your Nana, you really like this farkakte show business?" she asked, brows furrowed skeptically.

"Yes, ma'am. I'm gonna be a superagent like Sue Mengers."

This predictably got an enormous laugh out of my knowing mother.

"I would also like to be a comedian," I said with what I hoped sounded like nine-year-old confidence, but definitely sounded coached, because that was what my mother, who was also my manager, had coached me to say to my grandmother, if and when she ever inquired.

"I see, I see." Minna nodded sagely.

"Mom! *Bad News Bears* is on after *Donny & Marie!*" Twin had jolted upright at the blaring promo announcing his all-time favorite movie. My brother was a handsome and stupid jock even then, so we had naturally already seen *The Bad News Bears* five times at the Eutaw 1-2-3. Yet still Twin piped maniacally, "Coach Buttermaker! Coach Buttermaker! Oh my God!"

In his defense, Walter Matthau was some kind of secular Jewish deity in this household.

Asshole squinted, coolly spit out a bloody fingernail he had been working all night, and kicked Twin right in the head. "Are you insane? Sit down. *Hulk* is on next, dummy, and love *is in the air.*" He grunted from behind his glasses, aggravated at his brother's betrayal of everything we stood for as a family. Nothing—*nothing*—got in Asshole's way of a rampaging monster in love.

"But—but—Coach Buttermaker," Twin said, wounded, casting his piercing blue eyes down to the green shag.

"Wrong. *Hulk.* Monster sex. *Idiot.*" Asshole glared, ending the discussion with his patented, thermonuclear sneer.

"The both of yous! Bist meshugeh?" Papa Joe shouted from the tattered reclining chair, ending Twin and Asshole's squabble. "Your Nana and I will be enjoying the season five premiere of *The Rockford Files,* a shaynem dank!" he announced, gripping my prized *TV Guide* fall preview so intensely that I was afraid he would tear the cover, and then I'd have to buy an immediate replacement for my hallowed collection of *TV Guides* that I kept holy and pristine. Joe Katz spoke with such a forceful, thick Bronx dagger one could not argue. His voice, when raised—and it was nearly always raised—was a 1970s New York City taxicab laying on the horn. *It physically hurt.*

"Hope you're happy, *dummy.*" Asshole glared at Twin, who looked genuinely confused, as baseball players always do in the playoffs, as to how he had brought this latest tragedy down upon our house. Fool. We could've had a monster in love *with Mariette Hartley.*

Nana Minna steered her lighthouse gaze back upon me and said,

"Ainekele, your Uncle Gig lives in Burbank, near a big fake lake called Toluca. A real big shot. He does show business. I'll give you his address, you'll write a nice note to your Uncle Gig. He works for Mister Big Shot Bob Hope."

Minna's thickly penciled eyebrows were cocked as she casually dropped the single most explosive and exciting morsel of biography *anybody* has *ever* said about *any* family member since my mother's mother, the vain and emotionally illiterate Marian the Hungarian, confessed privately to me over one of her astonishingly light angel food cakes the summer before that she used to babysit for legendary celebrity facialist Georgette Klinger, back in the old country.

My mother was rocking and nodding at me so emphatically she nearly spit out her current chunk of one of the four tender, delicious chocolate babkas Minna had already proofed and baked since her arrival, which Renay seemed determined to eat single-handedly, all in one night, as if to prove a point.

"He would *love* that!" Renay roared between bites, elbowing Bernie, who had appeared in the living room a short while before, now dry and, tragically, overdressed. "Won't he *love* that?" she said to him as she delicately picked crumbs from her decolletage with her long nails, sucking at them like prized oysters as she pointed at me approvingly, goading me on.

"I would love that, Nana Minna!" I said, taking my mother's emphatic hint. "I'll write to him tomorrow!" Then, demonstrating some of my father's legendary suck-up skills, I added, "I'll get my entertainment industry notebook!" I had a spiral notebook for show business notes, and so far the only name penciled in under "Show Business Notes" belonged to a remote Czech skincare maven named Georgette. Things were looking *up*!

"You will write a nice note. He's der groyser tzuleyger, but you're mine, and he's married to my sister. You're a smart one. He'll write you back," she said with such pertinent finality I believed her the way a man lost at sea believes his rescue as he's lifted, burnt and starving, onto a fever-dreamed-for shore. "You'll tell him some nice things about yourself, and he'll tell you what it takes to have your own show." Minna then shrugged her thin, indomitable shoulders. "Ganseh macher, too big to join his sister-in-law for a holiday, but maybe he will answer your letter."

"Bob Hope is on *Donny & Marie!*" I whispered, shocked to my core. "Bob Hope is on *tonight.*"

Up until this moment I believed that standing before a naked paratrooper had been, and would forever be, the greatest revelation of my life. *I was wrong.*

"Your Minna has eyes, boychik. I'm sure your macher uncle had a little something to do with it. When that one"—here she points to Bob Hope on the TV—"opens his mouth, it's usually Gig with the hand up the tuches," she said, to the braying laughter of Papa Joe and Renay.

I had an actual relative who was one degree removed from *Donald Clark Osmond.*

That made *me* two degrees removed from Donald Clark Osmond.

"Maybe you can just go ahead and move to California now," Asshole offered helpfully.

"Yeah, get started, I'm sure he's got a room for ya in Topeka," Twin said stupidly.

"*Toluca!* It's near *Burbank*, dummy!" I screamed, offended.

"Your kid knows where Burbank is," Bernie Alphabet rasped to Renay in awe. "I don't even know where Burbank is."

"He studies *maps.* Ann is going places," my mother said, nodding at me proudly, and I didn't even mind that she used my private girl name in mixed company.

"Could he go now?" Asshole asked, with a wave to the door. *He's such an asshole!*

"I would love to be a joke writer," I said, ignoring Asshole, plastering a wide, showbiz party smile on my face, and turning my full attention to my important, showbiz-adjacent grandmother.

Minna struck up another Pall Mall, and I saw her considering me in her Talmudic way, really studying me in the TV glare, deciding whether I was a diamond or a zirconium.

"So why don't you have a show?" she asked.

"I'm—my show?" I stammered. "Why don't I have a—"

"Yes, idiot, a show," Asshole said, making a monkey sound and rubbing his stomach and head at the same time, Twin pathetically joining in on the monkey laugh, too.

"Why. Don't. You. Have. A show?" Minna repeated in her deepest, most ancient, thoroughly unwashed Brooklyn subway car announcer voice. Then, irritated by my brothers' atrocious manners and obvious lack of deference, she stormed over from the sofa to stand towering above where I lay on the shag, all five feet of her, her Pall Mall Gold dripping three inches of ash, her jelly glass sloshing over with the white wine she couldn't survive after five o'clock without. Her rust-red hair was streaked with white, like falling stars through the red skies of her past. Her eyes, so fierce and black as coffee, interrogated my soul, demanded to know right there, in front of my Mormon TV god, my Jewish family, and my good Christian WRAL TV-5 Raleigh, why I, her nine-year-old Fayetteville-based grandson, didn't already have a variety show in our tiny North Carolina media market.

"Donny and Marie have a show," she enunciated slowly. "So why don't you have a show?"

Bernie slapped his hands on the table, whooped in agreement. "Yeah!" he said, startling us all. "Do it! You can do it!" he shouted, I thought perhaps a touch too loudly, overcompensating no doubt for our erotically charged encounter in the guest bath.

"He could. He could have his own show," Renay said with grave seriousness, two babkas down, two to go. *She was going for it.*

"Why—why—" I stuttered up at Minna, flummoxed.

She leaned down, a stern half grin, half grimace on her thin, pressed lips. Close like this, you could see the burn scars that played across her brow and cheek, faded but not gone. Puckers of tragedy past, a map of hardship overcome, of defeat *defeated*. She was scary as shit.

"You're not like these chamoole brothers of yours. Why don't you have a show? Donny and Marie do, so why not you?" she demanded.

I couldn't tell in that moment if my grandmother was asking me, *Why don't you already have a television show, you obviously gay clown?* or if Minna Katz was telling me, *Hey, why don't you, Andy Corren, my smartest grandchild, go ahead and have a TV show? You're good!* or if Minna Klatskin Cohen Katz of Brooklyn, Miami, and, briefly one night, high over Elizabeth, New Jersey, was asking me, an impoverished Jew stranded on the ass end of a broke-butt Southern town, who had just found out what a dick was, *Hey, schmuck! Get up! Get busy! Get a show! Options!*

I knew I had options. Under Renay's tutelage, I had learned to *always* have options.

Being Renay's youngest had conferred upon me many advantages, mostly in terms of being closest to her and, therefore, closest to jokes told the first time and first servings of food, which was very helpful when the starving animals I was genetically similar to were seated at the same table. But in almost all other ways my size and age had been a distinction without a difference—and so I saw to it that there was, at least to me and Renay, *some* difference. Like her, I read. I retained. I learned. I liked maps. I liked *TV Guide* and my mother's gossip magazines and the stories behind the stories that we loved. I memorized arcana so Renay and I could talk into the night. I became a repository of useless facts, primarily show business stuff. A gossip. A friend. An indispensable, content-dispensing fiend.

I was the only one of my brothers who regularly sneaked into our mother's shiny casino clothes and semi-kitten heels, who knew who all the Warner Brothers were, all of them, literally every single one, by name (Harry, Sam, Albert, and Jack Wonskolaser). I knew what the William Morris Agency and ICM were, who Freddie Fields and Sue Mengers were. Hell, I knew who Sue Mengers *represented*. Sue is now an angel in Jewish heaven, but she briefly lived *right here* on *this* earth with us, and she was the most powerful talent agent in the world, which is really just a few small blocks of Beverly Hills and Century City. My mother and I adored Sue Mengers, her amazing floofy hair, her soft pillowy lips, the way men were both *frightened* of her and *turned on* by her, the way it seemed certain she got high and fucked all her clients. We would go on to emulate Sue Mengers our whole lives, particularly her high regard for hand-rolled joints, hot brisket, and bright, wide muumuus for all occasions.

I knew the difference between a highlighter pen and pancake foundation.

I knew how to pick Renay's hair up and out so it created the perfect silhouette for her shape.

I could tell you what was airing on what network, at what time, seven days a week.

I knew how to panhandle in a bowling alley.

I knew how to make you feel like *I* was doing *you* a favor, when *you* gave *me* money.

I knew *so many* useful things for a poor son of Fayetteville. I had a lot going for me in terms of primitive, nine-year-old intuition.

But I did not have backup dancers.

Despite all these brothers, I was the one with talent, and it was just me on this stage. And it wasn't even a very nice stage. It was just a nutshell-strewn, shag-covered platform, and there were no disco lights. Sometimes there were no lights at all.

I was alone, in a very small media market without its own TV station.

"But how?" I asked, aching for somebody, anybody, to tell me how to get out of here and get my own show greenlit in beautiful downtown Burbank.

"You're a *Litvak*, ainikle. It's never too early to start," Minna said.

"Plagen!" Joe Katz shouted from the reclining chair.

"Plagen!" Renay shouted back at him, babka-drunk now, laughing, delirious with righteous, yeasty carbs.

Then freshly combed, hot-ass Bernie Alphabet joined in, screaming "Plagen!" and pretty soon it was a Yiddish call and response, everybody batting about this nonsense word, over and over my head. "Plagen! Plagen! Plagen!"

"Work hard, suffer." Minna nodded grimly. "A brocheh, plagen zich is suffering, and suffering is a blessing." *Man, Jews are working with some fucked-up shit.*

It was at this precise moment that Joseph Katz absentmindedly reached his hand down behind the big, ripped recliner in which he was ensconced to do something he had done a thousand thousand times: lovingly stroke his beloved poodle, Licorice Katz. How many times had Twin and Asshole and I chased that dog around the house that day, playing with tennis balls and fat pink grapefruits Miami-fresh from the Katzes' front yard tree? There we were, all happily together, Bernie in his halo of glistening, gay-making sweat, sitting next to his best friend, my mother, both of them stoned as shit on the sofa with stern Minna and curious Rabbi looking on, all of us contented, bellies full of righteous, gaseous, schmaltz-infused gastronomy, all that babka and kishka Minna had spent the day whipping up now inside us, rendering us prostrate on sofa cushions, on pillows, on the floor, all of us happily gathered for primetime TV, just like a *real* family. How could we know, as Joseph Katz's calloused hands—seasoned by a lifetime of wars and labors at the tool and die tables of Marshall's Bolt & Nut Company—delicately grazed the fur of his beloved Licorice Katz, that our lives would be indelibly altered in this moment?

Every Osmond on earth—and that's a lot of Osmonds—was gathered on that disco UFO stage. I was more engrossed than usual in that glittering disco sendoff, feeling an especially blinding light of revelation bounce from the tight gold lamé butts of backup dancers, through camera lenses and satellites, beaming its gay way directly into my gay heart. It washed over me like a liquid rainbow test pattern, a complete and total *joyful* surrender to who and what *I really was*. A knowing. As top-billed guest star Olivia Newton-John warbled "You're the One That I Want," and Papa Joe leaned down to caress his beloved Licorice Katz and realized in a single devastated instant that his dog was dead, I knew—*I knew*—with Bette Davis conviction and Joan Crawford flair, that I was not just Renay's most different and special son.

I was a show business gay.

Papa Joe lurched his chair forward and slammed down the footrest with a finite bang, raised himself stiffly in the glow of Orem, Utah, a stunned look etched across his broad, deeply lined face. I saw his hands twitch. I remember staring up at him, afraid that my gayness and commitment to variety entertainment had somehow been exposed. Because it was clear Joe Katz had something to say, and it was *bad*. He stared into the middle distance, his eyes flooded with tears. I remember not just being scared of *what* Papa Joe would say, but registering that this garrulous, abundantly joyful man suddenly could not find words at all. *That* was the biggest horror.

"Minna," he said quietly. His eyes blinked slowly behind his chunky, socialist glasses.

"Minna," he moaned again.

"Joseph," Minna catcalled from her perch on the couch, painted eyebrow arched, waiting to accept whatever zinger Joseph had at the ready.

"Minna, I am sorry. Minna. Licorice Katz has died," he croaked.

The announcement of the death of Licorice Katz sliced through the thick summer night, stilling those gorgeous, clean-skinned Mormons, the Sunshine Band, muting the gold lamé shorts and the Black backup singers who were obviously flown up from Los Angeles because there were only nine thousand Black people in all of Utah in 1978. The sulfurous Fayetteville sewer night air had come swamping into our living room and choked us all in a long, stunned embrace.

Licorice Katz had died.

He followed the voice of Olivia Newton-John and her lovely, outstretched arm all the way to the sun-dappled corridors of the celestial kingdom, which is located, as it turns out, in Orem, Utah, this whole time.

Licorice Katz left me behind.

He left me alone and newly gay and newly connected to show business royalty, alone in stifling Fayetteville, with my newly awakened gay downstairs and a glassy-eyed mother stumbling onto the brink of, I was certain of it, her third entire babka.

It was the first full week of the fall TV season of 1978, and it was ending on a terrible and important note.

"Joseph? What am I hearing?" Minna Katz asked. Here was a fantastically courageous woman who had sauntered away from crashed planes, foul marriages, financial ruin, and, once, even, a fight with Barbara Walters inside Lou Walters's Miami nightclub. But Minna didn't look strong enough to fight Barbara Walters tonight. She was white as a sheet. She was pale, ancient, and extinguished by a sudden and irrevocable wave of grief.

"What are you saying, Joseph?" Her pitted, speckled hands reached for her face, and she asked the room quietly, "Has my head fallen off my body? Am I falling? Am I falling? I feel as though my head has fallen off my body, and"—pointing at the television, she cried in horror—"it's staring at me from over there. I feel faint. Am I falling? Am I falling, Joseph?"

Renay leapt into action, grabbed Minna, yanked her close. The two of them stared wide-eyed at Joe Katz, shaking their heads in tandem, a unison of denial, of shocked, pale horror.

"No!" Renay said, her lips making a fish-flopped-on-the-pier-sucking-at-air sound. "It can't be true!"

"Minna," Papa Joe said again, a long, unbearable tightness wrapped tenderly around her name. "Minna," he repeated, and as deflated as it was, there was no mistaking the truth behind that one sad word.

"Licorice has left us. Licorice is gone, Minna." Papa Joe groaned, leaning over the back of the upright chair and regarding the stiffening, inert body of Licorice on the floor. His little furry legs had already gone rigor, paws leaned against the slick faux wood of our dirty living room wall.

As we stared at that still, dark body, it was incontrovertible.

"Joseph, this cannot be. Our boy. Our baby boy is gone." My grandmother sobbed, her face in her hands.

"I am so sorry, my darling Minna. I am so, so sorry, my love."

Then Joe cried, too.

In Orem, Utah, sexy, sexy long-haired KC, from the Sunshine

Band, had stepped onto the UFO stage with Marie Osmond on one arm, both wearing white, he in a white tux looking like the hottest prom date in all history. My mind a blank, I wondered distantly how Oscar Goldman from *The Six Million Dollar Man* would look in such a nice, clean white tux. *Perfect, I bet.* I wondered, too, if I would ever go to a prom with a date as handsome as KC from the Sunshine Band, wear a white tux like that, dance like that. *Probably not.*

"Terrible," my mother was saying over and over, her red-rimmed eyes wide and angry, the look of accusation etched deeply in them that appeared when things spiraled out of Renay's control, as they always seemed to do these days. "Terrible," she said again, gathering Rabbi in her arms, all three of them quietly crying, shocked, a dead dog at our feet while KC and Marie danced on and on at the TV prom that I would never attend.

"He just up and died," Twin solemnly marveled, bravely peeking over the back of the reclining chair, his freshly shorn black hair shiny and clean, combed and parted perfectly straight. *Funeral hair,* I thought.

Rabbi loved that dog like a brother. He violently jerked Twin back from the chair to get a look at Licorice for himself, then pulled back, wrinkling his nose, dismayed. Wounded, his face grew solemn.

"Mother," Rabbi said in that endearingly formal way of his. "Licorice is dead, Mother."

"Keep back," Renay warned Rabbi and Twin, who stared at her in amazement, fear suddenly splashed on their faces. *Did she think Licorice would suddenly leap to life?*

"Mother? Nana? May I pray?" Rabbi requested solemnly.

Minna, lost to shock, too far away in her grief to hear, was encircled by her husband's strong arms and was weeping deeply, and so it fell to Renay to nod permission at her curiously observant son.

And so Rabbi, in that perfect Hebrew he retained, began intoning the Mourner's Kaddish over the stiff, elevated paws of Licorice Katz.

"Yitgadal v'yitkadash sh'mei b'alma di v'ra chir'utei," Rabbi intoned, davening like a pro.

"It's not right, it's not right," Minna said, her tiny, scarred fist balled up and pounding the air, shaking her head against Joe's broad chest. "This is too much. Hashem asks too much."

God asks a lot. Always has. Always will. It's what *God does.*

"Minna," Papa Joe said quietly. I think this was all that he could say.

"Joseph," she whispered back. "Haven't we given enough?"

As if he were returned to us from his long and strange exile of living in a camper in Shithead's Pine Bluff driveway for just this very reason, this act of grace, Rabbi cantored quietly, gravely, "May there be abundant peace from heaven, and a good life for us and for all Israel, and say amen." Rabbi closed his eyes, concentrating, *remembering.* "He who makes peace in His heavens, may He make peace for us and for all Israel, and say amen." He had pitched it with just the right amount of singsong Jewish dignity and enough volume to be heard above the TV, which had continued playing quietly throughout the entire discovery and subsequent shock of finding Licorice Katz dead. In the background I could hear Donny and Marie crooning the end of "May Tomorrow Be a Perfect Day," their Friday night goodbye song, just the way they always did:

May God keep you in his tender care
'Til he brings us together again

And then those two beautiful, gifted goyishe superstars beamed their wide, expensive smiles out to Raleigh, then to the much-smaller media market of Fayetteville, and said as they did every single Friday night, *to me,* "Goodnight, everybody!"

"Goodnight, Licorice," Minna whispered. "Goodbye, my darling."

Minna Katz then did the most Minna Katz thing imaginable.

She ran her scarred, bejeweled fingers through the well-earned stripes of silver that shot through her fading red hair, dabbed her eyes dry, and fixed her shoulders back *like a true star does.* Blowing air from her mouth as though she were about to swim a triathlon, Minna turned to her husband Joe and said, "We'll leave in the morning, Joseph. You know what to do."

"Yes, Minna," Joe Katz agreed. "I'll get the cooler."

So it was that in the wee hours of a dewy late-September morning, a mere day after arriving from Miami and cooking nonstop in a greasy, shag-carpeted kitchen; sweeping up nut shells and hair; leaving behind groomed grandchildren, freezer shelves packed with chicken soups, trays of noodle kugels, sheets of frozen latkes, hundreds of hand-stuffed holiday kishkes, and a thousand perfectly round cabbage rolls; and swabbing a monstrous pigsty of a redneck home that had descended into reefer madness, Minna and Joe Katz turned around and took their leave. Minna embraced her chosen daughter Renay and then she perfunctorily rended the garment of her hand-sewn house culottes, wordlessly telling Renay in this short, savage rip of an ancient gesture, that her son, our father, was now as dead to her as Licorice Katz was, and it would stay that way until the end of time.

Renay nodded, understanding. "Thank you, Mama. *Thank you.*"

With one rip of her culottes over her dead dog's body, Minna *chose.*

Her choice was Renay.

Her choice was all of us ferkockteh meshuga kids that she loved so goddamned much she couldn't stand it.

Her choice was to never see or speak to her only son again.

She chose us.

The Katzes reloaded their Cutlass with all their recently unpacked belongings—two weeks' worth of clothes, all of Minna's cooking supplies, her meat grinder, her unused cow intestines for holiday kishke, a trunk full of cartons of Pall Mall Gold 100s, a crate of Cheerwine. Stray oranges.

Strapped snugly into the back seat a Styrofoam cooler sat upright.

It was packed with ice, fresh pine needles, and the cold, dead body of Licorice Katz.

6.

Licorice Katz was buried early Sunday morning, the twenty-fourth of September 1978.

It was 22 Elul 5738 on the Jewish calendar, the week before Rosh Hashanah, as Licorice was laid to rest in the warm, carefully turned soils of the organic garden of Minna Katz on Southwest 21st Terrace in Miami. In keeping with her strong Jewish faith, Minna Katz repatriated Licorice to the naked earth within three days, bathed fresh, wrapped in a simple sheet. The words were said, and her and Joe's spirit child was set free beneath Minna's precocious avocado tree, a fertile and productive wonder raised from a single Israeli Nabal seed Minna had illegally spirited home from her first trip to the Promised Land. There Licorice would stay and roam, to nibble on the avocados and the grapefruits, the tomatoes and oregano, to frolic among the cucumbers and the squash, chase the oranges and the figs that he loved, endowing the mulch that Minna and Joe so tirelessly turned and turned, for the rest of their long and natural lives.

Five days later in an Arkansas courtroom, on September 29, 1978, Renay and Shithead Corren's divorce was finally decreed. The marriage was done.

Indignities, they called it back then. The reason for the divorce. The one he had to give.

Indignities.

7.

I never did get Uncle Gig's address.

MY BEHIND

We are bobbing like dirty lake lures on Renay's heated, queen-sized waterbed.

Dressed in the same clothes we had worn the previous day, we are both stained ink-black from shoveling newspapers out the car window, three o'clock till sunup. It has been not quite three years since Renay and Shithead's divorce, and we have moved twice already, already always just a step ahead of the next eviction.

She is good at math, solid at cards, fantastic at fingernails. *Really* bad at bills.

Ever since that judge set my mother free, Renay has scratched after pretty much any old dirt job that didn't require a background check or much more than a strong back. Her back. Sometimes ours, too. Renay never hesitates to bring me and Twin and Asshole to work, bundling us up with several dozen stacks of the *Fayetteville Observer-Times* in the rear of the rusted Nova. Asshole joins us less and less, as, at fifteen, he has finally found his footing among the greasy jet set of Fayetteville's lower depths, running with ducktailed dirtbags in souped-up Camaros and spoiled Cadillacs all up and down Yadkin Road, stealing cigarettes from bar machines, raising hell with his friend Dicky, and drinking stolen beer from Bev's Place, Dicky's mom's famously seedy tavern down on Bragg. Twin is tall, a handsome thirteen, fully absorbed in many sports, quietly tempted—as all military town teens are—by the approaching seductive blare of the bugler, since ROTC, and all those practice rifles spinning in the air over Westover's track fields, command a lot of attention in our circle.

Twenty-year-old Rabbi has ditched us for his own shack, up near Bonnie Doone, which is a neighborhood, not a girl. If she was a girl, you'd dump Bonnie Doone. Bonnie Doone is so poor and raggedy, it makes the rest of Fayetteville seem like Greenwich Village. Rabbi is slinging speed at night at the Town Pump and driving daytime hookers in a cab financed by a Baptist deacon named Brown. Rabbi is trying to eke out a GED and trade certificate from the Harvard of Cumberland County, Fayetteville Tech, itching to land a job in far-off Fuquay-Varina, at the shiny new, hardly leaking nuclear power plant towering like a Japanese fish monster over Raleigh. Cathy Sue, now a wise and seasoned twenty-four, is divorcing her first husband, Benny, and clocking in on marriage number 2, a guy who promises to take her all the way out to the mythical, sleepy island nation of the Outer Banks, where an empire of sewage, tourism, and cement bridges is slowly rising out of the hot coastal forests and low sucking sands.

If you asked me where my oldest brother was at this time, I would not have had the first clue. At this point, I knew I had an oldest brother. I knew he lived far, far away from us, in Chicago. I knew my oldest brother had joined the Navy, which was an entirely weird thing to do in an Army family like ours. I knew that if you had said my oldest brother's name out loud—Bonus—it was like saying "Bloody Mary" three times quick, and the room got dark, and the vibe got killed. Ass-hole, Twin, Rabbi, my mother, my sister—they didn't seem to think

Chicago was far enough away. I'd only visited him once, six years ago, after a disastrous trial run of his living with us, when I was about six. I stood in the darkened lobby of a Gothic asylum deep in the woods of Southern Pines where he had been banished yet again, waving goodbye to a terrifying and handsome young man my mother told me was my brother.

If you've never visited a brother for the very first time at a golf resort–adjacent asylum at midnight, let me tell you I do not recommend it, but to make it extra Gothic: take the train.

We did.

Bonus was farther away and more unknown than ever, and that's the way my family seemed to prefer it. He had his own family now; we had ours. There was no overlap between the two. It was an estrangement that merely *was*.

What *is*: is Renay.

My whole world is this insanely funny, beautiful, fat, wickedly hilarious, locally beloved, always exhausted, and ravenously hungry-for-stimulation mother of mine. I must feed, entertain, and comfort. I must protect the queen-sized, heated waterbed universe that I am lucky enough to occupy alongside her. It is books. It is farts. It is gallows laughs.

She is never off work, so I am always on the clock alongside her.

This is what she made me for.

I am Renay's biggest fan, like so many, many others, but I am also her private chef, her on-demand baker, her food taster, book valet, loyal lieutenant, best friend on call, medic, personal shopper, housekeeper. I am her Employee of the Month, and I go where the Big Boss tells me to go. Renay heads out every Friday and Saturday night after work at the B&B Lanes to deliver the newspaper. This is our regular after-hours routine, how Renay catches some gas money, maybe enough cash to stop a utility from being shut off again, or for a Wendy's run on Sunday for a rare Frosty dinner treat. Maybe enough to stake a game of hearts at B&B, or slide some discount meat and some macadamia past the PX cashier. She empties and refills yellow boxes all over town while me and Twin, and sometimes Asshole, ride along. Renay at the wheel, one in the bucket with her, two in the back, bagging and tossing papers all night long onto the lawns of the Fayetteville elite.

We finished dropping off newspapers around four a.m., hit Shoney's to pile up our plates at the all-you-can-eat breakfast buffet, and then wended our way back home to Roach House—the weeping-brick ranch we'd washed up in on Brainerd two houses after Pamalee Drive finally, inevitably, slipped through Renay's shapely hands. Twin zombie-walked straight to his bed in the room we shared, but Renay and I had posted ourselves up on her warm waterbed, as was our habit. Hers are, of course, the finest accommodations Roach House has to offer: not only the biggest room, but also the only one without water stains blooming on the ceiling or namesake bugs in the corners. I had been dreaming I was fishing with her on Eastover Lake, a pretty regular thing, and a pretty regular dream, understandable when you sail the dawn seas on a warm waterbed next to your mom. Our boat was leaky, however, and Eastover strangely storm-tossed for such a quiet, albeit notably haunted, lake. I awaken to one of Renay's fat toes poking through the holes of Nana Minna's scratchy old afghan, the radio softly drilling "Bette Davis Eyes" into my fuzzy brain. I feel her stirring next to me, rising from her own state of semi-rest, demi-slumber, the half-lidded trance that passed for Renay's dreams.

She never really slept. She only paused.

Her hands would arise before her eyes, floating naturally back into the same position they'd held before she had dropped off: reading her book with one eye on the muted TV, casually plucking at a raised eyebrow, sipping a Pepsi, fiddling with some Pringles chips. One minute, she was dead to the world, and the next she had five things going at once. Press Play.

Renay's eyes are red, her flaming red hair dented on one side, on two front teeth a ruby comet's tail of last night's lipstick still glow. Maybe an hour or two of sleep happened on this woman, or maybe it didn't; it mattered little to her. If she caught a wink, it was a win. Now this overturned carriage of motherhood and mayhem sprawled before me gets back to her books, her brows, her business. The exfoliated, shining skin on her plump face *glows*, and Renay's buffed nails *sparkle* like cold, waxed-up grapes fresh from Kroger, and she still manages to seem *resplendent* to me, even after three long, dirty shifts that stretched from noon yesterday to now, from manning an oily gas kiosk at the Sunoco by day to pounding leagues and pins at the B&B by night, to the sunrise news boxes on Hay that we've only just finished filling with yesterday's bad news.

This Sunday morning, the final hot Sunday of May, there are two matters foremost on my mind, creeping like those water stains down from the Roach House ceiling. I cannot escape this terrible feeling deep in my soul. This *certainty*. This *knowing*.

I would be underdressed for an awards show.

Recently it was announced at school, much to my shame, that I am to collect a poetry prize—not a school-wide prize, mind you, but *county-wide*. The prize is considerable, fifty dollars, and that part is *fucking great*. Fifty dollars is a ton of money, the Corren family equivalent of striking *gold*. My poem, hastily composed during an arts assembly with a prestigious visiting poet from esteemed Chapel Hill, had been scribbled with the express intent of making my mother laugh until she farted, which, as everybody knows, is the best kind of laugh. Called "My Behind," it was littered with in-jokes about distant fathers, cold butts, a functioning toilet seat. It was so stupid, I knew it would make Renay guffaw-fart. And lo and behold, I won a contest for it. But the Fayetteville Arts Council seems determined to deepen my shame by placing my stupid butt poem onto every bus in Fayetteville. My butt poem, just circling and circling around Fayetteville on the side of all nine buses. With my name attached to it for all to see.

And I have not a thing to wear to the Arts Council awards.

All my clothes are rags or hand-me-downs. I don't own a stitch of couture. Not one Valentino. No Balmain. Not even a fucking Wrangler. Nothing you'd want to wear in front of a prestigious Chapel Hill lady poet *who smoked a corn cob pipe.*

"I need *jeans,*" I moan somberly to my mother's ceiling. "I need some *Jordache* jeans."

When I thought about simply holding a pair of freshly ironed Jordache jeans in my ink-stained hands—not the ratty, label-less hand-me-downs from Asshole and Twin that I begrudgingly wore—actual, new-smelling, stiff Jordache jeans directly off the rack, I physically ached with longing.

Renay thumb-cracks a crisp page with a practiced flick of her reading wrist, ignoring me while juggling the hardback copy of Judith Krantz's *Princess Daisy* and her eyebrow-plucking mirror.

"Uh-huh," she says in her noncommittal and unhelpful parenting mode.

Published the year before, *Princess Daisy,* a thick, juicy, semi-incestuous saga, is still seducing women and closeted pastors from every newsstand and Winn-Dixie in town, and Renay has finally, triumphantly, carried it home from Tyler's half-off. But instead of plowing through it in a single night as she ordinarily would, Renay has lingered over this book for an entire intolerable weekend. Two whole days. For one book!

And so I do my best to become part of the experience of reading it with her, gazing at the clearly postcoital blonde on the jacket, who coquettishly peers over her shoulder at me while clutching an expensive, diaphanous sheet. I slow my own breathing to match Renay's as she thumb-cracks another page, and soon it is as though I was reading alongside her, inhaling every word, exhaling every scandalous twist and turn until our heartbeats become one and we are joined, a depraved metronome of book-inhaling trash and lust and sin, all of it flying off the page as we cram those creamy, delicious scenes into our mouths like rich, buttery scones. She and I have never had a scone, but it matters little, as we are suddenly skiing down the Alps together, and then the slopes of Biarritz together, places we have never been and will never go, but navigate now with insouciant ease, and then we are chauffeured off the base of this powdery mountain, soon skimming the brisk waters along the Monterey Bay coastline, laughing beneath the Santa Cruz lighthouse on a three-masted sailboat of a type we will never board, and have never even seen, but there we are anyway, sailing, skiing, *schussing* together, rich-as-shit best friends dripping in fur, loving every buttery second.

From my earliest days, I read what she read, as soon as she put it down. We had an ongoing book club that began when she opened her eyes, still smudged with purple or scarlet shadow, and ended when she was finally released by her kidnapper, insomnia. We read every moment we could. In addition to Judith Krantz, we were ardent admirers of the great Jackie Collins, Sidney Sheldon, and of course the Edith Wharton of incest, Miss Cleo Virginia "V. C." Andrews. We just loved to curl up with those Dollanganger siblings, a family that was, at a minimum, eleven or twelve thousand times more fucked-up than our own—and they had money and doughnuts!

At twelve, I read as fast as Renay, and as wolfishly, indiscriminately.

So I am of course desperate to pry the flashy, filthy new Judith Krantz out of her sharp, perfectly filed claws. Renay *knows* how much I love Judith Krantz, and she *lords* that racy tome above me in a ritual of withholding and ostentatious slow page-turning by indolent thumb-flick, thumb-flick, thumb-flick.

A real Krantz bitch-heroine thing to do, if you ask me.

Renay, like me, has been waiting a long time to have this new, exciting Krantz in her mitts, and after such a lustful and suspenseful wait she isn't about to waste the special effect of being *seen* carrying it around. To be *seen* with Judith, may her name forever be a blessing, to be seen with Judith in hardback—well, you must be some kind of classy, in-the-know Fayetteville society lady from up in Haymount, probably, and you are just lost or stumbled your way behind that counter at B&B Lanes by accident. You are danged right Renay took her time being seen with all that. *Princess Daisy* was *power*.

Renay could read anywhere. At work. At home. The toilet, obviously. But less obviously, and of course *dangerously*: in her car at any length of stoplight, out delivering newspapers, at the Sunoco, pier fishing, at the casino, at the Shoney's, watching TV, standing in front of a microwave, seated anywhere, because that woman loved nothing more than a good, long sit. My fondest memories of childhood are of dozing like a curled shrimp against my mother's big butt, my toes wrapped inside her massive, gnarled troll's feet while she *flick-flick-flicked* her way through a book a day. A *Pietà* of mother and son, afloat on trashy worlds, heated beds, and sultry words fashioned by wealthy women ensconced in far-off, cultured Beverly Hills.

We made monthly pilgrimages to *our* cathedral, that corrugated palace of pulp on the Champs-Élysées of Fayetteville, Yadkin Road: Edward McKay's Used Books. There we would sell off Renay's discards—usually, thirty or more books—and load up our wrinkled grocery bags full of other people's cast-offs, one bag for Renay, one bag for me, books we paid for by the pound, not the title, and which we would then spend the next month haggling over. "I'll trade you my copy of *Cujo* if you give me your copy of *Bloodline*" is usually how this great game unfolded, before we descended into bitter recriminations over who *really* had the temperament for Tom Wolfe and who didn't, and inevitably an unseemly screaming match over the single prized copy of the magnificent Shelley Winters biography *Shelley: Also Known as Shirley.*

Renay is humming and plowing her way through the final three chapters of the new Krantz and she seems…happy? It is, after all, not *her* name that is going to be appearing on buses all summer next to a poem called "My Behind." *She* isn't the one begging for a pair of fresh Jordache jeans. She kicks me a little with her stuck-in-the-afghan foot, wiggling a pungent toe that still steams of sweaty bowling alley sock, urgently whispering, "Ann, rub my feet. Please, my feet hurt *so bad*."

Now I am definitely awake.

If my mother's hands are the beautiful people at the Biarritz ball, Renay's feet are the flowers in the attic. It isn't just that they are extra-extra wide, 10EEEE; it is because, between her job at B&B and managing the Sunoco, Renay stands on those planks more than sixteen hours a day, six or seven days a week. She is *that* person, doing the jobs that you have to stand for, that big lady doing that thing for you that you could never do, at that store you always go to, that lady who always makes you laugh. That lady made *these* feet, and they are treated as harshly as the bed of an old pickup. They are wider than they should be, calloused, her ankles strafed with deep, inflamed depressions from the straps of her shoes.

I get to work on massaging them—and am promptly rewarded with an enormous fart, rolled languidly upon my head. From my own mother, and with no warning at all. Renay's farts were freely given, a benefaction unto all, always generously dispensed with her jovial wave. Hers were happy farts, and one dared not recoil. Renay's bleats were the beefy, thunderous variety, delivered upon cloudy blats of sound and fury typically only found in certain roomy, Ashkenazic women of the diaspora with those fashionably bulletproof bowels lined with decades of schmaltz.

"You will pay for this," I whisper, glaring a low curse up at her.

"*There.* Yes!" she yelps. "On the knuckle. *On it!* Press *harder.*"

I bear down, but I am just a weakling, the runt of Renay's brood. Even my farts are tiny peeps. Her big toe is swollen beyond recognition. The help it requires is far outside the reach of my meager, albeit celebrated, massage skills. Yet just when it seems like I will have to give up, I manage to wedge one of my boiled chicken bone-weak fingers deep into Renay's toe, and she sort of seizes, then kicks her head back against the waterbed frame, moaning in *Princess Daisy* levels of surrender and ecstasy, like she is thrashing in a Park Avenue penthouse, not on a ripped corduroy husband pillow half off from Kmart.

I get it.

I was a boy who called his father Shithead and massaged his mother's toes.

I have cross-referenced all of these acts with my appropriately pricey but still wrong side of Union Square–adjacent therapist. Sam has helped me to understand that I was *not* in love with my mother, nor was I merely doing her bidding. I was acting *responsibly*, responding as a child would, to a dire need for maternal survival, doing it as urgently and as often as required, as I was taught to do from my very first minutes on this earth, when I was pincered from Renay's womb and was not seen or touched by her again for the next two weeks, as she recovered from twin shocks of the neck-to-butt gutting Cesarean and the disappointment of another boy child. As Sam has explained, my own future happiness—my own survival—was *highly* contingent upon Renay's, so much so that my own dreams and my own sense of self, pleasure, or intimacy was practically nonexistent in the face of hers. Sam has reassured me that during episodes like this, I was just getting the tension out of my mother's toe knuckle.

Because that made me feel better, too.

A potent cocktail of servitude and congenital desire to please the woman who had nearly died bringing me into the world and never let me forget it. Not once. Not ever.

Our massage sessions were therapeutic for *both* of us. Renay had a high threshold for pain, and I could use that as an outlet for expressing my rage. I would beat those garbage digits of hers *down*, making Renay's toes the repository for all my emotional manifesting, our poverty, our used paperback books, the loss of our house on Pamalee Drive, the fact that we all called this place Roach House, *and it wasn't ironic.*

"I am not going in front of Chapel Hill's most important living poet wearing Asshole's old jeans. It ain't happening," I say, bartering with two swollen toes smashed flat between my palms.

"Harder! Dig!" she shrieks into the calm of our Sunday morning, waking the roaches, but not my brothers.

"You're coming tomorrow night," I say, slapping at her ankle. It isn't a question.

"I *know*," Renay says, affecting an unconvincing offense that I would suggest otherwise. But I know better. My mother is not the *plan ahead* type.

"You forgot. It's fine. I'm reminding you." I sulk.

"Would I forget my little *poet*?" Renay's mocking tone is appropriate for a poor poet who has written a terrible nine lines about a butt and a toilet, so I take no offense.

"It would be very *poetic* of you to forget your little poet," I mock back, triumphantly.

"Forgetting that my distinguished poet child won a poetry award? That would *not* be poetic, son. That would be *ironic*," she corrects me— I would add, *vindictively*. But she speaks often in such a key when any of our accomplishments threaten to outshine or upstage her aggravation.

"Ow!" she yelps as I stab maniacally at her prematurely old-lady toe, the one that looks most like Popeye in repose, shoving the sharp end of a blue curling brush deep into what I now can only assume was her liver meridian.

"That! There! The fascia! Do it, Jewboy! *Do the fascia!!*" she screams.

As if I know what a goddamned *fascia* was.

2.

As I lie there Sunday morning, drifting alongside my mother on her heated waterbed, surfing small waves she makes with every tiny disturbance for refreshment or a thumb-flick-flick, as I watch my mother ravish those final chapters of *Princess Daisy*, I replay in my mind our entire previous night, which was a three-act play far livelier than anything Neil Simon could ever write, because Neil Simon never wrote about bowling in Fayetteville, my mother's feet, or the ladies of the night down on Hay.

3.

If it was Saturday night in Fayetteville, then Renay Corren was coming off a double, which meant it was most likely a *triple shift* kind of a night, and Twin and I were going along for the ride. She needed us to keep her up, to keep her company, and to keep those papers flying.

So we went.

Sunoco shifts—any gas kiosk shift—are monotonous, plodding, the same sounds, fumes, questions, transactions, over and over for eight hours under bad lights, on bad feet, with bad ventilation. You want to talk hard gigs? Go sit inside a gas station kiosk without air conditioning in May, or with only a portable heater for your feet in December. Try making *that* job fun.

Renay made it fun.

All day Saturday we'd sit in that kiosk entertaining each other, watching TV on the tiny black-and-white screen, making the customers who never stopped rolling through laugh and laugh. The Eutaw mall was long, colonial, and spread out in two big pavilions, its most notable feature plentiful parking. It looked a little bit like a tired, colonial-era marketplace, except after the French had sacked it good.

We stood together in there trading jokes with customers, as well as sports scores, credit cards, cash. She sent me back and forth to Morris Cohen for sandwiches, Tyler's to pick up her "adult" magazines, to the store for a Pepsi. Honest to God it was *fun*, and it was over before you knew it, because you laughed with Renay the entire day. She always had something to say, an observation about that day's news or yesterday's scandal. I hated leaving that kiosk, her stage, her hours-long standup set. It was a fume-filled confessional, and Renay was the high priestess. But a second shift always beckoned.

Renay would roll into B&B Lanes from Sunoco by five o'clock. She would swiftly take command of the front desk, which floated in the center of the bowling alley like the battle bridge of the *Enterprise*, greeting one and all as they entered through the glass lobby and passed her royal personage on their way to fun. She couldn't be ignored, her red hair a shining beacon, her welcoming laugh a booming foghorn. And that hair said *Obey the Big Red Lady behind that microphone, or you will not bowl this Saturday eve.* She counted out her cash drawer, pulled the first sweet draw of her many fountain Pepsis, and banished Twin to a faraway lane or, much worse to a teen, to the nursery to watch TV with Big Wanda or Red Mona, the brassy Germans who guarded all the B&B babies, two steely Krauts who didn't give a Salzburg shit how pretty Twin was, they weren't watching Putt-Putt or Mid-Atlantic Wrestling, it was *Kung Fu* and *Hee Haw* as far as the night would take them. I was at my usual station behind the battle bridge, kneeling below my mother at her feet. I was on shoes.

I was always at her feet.

She would send down an endless procession of funky bowling shoes reeking of sock and sweat, which I was in charge of spraying with disinfectant, retying, and organizing. We would do this all night, a conveyor belt of used and fresh, then fresh and used, two pairs for a dollar. From my floor perch I could marvel up at her, so suave, so confidently running the whole packed bowling alley, leaning over her microphone with unquestionable authority and jovially singing out like a Mardi Gras parade barker in a voice you want to follow deep, deep into Bourbon Street, so full of scratch and singsong, "Ball on 6! Ball on 12! Reset 8! Ball on 12! Hayes, your lane is ready! Gordon, your lane is ready! Pickup 12! Thomas, *ball on 12! I said ball on 12! Thomas, where the hell are you? BALL ON 12!*"

We would be like that all night, me listening to her seven-plus hours of monologue as it dipped and weaved in between taking money out of outstretched palms, taking names for the waiting list, taking sip after sip of Pepsi. Open bowling was always packed, with a line out the door all the way to Bragg Boulevard, to the Flaming Mug across the street. The candied, kaleidoscopic carpets of B&B would be teeming with packs of horny high schoolers out on dates, raucous birthday parties, soldiers with their new wives, soldiers with their new mistresses—they were all there to forget their troubles, their deployments: *to bowl.* They were there to hear my mother's latest dirty jokes, to bet on tomorrow's Steelers or Dolphins game, captivated by Renay's siren song of ball and return, ball and return, which seduced them into staying longer and longer, and paying more and more. After ten o'clock the lights dimmed and the pink and yellow glow-in-the-dark midnight pins dropped into the racks, sometimes just the single red pin, that lucky, astonishing one falling on a random lane, and there would be screams of joy when the next ball was a strike, or the red one went down for cash or prizes. Sometimes there was disco, sometimes just white people rock: ELO. Judas Priest. Grand Funk Railroad. Renay's best friend Doreen would fly in and out of the one-way mirrored door of the B&B bar, the Groove, pitchers of beer and trays of fried food raised high above her as her blond sausage curls jiggled and twirled. Doreen easily navigated the mob of bowlers, moving like a ballerina through the thick layer of ever-present smoke that swirled above us all like a stalled hurricane. I stayed below as my mother above completed her transformation to Rosie. Renay was always Rosie at the B&B, or Rose, or the rose-covered, rose-smelling, thorny, horny Red—and Rosie led from above, never moving; we did not move all night, either of us, not until that last red pin fell before Rosie, that last empty pitcher was piled onto Doreen's tray, the last cigarette got crushed, the last tidbit of gossip floated out of the Groove and filtered up to us by way of Fayetteville's very own Voltaire, Don, who everybody called Butt Check.

Eight hours. Second shift.

No breaks.

Then B&B was *closed.*

Rosie would take her cash bag and her Pepsi to the ratty back office that hadn't been painted since Howard and Dave opened the joint in August 1959. She sat for the first time in twelve hours, and we sat with her. We kept her awake and laughing as Rosie smoked and tallied up the cash bag, and her mop-up crew bussed and hosed down the whole front and back of house from snack bar to the Groove, lanes to arcade, slopping out the sloshed beers, the ashes, the drips of nacho cheese and ketchup smears, the lipstick-stained napkins and mascara-stained towels. An hour passed. Then a table and chairs were dragged close to the front desk, the battle bridge. An altar was constructed.

The Church of Hearts was in session, Her Excellency, Right Reverend Rosie, dealing.

Rosie and Pig, Porky and Gator, Mucket, Doreen, Butt Check—anybody awake or lingering on the street with a nickname, anybody willing and walking with some extra cash in the pocket, is invited. It was time to play.

And for the next two hours, *Rosie played*.

This was my mother's religion. Midnight hearts and after-hours spades, a little rummy, a little 21, a lot of cribbage, filthy jokes, shit talk, bets, and bluffs. I'd sleep under a table or in the nursery beneath a crib opposite Twin, both of us hiding from Big Wanda and Red Mona, finding the only darkness to be found in a bowling alley full of lights and machines. I would wake up disoriented, staring at the coils of a pee-stained mattress pressing down above me or, if I'd passed out beneath my customary end lane scoring table, up at the wads of hard gum stiffening under a scoring sheet, stray cigarette butts smashed accordion on top. I was always confused waking up to the sounds of cards in the darkened B&B as an abandoned feeling washed over me— *Did she forget me this time? Is this it? Do I live here now?*—and then I would hear her joy sound, her cards belly laugh, my mother at the table. Rosie was *winning*. I heard the flat, flapping *SNAP* of the cards hitting the table like gunshots in the night, momentarily overtaking the eerie electronic *bleep*s and *splork*s that came at me from all corners, the humbled arcade games standing midnight sentry to Renay's sacred after-hours communion. The lanes were hers, gleaming in their night-time glow, slick and glassy, every red-crowned pin stood at attention, every sweeper sentinel down and at guard, every ball polished, counted, and stacked.

Twin was awake now, too, and Rosie casually tossed us a roll of quarters from the cash bag in front of her, something I knew every child in every nation dreamed of, but the bowling alley child dreamed of most of all. Then she handed me the big metal ring of B&B keys that unlocked every one of the candy machines, an astonishing codex to be entrusted with, a massive responsibility, an incredibly dumb thing to give two sugar addicts. But that's what she did, every Saturday night, and Twin and I would descend into a lunatic, ritualistic madness of sugar and chocolate, *gorging* ourselves, devouring all the Whatchama-callit, Bottle Caps, Good & Plenty, Twix, Fun Dip, and M&M's that we could fit into our slobbering, sleepy, murderously sweet mouths.

There were *no limits* and *no rules* except "Stay the fuck out of Mommy's red hair."

Me and Twin jumped on Galaxian, played until our eyes bled or until we were bored enough to switch to Asteroids Deluxe, both of us high as kites on SweeTarts, the original ones, so sour and vile our tongues and bottom lips bloomed instantaneously with canker sores. We played into the dark of night, our eyes shot through with red streaks, our mouths stained by Fireballs as we drooled over a pinball machine, whacking at metallic flippers like wild horses bucking trails, while we talked shit to each other and violently tilted the console like we had not a care—because we did not, because we were *Renay's sons*, we were *young*, wild and high as fuck on fructose, and everything was free and we had unlimited quarters and the keys to the whole mother-fucking midnight kingdom. We would *always* be in this bowling alley with our laughing, gambling mother, who was finally, at long, mercifully last, thank you Lord, *sitting*.

Mucket, Butt Check, and Porky were pissed. None of them wanted to quit, they could've gone all night, and they usually did, but Rosie's got to get to her *Fayetteville Observer* drop-off spot to fill up the Nova with papers and deliver them to all the people who needed yesterday's bad news today.

Soon, me and Twin were alternating throws, him from the front seat, me from the back, chucking the bagged Fayetteville news out of rolled-down windows. First, we covered our own neighborhood, where we lived with all the poors of Ramsey Street in the shadow of bread, milk, and chemical factories, families like ours who couldn't really afford cable but couldn't *not* afford the *Observer*, because how else would we know if one of our own had been arrested? This side of town was sprinkled with dilapidated, single-story ranch houses that slipped and sighed in front of patchy dirt yards, some of those shacks daring you to call them a double wide. We crossed an invisible dividing line known only to taxpayers, and suddenly we were throwing papers onto the deluxe estates of Haymount, soaring homes raised of privilege and stone, all of them with shingles, homes so big and clean, my aim grew automatically true, my arm knowing it was *an honor* to drop the paper squarely on such stately lawns. Those Haymount places looked like mansions to me and Twin, mansions for fancy Fayetteville people who did not bowl, who did not do time in county, who did not steal electricity or food or have to burn old bowling pins for firewood in the dark of winter or share a bedroom with strippers in the spring. On those early Sunday mornings, in those third-shift hours along the manicured lawns of Haymount, I had to blink away jealous tears as I imagined all the fancy children of all the fancy people, bellies full of packaged lunch meats and bespoke cereals, sleeping in their nice houses with good sheets from the Thalhimers. No bugs on the wall.

Central air conditioning turned up high.

I stared longingly at a passing house with a cupola, wondered what it would be like to live in a house with a *cupola*. I didn't even know it was *called* a cupola. I didn't even know what a cupola *was*, or why I *wanted* one, and that was enraging to me, that those people had something like that on their house. I read Judith Krantz, for God's sake, *I should know what a cupola is!*

Not five blocks away we were downtown. In another world. The infamous 500 block of Hay Street. Renay's Jerusalem. Old Fayetteville's very own, very dirty, Down South Old Times Square.

Her eyes *lit* up. Renay was suddenly alert, alive, *and in the wild.*

This is what *she* was made for.

Hay Street was her place, an electric night district that revolved around fights, pussy, and drugs, usually in that order. Renay loved it all, the blood and the guts, life and death on every corner. Her gambler's heart and her pulp eye aligned together in a conjunction of funk. They *twitched*.

Her place was a world that revolved entirely around women.

Women from half a dozen South Asian nations stood outlined in every shadowy doorway on both sides of Hay Street, reeling in rowdy soldiers, flirting with all the cops and the MPs from Bragg, and even the broke farm boys, too, but only the ones riding by on their polished hogs or shined-up pickups with a clear few extra dollars to burn. Everybody on Hay was cruising for a deal, or dope, or a dick down. If you are out on Hay on a Saturday night, you are out to get fucked or get fucked up, no two ways about it. It was a neon crossroads of midnight peddlers and twilight fixers, of pimps in the shadows and hustlers in the low lights, dealers dealing, workers working, soldiers spending every last dollar in their wallet.

"Look at 'em. Butts, scutts, mutts, and sluts." Renay nodded approvingly, dropping the car to a crawl as we cruised past the sinister-looking Town Pump, which would soon figure prominently in one of Rabbi's upcoming downfalls, and the legendary Rick's Lounge, where it is rumored Brooke Shields once took a turn on the pole, and there goes the delightful Sassy Lady, a modest bôite by compare, where ladies wore pasties, but not much else. There was Kings Den and the Nite-Cap, the Seven Dwarfs and the High Top, Oasis and the fiery, perfervid awning of the Foxfire Lounge, a glorious, red-hot hole of redneck desire.

Those bars on that one block of this shit-ass town were the talk of the whole danged world. And for a reason.

"That boy done got his boots stole o'clock," Twin said, hanging wide out the Nova passenger window, as he pointed to a soldier in parachute pants stumbling down Hay in his socks, screaming into the night air about his stolen jump boots.

First rule of Hay: jump boys get jumped first.

He'll spend most of his Sunday afternoon limping hungover and shoeless into and out of every pawn shop on Yadkin Road looking to buy back his stolen jump boots that some pimp hocked for cash. Yadkin Road is pretty much only pawn shops, so that's a full day's work for a flyboy.

"Shoulda wrote a poem about *that*, Joyce," Twin mocked me, with the one and only poet he and I both knew from school, Mrs. Joyce Kilmer, who once wrote a long, boring poem about a tree.

"I don't write for the *common man*," I clapped back, but without malice. No need to escalate with Twin. He was not worthy of my wit.

I dreaded the coming waves of attention for my silly butt poem, bound as it was for the buses of downtown Fayetteville, but I was quietly, even poetically, enchanted at the notion that I, Andy Corren, locally sourced butt poet, would soon be published in the very paper that Twin was pitching into bright-yellow boxes in front of all the enterprising whores and thieves of bustling Hay Street.

Now that's poetry!

"I think that I shall never see, a poem as lovely as your stupid Jew-boy face," Twin drawled, darting out of our rolling Nova like a little Dan Marino, feinting and weaving this way and that to the next canary-yellow *Fayetteville Observer* box, then the next, replacing today's terrible news with tomorrow's terrible news, all the while dodging the demimonde of downtown Fayetteville Saturday night.

We worked our way down Hay past the festive Pop-A-Top, the sinister and frequently shuttered Bunny Club, the curiously dim Moonlight. Occasionally, when we were pulled up to one of the news boxes, Renay got offered a bag of seedy shake or a small block of cheap black tar, but she would demur with a knowing look thrown back at me, her watchful, back-seat narc. She yelped over the wheel when she saw the Korean Lounge had been busted again and the Vietnam Spa was somehow reopened. We loved spying on the soldiers who leaned drunkenly in neon-dusted doorways, and we loved spotting the teeny, shiny stars or glittery flags glued to the waitresses' nips, sparkly miniskirts hiked higher for tips. "Nips for tips," my mother softly repeated behind the wheel, an incantation, a prayer. "Nips for tips," she said again.

The women were always warm to me, painted eyebrows dancing high and delighted when I, this hungry-looking, ratty Lord Fauntleroy varmint, came prancing by them with newspapers shoved under his arms, loose paper box quarters jangling his pockets. Renay drove right next to us, directing me and Twin out her window, languidly smoking a Slim 100, maybe a joint, landing us at canary yellow box after canary yellow box like an ace air traffic controller.

We never felt in danger down on Hay. We were with Renay. We were *safe* with Renay.

We were in *her* place.

"Hustle your fuckin' muscle," she yelled out the window, half a joint in. It was now long past three o'clock in the morning, and most of the bars were closed or closing, and it was sidewalk sale time down on Hay. The straggler soldiers and the puffed-up farmboys were *drunk*, and they were ready to brawl or fuck. Renay urged me and Twin onward, moving the car faster, telling us to empty those boxes faster, fling the papers in, lock 'em all back up quick! *Tighter, faster, move it, move it!* I loved the thrill and excitement in her voice on our downtown Saturday nights.

By three o'clock in the morning on Hay the boldest and most entrepreneurial women of Fayetteville's night kingdom have all come out in force, and they welcomed me and Twin to their corners with warm smiles and glittering faces, all of them gussied up with big fake eyelashes, wigs from Eutaw Village, with florid fake names like Sugar or Miss Peaches or Lady Savoy. There was a feisty and corpulent lady that I particularly adored. She was funny and wore thrillingly styled blond babydoll wigs that got her a lot of attention. She was always posted up at the pay phone booth near Hay and Bragg, where, fittingly, the US Army Airborne & Special Operations Museum is now located. She worked *her* "special operations" right there near our regular paper boxes, wearing the tightest skirts and loosest mesh tops we had ever seen. She didn't have a care in the world and would jokingly wave me over, pretend to sell me on her wares.

"You want some pussy, baby?" she shrieked, her wig only slightly askew, her sweat-streaked makeup otherwise perfect, especially miraculous on such an oppressively hot summer street. "You want some pussy tonight, baby?"

With an extremely nervous and high gay giggle, I would duck my head and politely titter no, but she never let me off that easy, every week giving me the same outlandish, satisfied guffaw, looking in both directions to be sure my rejection and her boldness both played to the crowd.

"Why not, baby?" she would press on, not satisfied with one curtain call, that scenery-chewing hog. "You don't like this pussy? Pussy's *pussy*, baby! Pussy's *pussy!*" she would affirm to me and to her audience, all laughing now, all in on the joke, and then she'd turn away in search of a soldier with money, or boots she could pawn before dawn.

I loved her acting technique *intensely*.

We could be real friends, I thought. *I could be her agent! That lady really knew how to pull off a sausage curl!*

I was no naif.

My mother subscribed to *Penthouse* and *Screw*, and not just for the articles.

I had seen plenty of dirty movies, including a double-bill of *Big Bad Momma* and *Crazy Mama*, my first and second films ever. I was five. *Five.* I had experienced an entire butt *and* a downstairs of a whole human commando stepping naked and lively from a hot shower.

But I had no real conception of what exactly happened on that sassy lady's Hay Street corner.

I just knew that jarheads gave her money, and she gave them a "good time" in return. I could no more tell you what a "good time" was than I could tell you what a cupola was. I merely understood that Roman legions of taut, freshly shorn soldiers from around the world, all who looked and smelled just like Bernie Alphabet, *rushed* into downtown Fayetteville each Friday and Saturday night on a paper pass from a nearby base, a pass that would expire at three o'clock in the morning. They were set loose upon Hay Street in shined-up combat boots and ironed white tees, a pack of Winstons in one pocket, most of their paycheck and an ID in the other.

"She said 'pussy's pussy,' Mommy," I told my mother, winded with delight and shock.

"She sure as shit did," she agreed, and she doubled over laughing, rocking and swaying, screaming *pussy's pussy!* over and over, banging on the steering wheel until tears ran down her plump, rosy cheeks like galloping, shiny foxes, and then the car was rolling, and Twin and I were laughing, too.

Every Saturday night, Renay ate it all up *live*. All of it. A buffet. She deeply respected the hustle down on Hay. Show Renay Corren you made money hand over fist, particularly money the government couldn't get its hands on, and it was 1-800-R-E-S-P-E-C-T.

"This is the real world, boys," she said, pointing at an Army Jeep weighted down with drunk cherries heading back to Bragg, a merrily twirling blue MP escort lightpole wobbling high on the back. "The real world is way more like Hay Street than Haymount," my mother quietly marveled.

"Rich or poor, it's nice to be rich." She sighed, dreamily and reluctantly pulling us out of the bowels of Fayetteville, leaving behind the dramatic back alleys and climactic public brawls, whisking us back up through the stately streets of Haymount, and finally into our grubby little slice of town, more mutts than sluts, but for sure some sluts to be found.

We spent our final hour before the sun rose at Shoney's buffet, reliving the whole night, every brawl, every whore, every turn that went wrong, laughing and eating, right up to the skirts of dawn. That buffet, just $3.99, was our last act after a long, hard night of performing by our mother's side. We filled ourselves with bowls of cheesy grits, gorged on plates of runny eggs, swallowed a pan of lard biscuits and a platter of syrup-smothered sausage and pancakes, all of it chased down with sixteen-ounce cup after sixteen-ounce cup of Pepsi. By the time we returned to Roach House on Brainerd, Twin was already balled up against the window, dead asleep. Renay and I would collapse on her waterbed, zombies now, with yesterday's news stained on our fingertips. We sleepily recounted one last time all the harrowing knockouts, the splendid manors we'll never see the insides of.

"Pussy's pussy!" Renay gasped, her belly shaking, her eyes closed, *Princess Daisy* sliding out of her hands. *"Pussy's pussy!"* Renay mumbled again, more quietly this time as she slipped at last beneath a wave of sleep, her eyes squeezed shut, her eyeballs darting back and forth beneath her thin, beautiful lids, still perfectly shadowed in a pearlescent cream-and-lavender Maybelline Soft Silk blend. Maybe her eyes were replaying the night, or maybe it was another night altogether, in another town. Maybe it was Miami Beach, maybe it was that hot, stupid summer day she fucked Shithead's brains out and got knocked up with Cathy Sue. Or maybe it was the New Year's Eve that Shithead took her to the Eden Roc to see Johnny Mathis, or maybe it was Havana that one time, or maybe it was the whole world spinning under those pretty, soft, silken lids.

"You awake, Mommy?"

She doesn't answer.

We were bobbing on the waterbed, scattered like buoys among the ocean of comforting mess she had amassed around her: the used paperback books and balled-up Kleenex, the brow mirrors and barbecue chips. Dark chocolate-covered pretzels spilled next to orange candies, two half-drunk Pepsis with the lids screwed on. All of it arranged around Renay, her whole world at her fingertips. A court. A queen. An ocean.

"That was fun, Mommy. You gotta buy me some damn jeans tomorrow," I begged softly.

When I heard her snore, I curled myself deeper down into the dark, comfortable crook of her heavy legs, and I pulled Nana Minna's scratchy old black yarn afghan over my head, finding a real darkness and a true silence at long last. I rocked wordlessly alongside Renay's heavy breathing, cradled by the gentle waves made by her long, expelling air, surfing the watery dream currents that flowed beneath us like a swim-up tourist bar in Waikiki. I thought about what a real poet's life would look like, feel like, sound like.

It isn't this.

It isn't this, I thought, before finally, too, letting go and plunging headfirst into the darkness of sleep myself, dancing along the water-fall's edge of her steady, raining snores. By her. With her.

I want to go where she goes.

My mother's bed was so damn warm. Maybe this was what a poet's life was supposed to be.

It can't be.

It can't be this.

It is this.

It is.

Reprinted below with permission (and with typos) from the June 2, 1981, edition of the Fayetteville Observer, *winning entry of "Andy Corrin."*

Winning poems were displayed on Fayetteville Area Rapid Transit System.

My Behind

Boy do I admire you
You let me sit on you
You let me lay on you
You save me from the teachers paddle
You save me from the early
morning toilet seat
You save me from my Daddy's hand
Boy, oh, boy, do I admire you!
You can take anything in your path.
Boy, do I admire you!

—Andy Corrin

THE FAYETTEVILLE OBSERVER, Tuesday, June 3, 1991

Poetry Exhibit On The Move

MY BEHIND
(By Andy Corrin)

Boy do I admire you!
You let me sit on you
You let me lay on you
You save me from the teacher's paddle.
You save me from the early morning toilet seat
You save me from my Daddy's hand.
Boy, oh boy, do I admire you!
You can take anything in your path.
Boy, do I admire you!

By MELISSA CLEMENT
Staff writer

"Being able to write poems pretty good makes me like myself better," said Andy Corrin, an Edgewood Middle School sixth grader. The young poet was at the opening reception Sunday of the Fayetteville/Cumberland County Arts Council's exhibit P.I.T.S. GOES F.A.S.T. (Poetry In the Schools goes on Fayetteville Area System of Transit buses).

In July, his illustrated poem and 50 others written by city and county school students, will go on display in FAST buses. They are all products of the Poetry in the Schools program, a joint effort of the schools and the Arts Council.

Carolyn Carlson, director of the Arts Council, came up with the idea to display the poems on placards; sometimes used for advertising on the buses. She calls the idea creative plagiarism because a similar idea has been used in large cities before. "It doesn't cost a thing and it is a good cooperative venture between the city agencies and the Arts Council."

Andy Corrin, first began writing poetry several years ago when a visiting poet came to his elementary school. According to his mother Renay Corrin, he has had one poem published and wants to write a book. Speaking of the poem he wrote, he said, "It was there all the time. The teacher just had to pull it out." He knotted his face up in distress when he was told that the program was being discontinued after seven years because of a lack of funds.

Also at the reception were poets Ellen Johnston-Hale and Ruth Moose, both five year veterans of the program in which visiting poets stay in town and work at one school for a week at a time.

"We are all born poets. We just have to loosen up and let out the magic of the poetry within." Johnston-Hale said. At 33, she stopped teaching school and went into the poetry program. Using Chapel Hill as her home base, she now teaches poetry to students and does poetry workshops for teachers about 40 weeks in the year. She has also written several books of poems using her teaching experiences as a springboard.

Taking a mile a minute, between puffs on a small hand painted pipe, she recites from memory, poems her students have written or ones she has written

about her students, some poignant enough to make your eyes water.

The "yuk, poetry," syndrome, as well as "page fright" are what you have to overcome in helping students write, she said. She often lets her students use substandard English because, "You have to start from where they live." Then you can slide into things like metaphors and similes. "You can't believe how excited these kids get when they find they can make a poem using their own words about their own experiences or their own terms. She recited a poem written by a class after a turned off student said, "I ain't coming to school tomorrow."

"I AIN'T COMIN' TO SCHOOL TOMORROW

Sposed to be our vacation for spring tomorrow.
So I ain't comin' to school tomorrow.
Got some pretty things to do.
Gonna sleep til noon
Watch the Gong Show
Going to South Square,
Northgate too,
'Gonna shop around
for a 3 piece baby-blue suit.
I ain't comin to school tomorrow,
'Gonna sit in the sun all day.
Watch little children play
Jump rope,
Hopscotch,
Watch a buttercup open up.
Sit and watch the grass turn green.
I ain't comin'to school tomorrow.

"Not being afraid of being alive" is how Ruth Moose describes the act of poetry writing. "I teach communication and try to help each student write clearly and concisely with enthusiasm."

Using natural objects like rocks, shells, herbs and spices, she encourages young people to use all their senses by provoking memories which they can tell about in verse. After smelling dill seed, one girl wrote about her mother putting up pickles in the kitchen.

She also clips words from magazines and seed catalogs and has students select five words each. The words "Grow Your Own" once inspired a poem about growing up and accepting responsibility.

A lot of her work is done on the individual level and she finds if she can get the macho guy or captain of the football team to loosen up and express himself, others will accept the idea.

When she is not staying in motels and eating in restaurants in Fayetteville during her work week, she goes home to Stony Mountain, her home outside Asheboro in the Uwharrie Mountains where she lives with her two sons and husband, well known artist Talmadge Moose. Her award winning poems and short stories have been published worldwide.

The show will continue until June 23 at the Arsenal House before the July bus display.

Ellen Johnston-Hale and young poet Andy Corrin

© *Fayetteville Observer*–USA TODAY NETWORK

THE PEPSI GENERATION

1.

Once upon a time, we were a poor-as-shit family in Okinawa, Japan, too.

We went to Japan. We went to war. We went to pieces.

And then we went back home to Fayetteville.

In November 1969 I was but a wee thing, wildly spraying feces and urine all over a rusted, plummeting C-130 cargo plane. I was inbound, alongside my mother, three brothers, and my sister, to Kadena Air base, from Hawaii via San Francisco, via Alaska, via two more planes, via Fayetteville. It was a lot of via-via, and now I was suffering from air sickness and a watery, wasting reaction to the buckets of tropical immunizations administered by the busy doctors of Womack Army Hospital, hardly a month before Renay's sudden relocation to the far Far East to link up with Shithead. In just the same way that I was ripped from her womb, Fayetteville, too, had only been my dark acquaintance for all of eight months before we were whisked away to Nippon, to start our life anew in the Land of the Rising Sun.

It was to be my first Fayetteville escape attempt.

At only eight months I was already quite canny, and I would soon discover that leaving Fayetteville was a tall and difficult order, one that required stealth and planning, or else you would take Fayetteville with you when you flew out that door.

Renay took Fayetteville with her, all the way to Japan.

My thirty-two-year-old escort and future best friend Renay Corren, a besieged Army wife and mother of six, had selected five of her children to accompany her halfway across the world over five nonstop days of bouncing, no-frills military flights to reunite and live under the same roof again with her estranged warrior husband, who had already returned to the scene of America's latest colonial aggression, this one being supplied from the tip of an island on the tip of Japan.

Where is Renay's oldest son in 1969? you ask. We will get to that in good time, Mrs. Krantz.

According to Corren family lore, upon our landing in Japan, my befouled airplane seat was immediately unbolted and yanked from the floor of the Hercules, removed by two rowdy soldiers who marched it behind all the Correns as we filed onto the tarmac in a solemn, single line, threw it into a dumpster, and, in what was probably one of the last joyful, defiantly life-affirming acts they would undertake before the jungles of Laos swallowed them whole: they set that shitty chair ablaze.

Yes, the white smoke of my smoldering feces certified to the Japanese sky, and all attending, like an affirmative papal declaration: Mrs. Renay Mandel Corren and her troupe of filthy, colonizing, shitty little troublemakers from Fayetteville had arrived. The travel-battered Corren tribe huddled together on the tarmac at Kadena Air Base while I, still screaming and shitting, was held at arm's length by my disgusted, yet devastatingly beautiful, nearly teen sister Cathy Sue. My brothers Rabbi, Asshole, and Twin gathered in a confused gaggle behind Renay's shadow as she struck her raspy lighter to her long 100 cig and waited for her husband to arrive to ferry us all to what was sure to be our delightful new home along the lively Mizugama-Dori District.

Shithead was a no-show.

He was an in-demand soldier and had been called away on TDY—Army temporary duty. Along with the Marines that he trained in the fearsome MACV-SOG brigade, Shithead was doing some dark deed or another, either here in Japan, or in Laos or in Cambodia, when we arrived.

Nobody was coming to pick us up.

Nobody bothered to tell Renay, and so she began this Japanese adventure of a lifetime on entirely familiar footing: her own.

It was an inauspicious start, but what unfolded after those confused arrival hours would be remembered by her, oddly, as the three happiest years of her whole, entire life. I know this for certain, because Renay fondly recalled many times over many years that it wasn't marriage, it wasn't motherhood, and it wasn't Miami that made Renay *Renay*.

It was Nippon.

My brothers and I, and Cathy Sue, would have a front row seat to the dawn of her joyful noise, but first we would all learn to survive, once again. Renay and the five of us found lodging in what my brother Rabbi charitably recalls as a "sleazy" motel in the Old Koza District, a maze of alleys, kitchens, and nightclubs that was primarily populated by the Black servicemen and women who didn't live on base, and the bars, clubs, and nightlife that catered to them. It was cheap and as close as Renay could find to a home. It had no kitchen, just a hot plate. There was not much schooling for the teens, and not much food for the littles. It was survival.

Yet somehow Renay found her footing in all of that.

Renay began working as a cocktail waitress and bartender at the Topper Club, an enlisted and spouse's bar on base, and then she found the bowling alley, and soon it became clear that Renay would rule Okinawa with one cocktail-clenched fist raised high, a bowling ball screaming in the other.

She found herself, then she found her people, and then she *glowed*. Renay glowed *red* in the Land of the Rising Sun.

Eventually Shithead rejoined us, found us a tiny little house in Kadena, closed up a carport to give teenaged Cathy Sue her own room, and when he wasn't teaching Marines how to kill Laotians, he joined his wife at the Topper Club, pouring drinks and basking in Renay's sharp, amiably rose glow.

Renay Corren was *so, so happy* to be living in Japan.

"Japan was my lucky place!" she told me. "I can't explain it. Japan set me free. From everything, from *him*, from my parents. It's where I learned that to be myself, I had to *love myself*," she said with the same note of wonderment each time, at the *very idea* of her not *ever* loving herself.

Renay's Pennsylvania and Florida girlhood had been spent under the thumb of her dyspeptic, neat-freak mother, Marian the Hungarian, a white-haired Slovak bottle cleanser obsessive who would periodically descend upon her shambolic teenage daughter like a wraith, armed with cans of Lysol, Yiddish recrimination, and a trash bag for all her daughter's smutty medical thrillers and potboilers. Renay was nothing at all like her vain, emotionally illiterate Old World mother, a woman wildly talented at baking but truly skeptical of human friendship. Renay was Marian the Hungarian's only child, and as such, this queer, intelligent, defiantly agnostic, lovable Jewish princess was the smothered center of stern Marian and affable Isidor's entire life. Her parents had nothing better to do than spend eighteen uninterrupted years alternately spoiling and shaming this lusty, busty, determinedly bad seed of theirs. They gave Renay everything, including a badly misspelled first name, an idyllic Jewish childhood filled with fresh pastries, and a lifelong taste for betting on anything that moved. Renay scandalized her parents in return by being an indifferent Jew, by stealing ham from the deli downstairs of their McKeesport apartment, and by getting knocked up and dropping out of college, then spending the next dozen years more or less permanently pregnant by a repugnant man they never did warm to, or approve of. It seems to me my father never met a person he couldn't, and didn't, eventually estrange, and in Isidor and Marian he did not disappoint. "Putz-head," they called him dismissively, or "Shtik drek shmeckle shtoonk," which is a whole lot of Yiddish nails in the Shithead coffin. But that was all behind her now. The parents were a far-off, retired dot down in Miami; her marriage was a stale, crumbling rice cake, merely a Japanese business arrangement by the time Renay and Shithead reunited in Okinawa.

What better place than Japan during a global conflict to explore at last the outermost reaches of long-suppressed desires? Perhaps it was *here*, on an island nation riven by war and intrigue, that was the *perfect* place for a fertile American woman to give birth one last time.

This time to herself.

The entire Vietnam War was supported from Okinawa. *All of it.* All the bombs, all the training, all the food, all the bullets and bodies, the stretchers and pallets, they all started or ended their journey right there on Okinawa. Renay, Cathy Sue, my three brothers, and I lived among the crates, darting about the refugees, dodging the wounded, the recruits, and all the others just like us—lost, bandaged souls adrift on the East China Sea. My first idea of "home" was this cacophonous place, an occupied Japanese island. My first memory was my occupied Japanese neighbors. My first spoken words were in rude, halting Japanese. We had *so many* adventures. Renay took us for picnics to Chibana Castle. We hid behind the couch during the Koza Uprising, couldn't leave the house for days; they damn near burned the whole base down. We went to Torii Beach at sunset, swam at Nishihara. I tasted my first ocean salt in the East China Sea.

I was born in North Carolina, but I was baptized by my mother in Japan.

During this period, Shithead was rarely at home. If not called away overseas, he was instructing teen Marines bound for the jungle on the arts of survival. His specialties were surveilling, field operation, and jungle swagger. When he was back in Kadena, his responsibilities to MACV-SOG kept him far from us, and he gave Renay half his salary, the grand sum of about five hundred dollars a month, to feed, house, and clothe us. We were led by a woman who, like her husband, knew how to live off the land. All her kids did. By the time our family arrived in Japan during Shithead's last tour of duty, queerly odd nine-year-old Rabbi was already on the make for girls and drugs; he had already been almost drowned twice, burned once by his own father in an unfortunate gasoline jar incident in Miami, and had spent several months in a coma. Cathy Sue, our leader, on the cusp of thirteen when we arrived, was a devilishly smart and mean little country girl. She could already pick a lock on a snack machine and the heart of a cold-blooded Marine. Cathy Sue had long, jailbait legs and gorgeous blond hair always pulled up in a bandana, perfect teeth and two lovely, piercing, blue eyes that saw *all*. She was prematurely wise, embittered from long shifts in the mommy position whenever Renay couldn't be bothered, and Renay couldn't be bothered quite a bit with all them kids. Asshole was three years old, Twin was two, and I was that eight-month old baby, the one shitting on everything in sight, on the tarmac, on the soldiers, on Japan itself. I will have moved five times before I was four years old.

That was me. That was us. That was all of us.

Well, all of us except Bonus.

Bonus was in Hialeah, Florida, at the Adelio G. Montanari School for the Mentally Retarded.

My oldest brother was not mentally anything.
He was just misplaced.

2.

Once Renay found the Topper and the bowling alley, she did what came naturally: she turned her three youngest children over to her daughter, Cathy Sue, and to two Japanese babysitters, sisters Yoshiko and Toshio, who made the journey to Kadena over the Mizugama-Dori to take care of us in exchange for five dollars a week.

While Renay was consumed by her raucous life at the lanes and the Topper, Shithead was teaching teenagers how to make war. We effectively no longer had parents. It was just Yoshiko and Toshio, and Cathy Sue with her watchful, piercing blue eyes. She still had both of them then. A date with destiny and a cursed glass bottle of Pepsi soon beckoned.

My first Technicolor memories of my mother are in that crusty little hilltop Kadena house, laughing boisterously, loud enough to peel the yellow and white paint, laughing in the setting Ryukyuan sun, smiling, resplendent, at home in herself—and headed out into the night, to the Topper, or to the lanes. My first memory of my father is from this time, too. Rough hands holding me up. His arms, strong, a soldier's arms—I knew that even then. A baby knows a killer's arms.

I remember my father's veiled eyes greeting us whenever he returned home, and I remember the jungle shadows that lived in those eyes and never left. I remember his medals. All of them. His Purple Heart. His Silver Star, still so shiny and new. His rows of ribbons; the dark, felt beret with the two swooping, broad *A*'s that stood for "All American, not Army Airborne," he would say proudly. The bright, gold patch with the three shiny yellow lightning bolts pierced by a golden sword pointing to the sky. To God. To him.

He would be home—and then he would leave. The house would exhale. And we would, too.

TDY.

It means goodbye.

3.

If Japan was an island heaven where Renay's soul went to be reborn, it was also a kind of familial heaven for me, a place where I had a family, a place worth defending at all costs. Upon learning that the United States would be winding down the war and bringing the entire Army Airborne home, I was, predictably, like my mother, devastated. I was hardly four years old, yet seized with an attack of severe melancholia that had already become typical of me when the fall TV season, or the tree pollen count, was too bleak. In such a state of all-consuming grief, I was perhaps not acting in a rational manner when I may—*may*—have vengefully released the brakes of our family car, and I might—*might*—have placed it in neutral, then waved silently as our boxy little Japanese wagon rolled slowly down the little hill of our Kadena drive, watching as the Corren chariot rolled slowly onward, *and perhaps over*, my darling brother Twin. The car knocked Twin to the ground and dragged him down the street. He was fine. Protected as he was, even then, by his gigantic jock-boy skull, Twin rolled to safety as our car slow-motion crashed at the bottom of our hill, right into traffic on Mizugama-Dori Street. Our imminent departure was at hand.

But first: a refreshing, ice-cold Pepsi.

4.

We went back to Fayetteville the way we arrived in Japan: in stages, and in pieces.

Cathy Sue had to go back to the United States before us *and* before the Army Airborne, as it turns out. She was accompanied by Shithead on a medical evacuation flight, because Cathy Sue required some emergency surgery on her doomed, soon-to-be-lost, beautiful, blue, right eye. This "incident with the Pepsi bottle" would stalk our family for decades. The accident itself was straightforward, but the recovery and the lawsuit were rumored by my brothers to be bungled by my father right from the start. A single, shaken-up glass bottle of frosty-cold Pepsi was released from a PX vending machine and unfortunately exploded in my sister's face. It sent her first to the hospital, then back to the United States on a stretcher, where she underwent extensive surgery. Just one more veteran in Henry Kissinger's war.

Once again Renay was compelled to sherpa her children—four this time—halfway across the world, by multiple planes, retracing her steps back to Fayetteville, by way of Miami to collect her wounded daughter, all without an escort.

It was Cathy Sue's date with that damned Pepsi bottle that blew up our final days in Okinawa. Our time in Japan was suddenly *done*. It had been the time of Renay Mandel Corren's life, and then it was over in a brown rush of fizz, and all those three years had cost her was one of her daughter's beautiful blue eyes.

Renay returned to Fayetteville, where she launched herself into a highly reenergized life at the B&B Lanes, determined to replicate her overseas social and personal successes.

Shithead returned, too, to a regimented and highly ambitious life of suck-up sergeant major, a universally loathed instructor, I am told, of soldiers up and down the pay line. Shithead stayed as far away from this family that confused and frightened him as he could.

Then he lost the house on Tempe Court to a foreclosure and moved us to a house on Pamalee Drive.

By the time I was six years old in late 1975, we had moved houses seven times.

Renay and Shithead then demolished what was left of their marriage before Shithead unceremoniously decamped to beautiful Pine Bluff, Arkansas, America's seventh-most deadly city, where, depending on who is speaking to who of these events, Shithead went willingly, sacrificing his esteemed Fort Bragg career in order to altruistically serve the underprivileged ROTC youth of Jefferson County, Arkansas, or, he was busted down to Pine Bluff because he fucked the wrong colonel's wife and Renay Corren was emphatic that she could not stay married to a man who had another whole family. She was old fashioned that way. I know Shithead didn't marry that colonel's wife, or acknowledge that new child—he certainly denied both the mother and the child to me—but others of my brothers, and my sister, refute the denial of the denier. The child remains unacknowledged. Shithead wasn't big on acknowledging his mistakes, or his children, anyway.

Renay was a single mother of five, and one of the five was out the door.

Recovered from her catastrophic encounter with Pepsi, and determined to bounce back higher than ever, Cathy Sue threw her arms and her legs around Benny, a Vietnam vet like herself, a hot and rangy recently discharged Marine. Together, and far more deeply than either I or Renay could ever have imagined, Cathy Sue and Benny fell in love and into teen pregnancy and then, deeper still, in an affront to all of us, to Virginia Beach. It wasn't drugs or teen pregnancy or dropping out of school that hurt us most deeply. It was moving to Virginia Fucking Beach.

Four Corren brothers and Renay Corren set up shop on Pamalee Drive, and then in a series of ever-diminishing shacks thereafter, concentrating on the business of surviving each day, and then each other, and then Fayetteville itself.

In 1973, Renay Mandel Corren returned to Fayetteville from Japan.

Her nearly fifteen-year-old son, my oldest sibling who I had barely known, moved to Fayetteville from Florida to live with us for the very first time ever.

Bonus stayed less than fourteen months.

BIGMOUTH

1.

"Hook it through the lips," she urges.

Renay purses her red lips out lewdly, kissing the air and puffing her hot, pink cheeks like a bigmouth bass, grabbing her painted upper lip with two fingers in a ring, indicating where I should slip the hook in, but I am too squeamish for such barbarity and delicately slip the shank through the dorsal fin of the tiny, shiny minnow squirming silver between my damp thumb and nervous palm.

We are fishing on Glenville Lake this Saturday morning, but not the *nice* Glenville Lake deep in that volcano of socialism called Asheville. The shabby, street-level Glenville Lake just off Bragg Boulevard, right here in plain old Fayetteville. The one out by the filter plant behind "the Murk." You can drive right up to Glenville, park, and yank a bass out of the water if you get lucky, then hightail it back to B&B Lanes to scale, gut, bread, and fry that tasty fish, right there on the snack bar grill.

We do it all the time.

I am thirteen, she is forty-five, but those thirty-two years between us vanish like a river mirage when we are back together after summer break, and we are just two best friends reunited, chawing away the day, trading skincare tips, gossip, biscuits, Wolfpack predictions. She is my only friend, and I am captured completely by and in her regard. Age matters little in such consequential arrangements, I have found. It is trust, good gossip, and *very* dirty jokes that keep best friends together and powering through the years.

"Hand me the biscuit bag, Ann," she says.

This is what she made me for.

A summer and a dock, a cooler between us, best friends dropping lines into a deep lake, hers always more expertly dropped than mine. Swatting flies off our wet necks, already slick with Fayetteville's August worst, eighty degrees and not even eight o'clock in the morning. Fatigue clings to us, but we rallied and drove up here early. Me and Twin have only just returned from our annual Miami exile, summering with the ancient Jews who gargle at us in guttural Yiddish. I have glued myself to Renay's side every minute since I got back. Last night was another raucous evening at the B&B Lanes, all the usual spread: the soldiers, the sexual intrigue, the found five-dollar bills, the free cheeseburger and milkshake from smiling Sarah on the grill. Renay was determined to get us up to the lake this morning, to take me fishing on her one day off. We sit side by side, trading war stories of our long, hot summers. Who's in jail now? What's broken in Fayetteville now? What are her parents saying about her weight? Did I see Lolita the Orca at Sea World? We sit, three biscuits in a grease-stained bag between us, bribing hot-shocked bigmouthed bass to the surface of a bathwater-warm lake. In three weeks, I start junior high at Westover, but three weeks in Fayetteville? In August? A lifetime.

After seven years of separation, four of those years devoted to a hard, protracted divorce, Renay is a single mother juggling four kids in and out of home, two in other states, and has three different jobs going at all times. She's pretty crap at keeping up with two-thirds of what she has to do on any given day, but she says all the time, "Ann, if we get one-third of our shit done after we wake up, take the win." We consider today a win. We got to this lake, even after she pulled yet another triple shift, even after a week of putting out fires. Renay is forever putting out fires at the bowling alley, where she's become the indispensable queenpin, and is always bailing out one or two sons from jail, or angry principals' offices. There's always a stack of frozen Jeno's and Totino's cardboard pizzas in the freezer to keep the wolves on the other side of our door. It's not a big win, keeping us alive, but it's a win. A respectable C+ for mothering this August.

I think she's *splendid*, A++ all the way.

While I do not love Fayetteville, and long ago began constructing a picture in my mind of what life elsewhere—any place elsewhere—would look like, I love this woman completely, and I love the life I get to share with her here, as itinerant as it is.

I hated going down to Miami and missing out. Renay's life was my life; her glamour was my light. She always shared so generously, kept us entertained and laughing, making Fayetteville feel, if not lovely, at least worthwhile, the place to be. She filled our lives with R-rated jokes, pirated cable TV, filthy books, bawdy movies, cheap gossip, late-night cribbage tournaments, and night after night after night of bowling. I didn't know any better, and I didn't *want to know* any better. Hers was a good life for a thirteen-year-old accomplice. I only wanted this life. *Her life.* I only ever needed her laugh.

"Did you ever think you would end up here? In Fayetteville?" I ask her as she adroitly threads her hook through another minnow's lips without so much as flinching. I am a simp for nightcrawlers.

"Nope," she mutters. "Not once."

I frequently wondered why our family chose to stay in Fayetteville, whining so often in my perfected sissy pitch how it came to be that we were in such low circumstance in such a low-down town, when so many of our far-flung family were thriving in cosmopolitan places like Metuchen, New Jersey, or North Miami Beach, near the Aventura Mall. How *she*, this spoiled, bright young light from Miami Beach, stayed *here* of all places, scrounging in bargain bins, not a decent black and white cookie to be found in a two-hundred-mile radius. We were growing up redneck to the nape of our dirty blue collars right there in Fayetteville. All my brothers shot shit: hoops, deer, even their friends once or twice. They gambled late into the night. They bowled for money. Sold dope for cash. Yet despite all that, we were still the outsiders, still those Jews from that shit house down the street.

"We could've been living in Miami this whole time," I say to her.

"And I coulda run the damn ball to help Shula beat the Chargers," she mutters angrily, stoically swatting away the still-painful memory of the Epic in Miami, and the telltale crumble of Biscuit Kitchen on her chin.

I always whined extra loudly that we should go back to our people on those many box-and-move nights, when we were fleeing ahead of another eviction. It was our chance to bail completely on Fayetteville. *This is it*, I would argue. *Let's run! Now! Tonight!* I had read too many tales of our ancestors fleeing the tsar not to be enamored of such journeys. But no, downward we stayed. Why was my worldly, articulate, funny, well-read mother, who could fish like Hemingway and quote public intellectuals like V. C. Andrews, taking us to yet another shithole, on her endless shithole procession tour across this endlessly shithole part of town?

"Who would want to end up *here*?" I ask, resentfully, squashing another blowfly against my sticky neck. At least it wasn't a flea. *I bet there aren't fleas in Durham!*

"I never think about endings, son. The house always has the edge, and I play the hand, not the house," Renay says, dropping another line, daring the lazy bass circling below. Glaring from behind her oversized, cheap Russian Mafia sunglasses, I bet that fish *was* afraid of her. She really looks the part of "fat gangster" sitting behind that pole, smoking a Slim, sipping a Pepsi. Her stained white collar and dented hair be damned, you would not fuck with this woman if you were a wide-mouth and saw her up on your pier. You would just *jump* on that line and spare yourself the terror of her approach.

Play the hand, not the house.

"Trust me, we could've done a lot better, me and you, in Vegas or Miami," I say.

"Whenever a man says 'trust me,' I think *run*." She cackles.

Renay liked homely braggarts and humble men. She had a soft spot for barely reformed bad boys. She distrusted men who made promises, those who trafficked in holy truths, boasters, and blowhards. She looked askance at the sweaty Swaggarts and the venal Falwells, dismissing television pastors and their blow-dried cousin politicians as all cons, grifters just looking to make a dishonest buck like her, but doing it in a suit or a red tie. Renay thought pornographers and casino operators were the only honest men left in America. At least they told you up front they were gonna steal from you, your money or your dreams. Everything was a fix to Renay, run by crooked men shaking women like her down every day so they could buy more planes, more bombs, more bimbos, more yachts, whatever. All of it was a con for the suckers, and Renay Corren *was no sucker*.

"So Fayetteville was just your *backup plan*?" I ask.

"*You* are my backup plan, Ann," she says. "All of you. Only one I ever needed."

She said this so often, but I would only ever truly understand what she meant at the very end.

What a baller.

"God damn it!" I curse at a fat bass rippling away, newly well fed and mocking me in retreat.

I am terrible at baiting, at all things fishing.

I have no patience for any kind of sport. I am barely thirteen, and I am passionate, just as she was at thirteen, about pulp fiction, dirty Jewish comedians, handsome quarterbacks, and heroic soldiers in tight pants. I retreat indoors to books and baking. I love reading the recipes aloud from the Fayetteville Junior League and Methodist Women's League cookbooks, letting Renay decide what I would bake next after Peggy Dunn wraps it up on WTVD. Rabbi may be a full-fledged idiot—*and he was, he absolutely was*—but at least he can shoot a rifle and tear apart a car engine, even if he does both things badly. Twin spends every Saturday on a field practicing in front of leering cheerleaders, and hot coaches I have quiet fantasies about, racking up trophy after trophy. He is tall and blue-eyed and popular now, and we are spending less and less time together. Asshole, shit, he could've turned pro at bowling if he'd wanted to—he is a *fantastic* bowler, ice-cold despite being far-sighted, rude, and intemperate. But Asshole has already been lured away into a minor life of crime, following Dicky, Bev's son from Bev's Place on Bragg, around town, racing one of Bev's many Cadillacs up and down Fort Bragg Boulevard, doing his best to out-fuckup his fuckup older brother, Rabbi. My mother stands at the top of this all-boy, all-fuckup heap, the fiercest of us all. Renay is the boss. She is tough as shit. She knows how to navigate a man's world to keep stupid boys like us in line and to grab some laughs and some burgers along the way. But she can't teach me all the ways of men in this world, and frankly, from what I can tell, I'm not missing all that much.

"Maybe just throw your minnows directly at the water, save yourself the trouble," she quips.

"Solid plan, Renay," I say.

"I never had a plan," she says. "Who has time *to plan*?"

Another thing for suckers: planning.

"Why plan for tomorrow what you can put off today?" She laughs, casting perfectly.

I gesture over the hot, mossy-green lake. "So Fayetteville? That's our plan?" I ask, inhaling the algae-brown fumes of the carcinogen-filled waters of Fayetteville's finest public works reservoir. *You're a queen!* I want to shout. *You are too good for this place, God damn it!*

"Fuck a plan. There wasn't one in sixty-six when I got here, or when I got back in seventy-three. No plans after seventy-eight, either. Never once was Fayetteville the plan, son," she says, a touch too proudly, digging into that warm paper bag from Biscuit Kitchen for the second of our three perfect chicken biscuits. I am already regretting not making her buy a fourth, as they are addictive, *particularly* silky and flaky, rolled with real Raeford lard, slathered with pounds of salty butter.

We're sitting on the rusted beach chairs she keeps in the trunk of the Nova, next to racks of unsold bongs and feathered roach clips she sells two for one outside the Cross Creek Mall. Renay likes how Glenville Lake smells, she says, even if it is a filter plant. Smells like a pool. Maybe it's all that chlorine. I don't know. She says it "smells rich." The muddy Cape Fear feeds right into it, and we can hear the intake valves humming in the distance, both of us waiting for the right moment to take our eyes off our lines to inhale just one more biscuit. Occasional bass strikes hit her line, but never mine. They ignore mine. I am Southern, gay, and invisible, even to catfish. We're hoping for a hit before it gets hotter than it already has and we have to call it quits, pack up our shit, head for home. I don't want to go. I love so much that I don't have to share Renay. On Glenville Lake, Renay, at least, is *mine*.

"Why *not* here?" she says.

"Because we could've lived anywhere! *Miami. Durham*," I say, desperately conjuring the second-most glamorous city I could summon. "But *Fayetteville*," I say, choke-barfing the very word.

She just laughs, casts her line expertly again into the last cool spots atop the dank lake water. Her raspy lighter strikes up another Slim 100, and she exhales a big plume of smoke and biscuit crumbs.

"You are in for a big surprise, son. You don't always get to choose where you call home. Sometimes home gets chosen *for* you. I'd of thought you'd have figured that out by now," she says, laughing. "You have to be patient with bass, son," she tells me after I lose yet another minnow. "They're aggressive. They dine and dash, so you need to be ready, be strong enough to fight 'em when they come up to eat. You gotta be tougher, son. Smarter. Be a mudcat," she urges me, I think a little unrealistically.

I don't even like the taste of catfish, anyway.

We weren't out there just fishing for fun, she and I. We were fishing for food. We were fishing for dinner. We were always thinking ahead to the next meal, because we didn't always know where it was coming from.

She tried, but with four growing boys, there was never enough for us to eat. Many days, me and Twin and Asshole walked down Pamalee to the Qwik Mart, almost a whole mile, and stole what food we could, mainly vinegar and salt chips, candy, and Slim Jims. Then we trudged home to our hot house, licking stolen, melted chocolate off our fingers until Renay got back after dark with something we could thaw, or microwave, or eat ravenously from a warm drive-thru bag.

"It won't work if you keep jiggling your line like that," she admonishes me sharply. Irritated, like Shula watching the Chargers eat their way to his ten-yard line.

I could never quiet my mind or my shaky, delicate wrists long enough to become one with the fishing wire and the fish below, not like she could. I have no idea how she took to it *so naturally*. Fishing was her thing, her third-favorite land-based activity on this earth, after gambling and, of course, lying down post buffet. So much of Renay was concocted before our very eyes, a myth that arose out of Florida mangrove swamps, awakened to itself in a Japanese mirror, and perfected on the riverbanks of the Piedmont. She molded herself out of the onslaught of escapes, births, deaths, and abandonments, and she fished her way through all of it.

"Let's go, I got a pain in my bass and the fish ain't jumping," she says, rising and packing us up. "You really are a terrible fisherman, son. But you're a good son. And I missed you. I'm really glad you're back. Even in *Fayetteville*," she says, eyes raised in mock disgust, laugh booming across the cruddy, green-tinted reservoir lake.

One thing about all her kids is—I think as I gather up biscuit bags and dead minnows—we all got Renay's laugh. When I heard my oldest brother, Bonus, laugh for the first time, I knew we were related. I knew he was her son. Bonus, who was not, and never was, in any way, shape, or form, either mentally retarded (as they called it back then) or developmentally disabled, had nevertheless been tucked away in 1966 in Hialeah, Florida, at the Adelio G. Montanari School for the Mentally Retarded.

Let's talk about Bonus, finally. You ready?

He had begun presenting some signs of severe hyperactivity and impulsive behavior as early as three years old. Back in the early 1960s, this was considered "abnormal" or "mentally retarded" behavior. Bonus wrought a lot of havoc on Renay's already havoc-filled life in Miami— spontaneous fights with her and his siblings, huge dish-breaking tantrums, screaming fits and thefts that would bloom out of nowhere, some light arson at home and in the neighborhood, smoking cigarettes by the time he was six. Six!

Bonus nearly burned their family home down by setting a hamper of clothes ablaze, which was apparently the last straw for Renay. Because of his father's impending TDY to the Vietnam War, and his mother's more or less permanent, decade-long post-partum, and because in 1966 there wasn't a name for what was happening to my brother Bonus—he had been repeatedly misdiagnosed by Army doctor after Army doctor—nobody knew what to do until my overwhelmed parents were steered by a family friend to a man named A. G. "Monty" Montanari, whose school for troubled kids had just been opened in Florida.

In 1966, Monty took seven-year-old Bonus, and Renay took the rest of her kids to Fayetteville.

Bonus was, by his own account, treated humanely and kindly by Monty, but the school was not popular with the surrounding community, and Bonus's time there was not a tremendous success. Nobody could fix what nobody could name. He was transferred in 1968 or 1969 (he does not remember, and records no longer exist) to a second institution, the cloistered Green Valley School for Emotionally Disturbed and Delinquent Children, located in Orange City, Florida, way, way up near Orlando. Opened and operated by a fringe reverend named George Von Hilsheimer—who was, it must be said, the reverend of an entirely made-up religion—Green Valley became mired in endless controversy. There Bonus would remain until 1973, when the school was raided by the Volusia County sheriff and subsequently shut down by the state attorney's office. It was from there that Bonus was finally set free to live with his family.

In Fayetteville.

In all that time, in both residential treatment facilities, Bonus had only four visitors: his grandparents. He says he did not receive a single call from his sister, his brothers, his father, or his mother.

Upon arrival to Fayetteville that fall of 1966, having left her oldest son behind with Monty Montanari, Renay Corren was plunged headfirst into a cold, bare-bones existence that both frightened and exhilarated her. She lived in the shadow of her husband's and her country's latest war. She found the nearest bowling alley, a still-relatively new joint called B&B Bowling Lanes, run by Blum and Baum, Jewish Wolfpack fans of the highest quality.

Renay found her people while her husband found his jungle war. Even if he was at home between tours, Shithead was always mentally moving up or moving on to another deployment, packing his pipe, his duffel, his CAR-15, and twenty-one magazines of bullets. He would put two more war babies into Renay before they finally called it quits, but each time he left her, he left Renay poorer, hungrier, and more post-partum than before. Twin and I, those Fayetteville babies, the two youngest, were told so often by our sister—so loudly and with no small amount of bitter jealousy—that we were the lucky ones, the only two who never had to live in the same house as Shithead.

Bonus, Rabbi, and Cathy Sue, however, they were not so lucky.

Rabbi recalls vividly those impoverished first years in Fayetteville when Renay, scrapping for a dollar or a meal, urged him and Cathy Sue into backyard gardens in Hope Mills, or darkened farms in Raeford, instructing her two oldest how to snatch the easy-to-reach corn, and the cucumbers and zucchinis lying on the ground, eventually graduating them to coins, and then stray bills atop bowling alley bars and cafeteria counters. She taught Rabbi how to boost steaks from the PX commissary while she distracted the cashier, and Cathy Sue how to expertly pick a lock on a vending machine, to grab the bills first, the quarters second, and a Pepsi last, and walk away calmly drinking it, like nobody was looking.

Renay didn't think twice about stealing what it took to keep her kids fed, taking whatever she could from Uncle Sam along the way. My mother got us our vaccines at peeling cinder-block clinics, our food rations from commissaries, our cheap Army haircuts and sadistic Army dentistry inside faceless huts named for bomb ranges, or Confederate soldiers, or old wars.

She did whatever it took.

It was a long way from Miami for a bawdy, bookish gal far more accustomed to bags of hot bialys and fast boys at the Fontainebleau. Not even a decade had passed since Renay was just a horny teenager who wanted to bowl, gamble, fish, and give blowjobs behind the Imperial Lanes on the West Dixie Highway. She had been raised to swan into and out of synagogues and the Hotel Eden Roc, and now she was a plump Southern housewife in Fayetteville stealing liver and onions from the Morrison's Cafeteria. (Yeah, she did that. All it takes is a baggie and some courage.)

Shithead and Renay left for Japan, where they lived their increasingly separate lives, staying for three bloody but weirdly happy years. Bonus was a problem that had been solved, a problem left far behind with professionals in far-off Central Florida.

Renay returned to Fayetteville after the Vietnam War completely transformed. A heavy married woman when she departed, she was now obese and beached on a wrecked marriage, but had nonetheless tasted complete, mature, *foreign* freedom for the very first time, a freedom fueled by bowling, pills, easy Marines, and bottomless cocktails. She could never go back to the woman she was. Renay was stronger now. Renay would need to be for what came next.

Because what came next was a series of unending catastrophes.

The union of Shithead and Renay was a grind, a daily, dangerous series of emotionally violent confrontations witnessed by her children, fights that descended into broken dishes hurled against chipped, laminate walls. Her weight had ballooned, her husband stopped loving her, her daughter was missing an eye and had one foot out the door, she had two toddlers on her hips, and her troubled, faraway son wanted to come home to a family that didn't know him anymore.

Bonus arrived on Fayetteville's doorstep one dark night in 1973, showing up on a midnight train from Orlando, to be at last lovingly reunited with his mother, sister, four younger brothers, and even Shithead. Nearly fifteen years old, he had not laid eyes upon his entire family since 1966.

It did not go well.

After his years-long separation and a fifteen-hour journey, Bonus can be forgiven for not recognizing his mother on the train station platform. He walked right by her. Rabbi, Asshole, and Cathy Sue, predictably, loathed the sight of Bonus, frightened of this unpredictable stranger dropped into their angry midst. Twin and I didn't know this person at all, and so we have no memory of this reunion.

His time with us would last less than a year and a half.

Within months, with no wacky reverend or temperate Monty to ameliorate his episodes, Bonus had returned to his undisciplined and dramatically explosive disruption. It wasn't long before his parents resorted to having Bonus reinstitutionalized, this time keeping him in state, sending my oldest brother briefly to the dreary and infamous Dorothea Dix State Hospital for the Criminally Insane.

Because Bonus was neither insane nor a criminal, and not nearly rotten enough for a life in Raleigh, the doctors at Dorothea Dix would not hold my brother for longer than a few weeks, and he was quickly removed to the much nicer-sounding Duncraig Manor for Emotionally Disturbed Youth, which was in a very creepy and run-down Tudor estate way out in a famed golf resort for white people, Southern Pines, North Carolina. Bonus would stay at Duncraig Manor, where, I am pleased to report, he was *very* happy, until he graduated from Pinehurst High School in 1976, becoming the first Corren to graduate from any high school in North Carolina. Then he left North Carolina, and this cold-shouldering family of strangers of his, for good.

Then came a *really* bad divorce.

There was no such thing as a "good divorce" in the 1970s. Just bad options and bad laws. Divorce was very difficult for a woman to contemplate back then—a time when a woman couldn't legally refuse sex with her husband or have credit cards in her own name. Staying married to a cold, violent, belittling, damaged asshole like Shithead was a really bad option—but it was, practically and legally speaking, nearly her only one. Renay had four kids at home and nowhere else to go. That's when things got interesting.

In the span of a single year, from 1975 through America's bicentennial celebration year of 1976, Renay lost a lot. She lost her left breast, her fight with diabetes, her oldest son to yet another Gothic institution, her husband to Arkansas, and, perhaps worst of all, her daughter to Virginia Beach.

Renay found a lump in her breast in late 1974, back when the public conversation around women's breast health was in the dark ages. But Renay came from Miami, so she knew a thing or two about healthy boobs, and fortunately caught her cancer early enough so that the doctors at Womack could operate quickly. They performed admirably, if a bit dramatically, removing her cancerous left breast and radically carving away her chest muscles and lymph nodes, too. It was a *profound* realtering of her body, and nobody, certainly not the United States Army, would be ponying up for any fancy breast reconstruction for Renay. That was for civilians who lived in houses with cupolas, not Army spouses on one half of an E-9 paycheck. It took nearly a full year for Renay's wounds to heal.

Shithead departed Fayetteville for Pine Bluff after this, either for his own personal, altruistic reasons, as previously speculated, or more likely, for pissing on the wrong colonel's lawn. Either way, he was nine hundred miles away, and that felt just about far enough for all of us.

The only daughter of Renay Corren had herself turned quite feral overseas, in all the ways recognizable to besieged parents of any generation, but particularly to the libertine 1970s. Cathy Sue had gone full teen apeshit. She was transformed by her Japanese misadventures, by the legions of Marine admirers and fellow unparented teens she consorted with on that magical island. Cathy Sue was now a dangerously beautiful, one-eyed, long-legged Fayetteville stunner, a wise, knowing blond hellion with an unquenchable thirst for hot Marines, Kool menthols, and cheap morphine. Having left behind a blue eye and all her inhibitions in Japan, she was now a *very* mature teenager who was ready to party, and no longer interested in being Renay's free, full-time, stay-at-home maid. Cathy Sue was the single most beautiful available hippie in all of North Carolina, and she and her best friend, Brenda, the *second*-most beautiful hippie in all of North Carolina, were on a mission of maximum destruction, to fuck all the boys, to have all the fun, to do all the drugs. Along with Brenda, Cathy Sue entered Seventy-First High School, but unlike Brenda, Cathy Sue quickly exited. It was shortly after she met her future first ex-husband (the astoundingly sexy and rangy West Virginian Benny) at a hot hippie party being held in the Ponderosa, that Cathy Sue decided she had had enough education, enough of Fayetteville—but not *nearly* enough fun. Cathy Sue cast her one good eye upon that eminently fuckable Marine, and that was all she wrote. They were married young, dumb, and in South Carolina, which is, I am aware, redundant.

The teen bride and her groom departed Fayetteville, leaving her family bereft, but her former high school exhaled a sigh of relief heard county-wide. Her brothers, all of whom blindly worshipped the ground their one-eyed sister walked upon, were utterly heartbroken. Cathy Sue had been our spare mother. We would all fall in line for her. She was our only sister, and the light of all our lives. And then she was gone.

By 1976, Cathy Sue was nineteen, a mother, married, and, worst of all, a Virginian. Because Virginia is and always has been so famously second-rate compared to North Carolina, Cathy Sue hopped in her car and drove back to Fayetteville every single weekend to visit her mother and her adoring brothers.

After separating from Shithead upon her return to Fayetteville, then officially divorcing him in 1978, Renay Mandel Corren would never again marry, take a man at his word, or let a man take anything from her that she did not offer first.

But she had some sex.

Renay had all the sex she wanted to have and had it on her terms. She wasn't always just about the dick—she didn't have that kind of time—but she loved being Bernie Alphabet's wingwoman and having Bernie be hers. She loved the dick; didn't care much for the men that came with it. Renay Corren didn't care if you were a four-foot chain smoker named Fran or a seven-foot Frankenstein-looking motherfucker named Randy, if you were Joe the Redneck down at Cobra or that big Jamaican fella out in Hope Mills. She got what she wanted off you, no debate, no entanglements, no returns.

Renay's radical mastectomy, her acrimonious divorce, her dramatic post-Japan weight gain, her kids going every kind of FUBAR—it all turned out to be a kind of keyhole to freedom for Renay. A reverse blessing in disguise. Renay Corren became the loud, lovely, large-and-in-charge B&B fun-time lady who could *get it on*. She was the broad who fucked with impunity, ate with a vengeance, surrounded herself with the kinds of friends who didn't judge, and wanted to die laughing at the card table, with the taste of Pepsi on her lips and a shoot-the-moon in her hand. Renay lunged at her new lease on life, pledging to catch the next decades' hardships and setbacks that came at her—and they would—all those stars of doom that flew over our family, and flip that shit right back, roaring her laughter right into its face.

She was Renay Mandel Corren, the red-headed, one-breasted warrior-queen of Fort Bragg Boulevard.

Renay Mandel Corren could not be killed.

You cannot kill *freedom*.

Freedom is a warm bag of biscuits by the lake.

Freedom is a bigmouth bass dragged out and fried on a bowling alley grill on a hot Saturday morning.

Renay was never going back to the way things were.

She misplaced one son, yes, but then she found *herself.*

Then she found herself *again.*

2.

Anyway, we were evicted from Roach House in June of 1982.

ROACH HOUSE

1.

Summertime in Fayetteville.

There will be no balmy, skin-caressing nights out on the lanai. No blossomy winds wafting along dew-dappled palms, no moonlight skirted demurely behind a crèche of clouds.

No.

A Fayetteville summer is a touch meaner.

It's more like your still-drunk cousin left her hair dryer on high all night, pointed at your eyeballs, then stuck rotted azaleas up your nose as her nineteen-year-old boyfriend with flaming pimples and amber pits—who irritatingly refers to himself in the third person as, for some reason, "Deadrock"—stands above where you've passed out on the hot Flaming Mug parking lot, swaying and whispering lyrics from Molly Hatchet songs as warm beer dribbles out of his mouth and onto your face.

It being June, the dogwoods of Fayetteville have lowered their drawers, lewdly spreading their spring bloomers onto the ground in a fermented tapestry of singed-black petals, blanketing the city in a seasonal rite as certain as the Burning of the Wicker Chair. Heavy falls the pollen from the longleaf pine, and every single thing will soon be sprayed with a fine coating of poisonous lime-green powder. Windows will smudge with thick, toxic tree smut, making it next to impossible to discreetly observe the waves of freshly recruited soldiers who thunder into our neighborhoods on their morning marches. Legions of young jarheads in dainty yellow gym shorts; formations of muscular thighs and combat boots and heads shaved to the bare, glistening nape; legs like iron pistons on speeding trains, rising and stomping, rising and stomping *HOO-AH* over sunbaked streets paved with pollen and dead flowers. Soon, too, the malodorous bouquets of ancient catfish seduced to the surface of the dirty Cape Fear, breaded in seasoned cornmeal, then fried in peanut oil with tart green tomatoes, will mingle with the spice of pepper jelly, hog farm, Army sweat, and road crew, an ambrosial cologne that can only happen here in Fayetteville.

I absolutely *loathed* Fayetteville in the summertime.

Especially when we got evicted.

And we always seemed to haul those cardboard boxes out right when summertime fell like a staggered axe.

2.

None of the many Fayetteville houses my brothers and I lived in looms larger in our imagination, and our nightmares, than Roach House.

I can't explain it, but somehow the memory of a place we stayed hardly even a year, from 1981 to 1982, still beats like a one-armed incarcerated serial killer against the stone walls of time itself. Was it the name, Roach House, coined in one of our gallows boys' efforts to cope with our despair, and the incessant boldness of our many, ever-skittering, hungry little landlords? Was it the lack of heat? The winter of 1981–1982 wasn't particularly harsh, but on our thin mattresses huddled beneath our thinner blankets, the high thirties and, yes, sometimes upper teens howling outside, the cold crawled inside and set a deep chill, feeling worse than a normal Yankee cold ever could. Even colder when you subtract heating and power.

Let's subtract heating and power.

Me and Asshole and Twin had to learn to make peace with the power being cut off, with the water being shut off, with our little bug friends in the dark. Asshole was in charge of keeping a roaring fire made of the used bowling pins that Renay had Rabbi surreptitiously shlep out the back door of the B&B. Asshole loved the druggy, chemical green and red of those melting pins. He loves a sour smell, and a lime fire.

Whatever it was: we all hated that fucking place.

We evacuated Roach House in the middle of the night.

I imagine you are asking yourself some questions. For instance, "*Why* leave a place called Roach House? You make it sound so enchanting." A house named after a roach can hardly go further to hell, you properly surmise, but nobody ever tells you, until you get Corren poor, that hell is a high-rise, a multifamily residence with many levels above and below "the roach line." We were always stabbing at that up button, desperate to change our elevator's directions, but Correns seemed built to go one way only, each time: another level down.

Renay was always prepared for shit to go down, and so, by extension, were we. This was our third bounce house since she lost the house on Pamalee. Renay worked longer and harder than ever at B&B, she's gone full-time, and up and left the Sunoco behind, quite suddenly it seemed to me, taking second shift at the Qwik Mart, which was absolutely spelled Q-W-I-K, and where Renay *definitely* boosted bags of terrible groceries for us kids every single shift.

Renay was middle-aged, obese, and broke. She had that yo-yo, sugary diabetes that she kept at bay with shots of insulin, and even though me and Twin and Asshole routinely burned piles of carcinogenic bowling pins for heat in our darkest months of Roach House winter, we did have a roof over our heads. A whole house. We hadn't ended up at the trailers on Cobra, which remained the lowest point on Renay's internal dignity meter. I have a feeling that the Cobra trailers were *a lot* better furnished, not to mention had heat and power, than this roach-infested, damp shit brick on Brainerd that made my mom feel superior to the poors on Cobra. She was doing her best to keep us all alive, mostly warm, and her nails done. We laughed with her all along the way. Laughed at hunger, at the mustard-and-lettuce sandwiches, at the conniving to pry snacks out of vending machines with coat hangers, at the low-stakes boosting of hot plates of food at the K&W Cafeteria. We laughed at it all.

Until the next eviction.

Subsequent to our midnight evacuation of Roach House, twenty-two-year-old Rabbi had returned to Fayetteville Tech to get his GED and go Fayetteville legit. He was still slinging speed at titty bars, driving a cab full of hookers and parolees, and flirting each day with every Fayetteville son's seductress, the county jail. Asshole, following in his brother's illustrious footsteps, had at long last defeated the principals of Westover and dropped out junior year to spend more quality time with the oversized pickled egg jar and the broken cigarette vending machine at Bev's Place on Bragg. He spent his days making a menace of himself alongside Bev's son Dicky, and while not a total crook, Asshole was a minor functionary in a gang of world-class Fayetteville doofuses. They all loved Renay, and understandably. Our house was open and nonjudgmental, and our mother probably sold them weed. Everybody stole from one another, got drunk and punched each other out in the parking lot, drove too fast, wrecked each other's cars, got busted together, bailed each other out, and started all over again, just as soon as they sobered up. *Family.*

Cathy Sue had finally and wisely abandoned those grotesque Virginia Beach shores for the sleepy Outer Banks, a bucolic arrangement of doomed and shifting North Carolina sand dunes. Cathy Sue's second husband had, like all men everywhere, fallen deeply and possessively in love with his fried blond Pirate Queen, my shrewd and sexy sister, and relocated her to an island kingdom known primarily for its amenable sands, flimsy piers, all-you-can-eat flounder buffets, and palettes of colorful saltwater taffy. All of this, and a boat-shaped house by the sound.

Cathy Sue was headed in a *very* different direction on the Corren family hell elevator. Her shit was goin' *up*!

Me and Twin are thirteen and fourteen, two ambitious, horny teenagers, boxing our busted Atari; bundling our besieged cat, Frisky, into a laundry hamper with one of Renay's torn nylon stockings stretched over it so he could breathe. Move after move, we carted our secondhand clothes and stacks of Renay's *Penthouse* magazines and what little furniture we had into and out of homes, setting up shop, making our way through yet another school, exploring another neighborhood, then leaving when Renay ran out of cash. We made the best of the homes that she found, the shacks that lacked heat, water, or a phone. We made the best, because we had each other, and while we were often the worst, we were better than nothing at all.

Renay continued to keep Bonus very much at arm's length. She only passed along the most minor morsels of her oldest son's life, whenever he managed to find her by phone. I am told that Bonus graduated Pinecrest High. I am told he went into the Navy for a tour on a submarine. I'm told that he got married to a nice lady named Emily, then went to Chicago with his wife and had some kids. I do not know

Bonus, anything about his family, or anything about his life at all. When I think of my oldest brother at all during this calamitous, itinerant time in our lives, it is only lightly and uneasily, a haunted shadow that skips frames, dashing across the blinking corner of my vision, a nervous, unknowable blur just out of sight.

It all went to shit at Roach House when Rabbi got our Sansui receiver stolen from Bonnie Doone, which, again, is a neighborhood, not a girlfriend. All of Rabbi's girlfriends back then had proper, Christian-girl disco names like Pepper, or Summer, or Season. Bonnie Doone is a neighborhood on the north side of Fayetteville that has been so notorious for so long it has become synonymous with phrases like "carried out on a stretcher" and "next of kin." It's where Rabbi lived in a shack he rented from an upstanding Baptist slumlord named Brown, who was not only Rabbi's landlord but was also a dear family friend and Rabbi's personal attorney—a handy combination in a town like Fayetteville. The house had four walls and was affordable on a cab driver's salary, and well situated, too, on that busiest part of the Bragg Boulevard corridor that slingshots around Fayetteville from downtown to Spring Lake to Fort Bragg. My brother was a very busy driver, picking up a lot of fares on Hay Street: drunk folks with suspended licenses, lost soldiers standing outside payphone boxes in a hurry to get back to base before their pass expired. Rabbi took a lot of folks to a lot of cheap dentists, and quite a few ladies seeking discreet abortions to the nearby township of Spring Lake. He also racked up *a lot* of tickets and suspensions, so I expect the on-demand legal services provided by Deacon Brown were an attractive inducement. Barely twenty-two years old, Rabbi was well on his way through the relentless churn of Fayetteville's fine institutions of justice and correction, and about to go further than any of us had ever imagined.

Your honor, I rise to offer this in my brother Rabbi's defense: it wasn't just *regular* stereo equipment that was stolen from him in Bonnie Doone. It was far more sentimental than that. This was the last, remaining *good* stereo equipment that Shithead and Renay had returned with from our family's time in Japan, and it had sat in a place of honor in the last family house, on Pamalee. We didn't have rich-people things like scrapbooks or family heirlooms or good memories, stuff we could reverently gather around when the cable or the water had been shut off again. Oh, we had a few stray things. A portable Brother sewing machine that my mother never, not one single time, figured out how to use. Two wooden screens that somehow made the journey from Japan, and that we now used to create privacy in stinky shared bedrooms. A melancholy and sincerely ugly pair of oil paintings, a mamasan and a papasan, who looked down upon us from a series of ever shittier living room walls, who seemed to grow more exhausted with each move. We had several dozen cardboard boxes of purloined B-2 unit c-rations which never made it to Vietnam. Twin, Asshole, and I—always ravenous—enjoyed tearing into those thick, greasy, green plastic cans of bitter spaghetti and devouring stale, flat soda crackers dipped into packets of oily cheese spread, which, to this day—and I have been to Paris thrice—is the best thing I have ever eaten. We fought over who got the cans of pineapple cake, and Asshole always took the little four-packs of cigarettes the Army so thoughtfully provided, while I always swiped the creamer and instant coffee, because you never knew when guests might arrive. That was it, the few, paltry artifacts we had left.

Somehow Rabbi, of all people, our speed-slinging brother, managed to hold on to Shithead's deluxe Sansui stereo system, the one he bought between the Tet Offensive and the fall of Saigon, and left behind, with us, after the fall of the House of Corren. Rabbi *loved* that stereo. We all did. It was *comforting*. The wood paneling. The Akai

GX-747 reel-to-reel player. The thick silver knobs that turned a quiet, electric green with a humming, thrumming current that sent every audiophile's heart *racing*. Those boxy, breathtakingly tall speakers that made the walls *quake* with Southern power rock. It was a *serious* audio system for a *serious* stoner, and it was Rabbi's prized possession.

Then it got seriously stole.

One night the Sansui disappeared into the dank guts of Bonnie Doone's fascinating ecosystem of pawn shops and mobile home parks. However, what might be considered a lost cause to nearly the entire human race was merely a speed bump on the way to revenge for a man such as my stupidest brother—by a landslide—the foolish Rabbi of Bonnie Doone. He was inconsolable—and filled with a rage and lust for recovery. He somehow managed to get a tip from our family friend and part-time paid informant, Detective Hicks, a hulking and likable Fayetteville cop. We knew Detective Hicks from the bowling alley, and he always kept us out of real trouble. Rabbi pried the name and address of the suspected Bonnie burglar out of Detective Hicks, and then did the stupidest thing one can do in the Doone: he shot at that burglar. Now just to be clear, Rabbi missed all three times. But he was arrested, and now we needed some bail money.

It's just that simple.

Quick recap: exploiting trusted law enforcement contacts from the bowling center, my mother's one legitimate job, Rabbi ferreted out the name and address of Shithead's Sansui thief, a known local crook, and using some logic known only to himself, Rabbi modified a rifle so it would shoot wide, a few inches off to the side. With this reasonable plan and modified shotgun in hand, Rabbi drove to the known burglar's house, entered this crook's lair, and fired his modified rifle at close range—*boom boom boom*—chest, knees, chest. All misses, blasted safely into walls and floors. Nobody died. Rabbi's immediate arrest at the hands of kindly Detective Hicks, the very one who had unwittingly led Rabbi to this Doone burglar's lair in the first place, was what most dramatists would call Chekhovian irony, where opposites unite to reveal their true character. But in reality, it was just dumb brother luck. Rabbi caught a few well-earned Class E felonies, including assault and battery, assault with a deadly weapon, and felony breaking and entering. It threw our family into a familiar spiral of disarray.

Second, shorter recap: My brother lost his Sansui and his damned mind, and we lost our rent money, so we had to move.

Rabbi was in jail for over a month. It took every nickel Renay had to spring him, but she did it. With every financial bridge laughingly long ago burned behind her and—spoiler alert!—zero savings, Renay understandably got behind on the rent. There would be no catching up.

Like the many before us, we fell behind, because one of our own had fallen. But like the Navy SEALS, or the fabled 1982 Dolphins, who famously carried their destroyed tight end off the field before losing to the San Fucking Diego Chargers, we Correns do not leave one of our own behind in Bonnie Doone. Much as we would've *loved* to.

Renay bailed Rabbi out, and now Roach House was in the wind.

3.

The power was out again.

We were packing in the dark, but we didn't care. We moved around by flashlight, emptying waterbeds and dressers and kitchen cabinets, getting one last glimpse of rooms stained with water and mold. You would've thought it was Christmas Day at the orphanage. Our move was *light and joyful*. The moving van Renay paid for with a hot check practically floated into our driveway on Brainerd and loaded *itself*. We were *giddy*. We did not dwell for once on how weird it was to be packing up again so soon. We *celebrated* the end of our Roach House era. We didn't care that we were moving by candlelight. Caring was for rich Haymount people with electricity. We were evacuating a house we hated and closing the books on a very sad year in a very sad shack. I was thrilled. Asshole was high from huffing burnt bowling ball pin fumes. Only Twin seemed disturbed, not enjoying our impending liberation. He seemed to be thinking, which for him was always so touching, and so *visible*. This move was a bit of a thinker, in his defense.

"Why *now*?" Twin moaned by warm, gloomy flashlight shadow, uncorking what was, for him, an entire sermon.

Renay hitched up the garden hose that was slung over her shoulder like a rubber boa and snaked through her chaotic bedroom, wending its way, darkened bedroom to darkened hall, before slithering outside to be uncapped and put to use draining her beloved waterbed, for the cumbersome breakdown and transport over to Docia Circle.

Not one living thing on this earth was more important to Renay than that waterbed. Not. *One.*

"Because dem's the breaks," she said, stuffing her face with a slice of cold Pizza Hut pizza and tripping over a badly taped box of her undergarments, spilling several of the rubbery mastectomy prosthesis inserts she had amassed over the years, which then bounced into the dingy, carpeted hall.

"Goddammit, Ann, find my boobies," she instructed, receding into the darkness like a German silent screen enigma.

It had been nearly a decade since Renay found that lump in her breast and her doctors radically remade one entire side of her body. Yet losing one good tit had not slowed Renay down, not a jot. She loved that body, was proud of it, and used every bit of it, all day, every day. She ate, fucked, fished, bowled, farted, laughed, and loved *hard*. Renay took that mastectomy punch on the tit, then she laughed, spit some blood, *and she punched back*. I never forgot that kind of strength and tenacity.

Renay's bedroom was nearly ready to go, and she nudged another box of clothes towards Twin. "We don't go now, it's gone tomorrow," she sang out to him in that carefree, la-dee-da way of hers that both acknowledged and denied hardship might be at hand, recognized the *possibility* that we, her sons, might have it worse than other Fayetteville sons, or *might* be feeling a midnight move sting, and that this *might* be a growth lesson for us, eventually, if we paid some fucking attention.

That, or she was stoned.

Honestly, she was probably stoned. It was *very* late.

We had to get out of Roach House by dawn and get our shit across town and moved in by noon the next day. While we were draining Renay's waterbed, our new place across town was being rid of its previous, likewise impoverished tenants, no doubt by similar force of eviction, and we were coming in hot on their heels, loading in as they loaded out, not even a day between us. *Hakuna evicta.*

"There's a Tyler's Bookstore at the Cross Creek," I squealed at Twin from where I was struggling over the vexing dilemma of how to properly organize my deluxe pull-string denim Legos blanket with all my Legos, my journals, and my underwear. Tyler's was a sanctuary, and not just for me—apparently for a lot of quiet Fayetteville gays, because I had found the discreetly tucked-away rack of saucy gay potboilers, titillatingly taboo pulp with lurid, illustrated covers half-hidden by brown wrapping paper, written by nom-de-plumes like "Dick Dale" and "Lance Lester," with titles like *Gay but Not Happy*, *Mr. Fancy-Panties*, and the electric *Cruising Horny Corners*. I was so *thrilled* to be moving next to a store that sold forbidden erotica and first editions of Judith Krantz.

"Imagine that," Twin sarcastically whooped, "a whole store *for books*. Yay." He's always been the pithiest of my brothers, devastatingly circumspect about his rigorous intellectual disposition.

To my knowledge, Twin has never yet gone inside a bookstore or read a book.

We don't have too much in common, him being tall and blue-eyed like Paul Newman, a big, dumb handsome jock, and popular to boot. Yet Twin and I shared one of the three tiny bedrooms at Roach House—Asshole was sixteen so he got his own—and so on the night of our joyful eviction Twin and I packed together quietly, he sloppily boxing up his baseball gloves, his athletic supporters, trophies, cleats, and his one clean shirt. I, his polestar opposite in all things, was delicately folding my school papers, then reverently organizing the pristine, museum-worthy *TV Guide* collection that I had been amassing since 1976, when my true biological sister and brother, Marie and Donald Clark Osmond, first graced the cover of the August 7 issue. My *TV Guide* collection would be the first, last, and only thing that would accompany me along every single one of our midnight moves.

It was around two o'clock in the morning when Rabbi showed up from his second job at the Town Pump, or maybe it was the Sassy Lady, where you climbed the stairs above a tattoo parlor to, as the sign says, "where the action is." Rabbi moonlighted between taxi shifts as the in-house speed dealer to the pasties-and-tassels crowd down on Hay. He came back to Roach House to help us load up the truck. After serving his month, Rabbi had been liberated from jail only days before and briefly moved back in with us. Rabbi's freedom was still so new that he was enjoying great gulps of sultry summer night air. There was talk that he'd be departing Fayetteville soon, to let all that Bonnie Doone heat cool off around him. It was quite something to have him back from jail—there was a reunion feeling in the air that night, along with the choking, dead azalea bush heat, the gunpowder, and the pollen. Frankly, we had all been pessimistic about Rabbi's chances of wriggling out of his latest misadventure. This wasn't thirteen speeding tickets and a Baptist lawyer. This was firing a weapon at a man who stole a Sansui. Either Detective Hicks was still looking out for us, or that bowtie-wearing Baptist rascal Brown had reserves of wisdom we had not yet been exposed to, but all of Rabbi's felony attempted murder charges had magically and mysteriously vanished, and he was one foot out of Fayetteville, a free man.

"You went from cab to murder to jail to freedom in one month. Please tell us your secret, Mr. Corren," I said, sticking a rolled-up *People* magazine with Burt and Loni on the cover into Rabbi's face as we awkwardly walked and dropped, walked and dropped the peeling green laminate dining room table up and onto the rented truck.

"Thanks to *Mother*," Rabbi said, continuing as he would his entire life to refer to Renay as "Mother." "Thanks to Mother's Sunoco bag, I don't do the time and she don't do the gas."

He danced his eyebrows up and down in a parody of vaudeville, a kind of ironical air I have always found touching when paired with that cracked, innocent, wide grin of his.

Something about the timing of the past weeks clicked at that moment: Rabbi's bust and bail; Renay's last day at the Sunoco, a job she had *truly loved*, completely out of the blue, followed just as suddenly by those first shifts at D.J. Ledford's Qwik Mart, which was followed shortly after *that* by our eviction and this, our latest, hasty, midnight move.

After three previous moves, it was such a natural rhythm for us, why bother trying to make sense of it? I hadn't been paying too much attention to anything the last year, not with the biggest season of *General Hospital* in the rearview mirror, and Laura still gone missing from her honeymoon with Luke! *Very* few people were paying attention to their own, normal, boring lives, as things in Port Charles were *bonkers*. It was difficult to keep track of all the dropouts and jails, mental institutions and failed marriages, the broken cars and bounced checks, when there were *beautiful* and *skinny* people having all those same problems on ABC! Last season, in addition to the latest obstacles in the romance between Luke and Laura, there was a plot line that had to do with something called carbonic snow, mortal terror of which continued to keep me up at night, and the energy required to stare so lustfully at Blackie Parrish that I could shatter the TV screen with my mind gripped me *far more* than our latest eviction farce, or wondering why Renay was suddenly working second shift at D.J. Ledford's Qwik Mart.

I simply retreated into faith in my best friend Renay. I *believed* in our mother. I had to. She could get out of anything. I'd listened in on phone calls between her and the power company. I had heard her cast a spell on bill collectors and the Charles Chips deliverymen. Once, when Bonus was visiting Fayetteville from Chicago, he had to call information for our phone number—you read that right, he didn't have his own family's home phone number—*and the operator knew my mother personally, and loved her!* My brother and a total stranger at the Southern Bell had an entire conversation about what a hardworking, loving sweetheart of a gal Renay Corren of Scotty Hills, Fayetteville, was. I have no doubt that this random telephone operator had met my mother on a very important day—the day Renay's home telephone was about to be disconnected. Renay was talented. If she needed something, Renay could *reach* through a phone line and *touch you to get it.* She didn't pour on the charm so much as drown you in it, waving her gleaming nails at you, hypnotizing you, making *you* want to help *her.* That's how she made any bill, any problem, *disappear.*

Renay coming up with all that bail money? Conjuring the enormous sum of several thousand dollars requested by Deacon Brown, LLC? It never crossed my mind to wonder how she'd done it. When she stepped down from her long-held position at the Sunoco, surrendering her title as Fayetteville's Most Beloved Local Fat 'n' Funny Gas Lady, I didn't interrogate. You don't ask questions in Roach House, because almost certainly you're not going to like the answers.

"Let's just say *Mother* might have *lost track* of things." Rabbi winked, huffing and somehow puffing on both a cigarette *and* a joint, which I know sounds *impossible*, but trust me: *Rabbi can.*

So *that's* why she was let go from Sunoco.

Renay had "lost track" of some dollars.

I was *stunned.*

That Sunoco cash bag was Renay's whole world. It was how she paid out fuel deliveries and kept track of gas meters. That bag was everything—receipts, change, credit card slips, the next day's register, petty cash, deposits. Every little bit of that little booth's business came and went out of that one, badly locked bag. Let's say, hypothetically, a talented grifter had been put in charge of that bag, and let's say, again hypothetically, that talented grifter was blessed with a nearly completed two-year degree from a Miami trade school in accounting. This talented grifter *might have been* able to pull off a slow, steady—and hardly noticeable—theft from a Sunoco cash bag over time, if so inclined. I don't imagine a few twenties here and a credit card theft there were all that difficult to manage. But when a diabolical person—I mean, *IF* a diabolical person—got the hang of spreading some grift by manipulating a few gas pumps and graphs here and there, well, that's a different story. Especially if she happened to have an enthusiastic and obviously gay literary accomplice, one with tiny hands and a lot of time, who never asked questions, but was only eager to please his mommy so he could get some dollars for his dirty gay Tyler's pulp books. If those tiny hands knew how to reset those old-school, hand-operated gas kiosk meters to "oops, no gas pumped *here*," one logically assumes that the child's mother would be *super* grateful. I adored the sound of those old gas meters punching backward, and I loved pressing all the little buttons to reset them; they reminded me of the temperature controls on Darth Vader's chest armor. Renay kept me out of school often to work those gas meters backwards with her.

Though I cannot understand how this kind of steady, drip-drip loss would go unnoticed for so long—even *she* had a supervisor—the dramatic uptick in business at that Eutaw Village Sunoco may have spoken louder than those pesky, inconsistent meters. Maybe the Sunoco folks saw more cars than ever, people going out of their way, willing to wait in long gas lines just for the chance to buy gas, cigarettes, and oil from that hilarious big gal who was good for a smoke and could *really* land a filthy joke. Renay was so beloved by Sunoco, she told me, that they awarded her an annual bonus of *$1,500 a year*! For three years!! From *Sunoco*! A very large, very multinational oil company. Sunoco's gratitude to her began, Renay said, when she thought up the name Sunoco in the first place at a company picnic.

"Their gratitude can never be repaid," Renay told me.

Probably not a lot of what my mother said about her time at Sunoco was true. What's *true* is that I believed it. I believed her *so much* that I repeated that humdinger for years. To classmates, to friends, to colleagues. I told that stupid Sunoco story to everybody I met all through college and all the way into adulthood. I really wanted to believe my mother named Sunoco. I *needed* to believe her. Today, many, many years after our Roach House midnight escape, I am willing to concede that maybe, *possibly*, Renay didn't collect an annual $1,500 honorarium for cleverly naming the former Sun Oil Company to Sunoco at a company picnic, and that this money *might* have come from another source.

Renay's can-do attitude and fuck-you-oil-companies grit kept us afloat. Long enough to get a son out of jail, and get us out of Roach House, that's for sure. It was that spirit of never surrender, or try never to get caught, that kept us nearly fed, often quite warm, and, mostly, bailed out of jail. If that's the case, I would like to be the first person in all of human history to say:

Thank you, Big Oil!

I'd also, for the very first time in my *family's* history, like to be the first one to thank Rabbi publicly for saving us.

Because of Rabbi's historically stupid fuckup one night in Bonnie Doone, my family got to leave Roach House, and I got to join a girl gang that changed my whole life and *almost* kiss a male stripper when I was barely thirteen.

So thank you, Rabbi.

You absolute idiot.

THE ALL-GIRL GANG

1.

I can still recall that electrifying moment when my family's rusted caravan passed below the ominous red shadow of the twelve-foot-tall, endlessly rotating Coble Dairy milk carton on Ramsey Street for the final time, as we abandoned Roach House for good. My mother's fist was raised triumphantly at the hot, setting full moon, lifted from the window of her Nova in that traditional, single-fingered, North Carolina salute of respect as our ragtag retinue sailed away over the sparkling All-American Freeway, to slingshot around the fresh-smelling, still-metastasizing spread of Fayetteville's newborn nucleus of trade, the Cross Creek Mall.

I can easily summon that joyful taste, a metallic bouquet of hope and truck exhaust mingling in the back of my eager throat, swallowing the delicious certainty that I would never again have to burn with the humiliation of shoving the stalled Nova against traffic to turn left and traverse deadly Ramsey Street, nor spend another frigid night in an unheated house with a stained mattress duct taped over the living room fireplace in order to prevent the roaches from feasting upon our stale Merita breads. The moment our rented van, crammed with what was left of our shabby family history, pulled off Morgantown Road into an area of Fayetteville both familiar and exotic, I was filled with a new feeling, something I barely recognized: *optimism.*

After emptying Roach House, we had made our obligatory pilgrimage to Shoney's all-you-can-eat to fortify ourselves for manual labor, and it was now late Sunday morning as we approached our new lodgings. Rabbi was in his Rally Sport Camaro, one he built himself, Renay in the rusted Nova, the dragging tailpipe showering processional sparks, Asshole illegally behind the wheel of the dented rental van, Twin and me shotgun. Our three-vehicle parade crawled past parking lots teeming with the Sunday morning faithful, bustling between service and fellowship, the usual Fayetteville spread of six houses of worship per square mile.

We turned right onto the woodsy embankments of Kendallwood, up a languorous bend of bucolic, pine tree-lined brick ranches that seemed, if not welcoming, at least resigned to accept us, and then, there she was: a grayish smear half hidden on a rise, set a touch below the street, as if its hopes were already sinking at our approach.

Our new home.

The Docia House was set precariously, seeming to descend into a madness of rolling, primitive forest that reared up behind it. It was a house that looked like it was on the verge of a major depressive episode, just barely hanging on, popping pills and impulsively changing its hairstyle. It was gray with a garish red door and a soaring tree out front, already heavily weighed down with the big white satellite dishes of early-summer magnolia blossoms that I knew, when sniffed, would stink of champagne and lime, lemon and reeking jasmonate. The yard itself, like a middle-aged homosexual struggling to accept he is a Norwood 6 on the balding scale, had not yet given up on the *idea* of grass, but would soon have to accept the inevitable: it would be planted deep not with seeds, but patio chairs, cars on bricks, rusted-out engines, and living room detritus. It was hopeless to dream of something better. The Correns were here. On the other hand, I sensed the *wildness* and the *purity* of the untamed, primordial woodland just behind, and all that it promised. This was the Docia House, on Docia Circle, in Kendall-wood: *our new, twelve-month lease on life*. Option to renew.

In the 1880s, Docia was a very popular girl's name. It is a diminutive for the Greek Eudocia, and a variation on the immensely unpopular Theodocia. It is a sturdy, Christian baby girl's name, perhaps the ideal sibling name if you already have an Agrippina, an Ubelia, or a Dorit. The word Docia has had three accepted meanings, all of which would soon be challenged by the recently released Correns of Roach House: God's gift. Good reputation. *Comfort.*

We coasted to a stop at last. Asshole slowly backed the truck down into the driveway that started high and then slunk along with the rest of the house in the direction of the overgrown woods in back. The truck kissed the wall of what had once been a garage but had been converted into a badly insulated bedroom suite fated to be an older brother man cave, for sure.

"Who. Is. *That?*" Rabbi clownishly whistled, a mewling Jewish dingus with dancing eyebrows.

That, it turned out, was Sherry Anne.

She waved shyly from her position between her brick ranch house and our brick ranch house, standing as though she had been waiting for us. Waiting *for me*, her noble bearing said. Petite with a messy pixie cut, she curled one hand around a smoldering Marlboro Light—the freedom torch of all Fayetteville women since 1972—and held a can of regional Royal Crown Cola in the other. *A girl who smoked and drank RC Cola for breakfast? Be still, my galloping heart!* Her gaze took us in with that forthright directness that Southern women seemed to be deeded by right of birth, a knowing smirk and a daring glare, the twin smiles of every Dixie gal. *Don't fuck with me*, scowls one side, but the other grins and graciously beckons: *Get in the car, bitch, I'm fun.*

"Howdy, neighbor," she said, shy and without a trace of irony. She was rocking a brown leather biker vest that had STANLEY stitched boldly on the front pocket.

Swoon.

She scratched out her cigarette on the heel of her boot—an act that I would witness a thousand thousand times and never be able to gracefully duplicate—fired up another, and leaned back with her thumb in her jeans, regarding us, this obvious rabble, her new neighbors.

Renay exploded out of the Nova, grasping at her gut, which had been loudly, ominously, and flatulently rumbling since we departed Shoney's, and dashed, keys in hand, to properly christen our new home in the most fitting way our queen knew how. Ear-splitting, tuba-like exertions could soon be heard blasting all the way out into the front yard, where Renay's four shell-shocked sons stood, detached and haunted, but ultimately resigned to their fates.

Sherry Anne strolled over our bumpy, nearly grassless yard, shaking hands with my stupid, leering brothers. I felt a touch of fate on my shoulder that morning. Did she know already? Did she know in that moment, under our dreadful Sunday Fayetteville humidity, that she would be the one who gathered around me my first, real tribe of girl-friends? I wondered if she knew, deep down, that she was sent by her Methodist Lord to teach me, not about the Heavenly Kingdom, but about smoking, kissing boys, and the vital importance of memorizing every single inch of Judas Priest's *Screaming for Vengeance.*

"Heard y'all was comin' up today," she said. "I took a flier on church *with Dad.*" She grimaced.

Later, we'd learn that Sherry Anne's father was the celebrated Knife

Sharpening King of Fayetteville, an honest-to-God, certified Fayetteville celebrity. He was also a Methodist deacon, and so I could not believe my new best friend Sherry Anne had the courage to skip Sunday service *on a deacon*. To meet *Jews*.

"Asshole over there." I pointed to my bespectacled brother, who had already figured out a way to poke an even larger hole through our one remaining Japanese screen. "Twin over there. He's not my twin." This was obvious to her because by now, Twin and I barely resembled distant relations, although our Jewfros matched. "And that's Rabbi," I continued. "But he won't be here long, and if you're smart, you'll ignore him completely. He doesn't even speak English," I added, getting the first of many approving chuckles out of Sherry Anne. She nodded in Rabbi's direction, then furtively made the internationally recognized "let's toke later" gesture, which Rabbi acknowledged with another one of his weird, high-pitched dingo laughs.

Rabbi and Twin began sloppily breaking down moving boxes and jamming our stained paisley couch and Renay's beloved waterbed parts through the door, all while being hectored by my mother, still barricaded inside commode command HQ.

"Get that wreck emptied and back to Yadkin Road before five or I'm bouncing a check!" she called from behind the poorly sealed doors of her bathroom.

My brothers were cursing at me for not helping, but I was not the manual labor type, and even though I would go on to hold many blue-collar jobs in my life, I always found a way to get bigger boys to do my heavy lifting. Asshole flipped both Sherry Anne and me off, and together we grinned, then we flipped him off in tandem. We really were instant best friends.

"Wanna take a tour?" I asked, offering her my elbow. I hadn't so much as stepped foot inside, and I was eager to take inventory.

"Sure," Sherry Anne said, effortlessly smashing another Marlboro Light on the heel of her boot.

I would follow this woman to the gates of Methodist hell.

It wasn't the worst house on the block, but it did have a roof that slumped dramatically in the middle, like a terrible book of history. The slump was above the garage-turned-living room-turned bedroom, and it looked like it leaked, but that would be some other brother's problem, *not mine.* There were two other tiny bedrooms along the hallway on the other side of the house, and one tiny, green-tiled bathroom for us all to share. At the quiet end of the house was Renay's large and airy lair, spacious enough for her queen waterbed, with its own privy where, at that moment, terrible, terrible sulfurous clouds had gathered. Everything in the kitchen looked like it had been set on fire at least twice, extinguished, painted over thrice, then burned again. But the stove worked, and the fridge, too, and the sink water ran clear. This was a mansion. Finally, on to the ass end of the house, which butted into the trees in back: a dank, tacked-on laundry room that had a concrete floor thinly covered by rotted old carpet, a hanging bare light bulb from unseasoned beams lending the room a meat locker vibe.

The Docia House was irrefutably an improvement over Roach House. For one, it didn't come with roaches. For two, it was close to my new school, Westover, so morning bus rides would be fast. For three, and most exciting to me, I could walk across the 401 Bypass and, if I survived that perilous passage, be inside centrally air-conditioned Cross Creek Mall *within minutes.* With our yellow paisley pull-out sofa, the house could reasonably sleep six, which meant that the eight to twelve bowlers and strippers and dealers who Renay routinely took in after they got evicted, paroled, or off work late would all have a place to drop their bags, stow their drugs, take a hot shower, and move on quickly before the cops or parole officers or ex-husbands found them.

"Ready to see the rest?" Sherry Anne asked slyly, parting the heavy sliding glass patio doors out onto the vast, primordial wildness that was the backyard of Docia. To my eyes, it seemed to go on forever before finally crossing a muddy little creek, then linking up to the much-better looking, manicured side of the neighborhood. *Landscaped for fancy people.*

"Follow me," Sherry Anne said.

I did.

We hiked to a muddy trail that snaked between our matching houses, taking us through the untamed jungle directly down a long, twisted tunnel made of hanging ivy, bushes of thorn and overhanging jasmines on both sides, before depositing us at the wooden fence in the split-level backyard of Sherry Anne's adjoining neighbor on the back side, Angela.

"Hey." She gestured, waving us over, gritting a cig in the corner of her voluptuous, lip-lined mouth.

Angela's heavy eyeliner sparkled in the hazy morning sun, and her full lips curled at the corner into a welcoming, daring sneer, lips that were Roman and strong, held up by a defiant, pointed chin that was always raised. She had that *presence*, the presence of a woman always prepared to do a monologue, or fuck somebody up. Or both.

"It's so good to meet you!" Angela said warmly and loudly, throwing arms around me like a long-lost cousin. Her amazing boobs bounced freely in a loose, crochet crop top, and her tomboy shoulders were muscular and tough, like a rock-climbing wall.

"I hear you got a bunch of brothers. You can feed 'em to mine," she snickered between puffs. Angela smoked with two tight fingers death-gripped on the butt, thumb smashed around and herky-jerked to the corner of her mouth like it was there to do its business *and git*. Angela's voluptuous curls bounced, warning the humidity to fuck with *her*, dazzling in the pine-dappled morning light.

"Welcome to the jungle. Got any weed?" she asked me.

I was barely thirteen and had yet to indulge in anything, including marijuana, but everybody I knew and was related to smoked copious amounts of pot, and it flowed freely throughout all our households. I always knew where to get weed: my mother's Nova ashtray. That woman never took more than two hits before she crushed a joint into the discard pile.

"My brother usually keeps a garbage bag next to his bed stuffed full of weed," I said. "Come on by and steal a bud," I offered.

Angela's street might as well have been in a different country for how stark the difference was between our side and hers. She was on the middle-class side of Kendallwood. Angela's parents were classy, fighting drunks who worked normal jobs and still smoked and entertained like it was 1973, which was when they had peaked, and they did not give *a fuck* what you thought of their heroic, bottomless five o'clock cocktails that emptied by seven o'clock and were refilled until long past nine. Angela navigated a rocky, brawling Korean-Southern household that seemed at once theatrical, loving, contentious, vulgar, fun, bitter, and always on the brink of nuclear meltdown. It was *divine*. Angela's parents—*she had parents!*—had some knock-down, drag-out fights in front of us, and you know what? They didn't give *a shit* who witnessed it. I *worshipped* them. Angela brought me into another kind of family altogether. A family that *stayed* together, no matter who screamed *what* at *who* in *what language*.

Angela was also the first person who told me about Westover's superior drama club, the Thespian Society, and the first one who would sneak me over from the junior high into the high school side, helping me infiltrate her exciting world of divine upperclasswomen, and the powerful drama troupe they had formed, one that was respected *county-wide*. Angela would be instrumental in bringing me to the attention of the mentors who would change the very course of my life. But without knowing any of that here, today, I already knew that Angela *was capital D Drama*. Old school, Italian opera, Sarah Bernhardt painted onto a Paris stage *drama*. If there was one thing my education by Dame Jaqueline Jill Collins, OBE, had taught me, it was how to spot a star. *Angela was a star*. Sparks *flew* from her knowing eyes when they fell upon you. Lord help any man caught in that diamond Korean glint. She knew how to hold a classmate or a raging drunk parent by the throat, and then strangle that bitch to the ground.

Two of those classmates of Angela's were currently outstretched on Kmart beach towels behind her, both seeking sun, lightly oiled up this fine, hazy morning with actual baby oil, because skin cancer did not exist in Fayetteville, not yet, not in the 1980s. Both of them were *so tan* they looked like candied bacon strips. They were leaning on their elbows, gazing up, tube tops rolled down, and *glaring* at me.

"Don't be scared, they don't bite. Come say hi to your bitch neighbors," Angela ordered, and I followed, laughing.

"Tammy," Sherry Anne pointed at the tall one. "And Honey," she said, pointing at the taller one. "They're both cunts, but the good kind." Sherry Anne giggled as Angela exploded her truck driver laugh.

Tammy and Honey were blond powerhouses in high-ass cut-off jeans. Just *knockout* pretty, and, like Sherry Anne, both sophisticated upperclasswomen at Westover. Here they were, deigning to talk to me, a lowly junior high pansy. I was honored. It was easy to mistake Tammy and Honey for sisters: both were leather brown, hard-jawed, and strong-limbed, with long, blond locks feathered to Xanadu.

"What's up, bud." Tammy raised a couple of "peace" fingers in salute, strikingly elongating the word "bud" at least three and a half seconds longer than it had ever been uttered before.

"I'm Honey. I'm not the *biggest* bitch," Honey said with a glare at

Sherry Anne, before turning her face back up to the struggling sun, daring it to hide from her glaring radiance.

All four of them seemed—to me—like they were lifelong friends. But this is Fayetteville—people come, people go; that's life in an Army town—so who knows how long this backyard girl band had been playing. These girls looked *tight*. They also looked tougher than my own brothers. Of tougher country stock, this much was obvious. Tammy's mom and dad raced cars up and down the drag strip and regional stock circuit, so Tammy definitely knew her way around a wrench better even than my brother Rabbi. Honey's dad flew planes over Pope Airfield, which meant he was smarter by a mile than my father. Her parents were on the rocks, but that was normal Fayetteville stuff. The girls quickly brought me up to speed on their lives, and left *nothing* out, so that, within minutes, I would know about Honey's parents' marriage, Angela's weird habit of dipping slices of cold cream cheese into jars of mayonnaise, that Sherry Anne was seeing Stan the Biker on the sly because her dad didn't approve, and that Tammy thought Angela might be the bigger slut of the two.

I did not think I could love Kendallwood any more than I already did.

Until Hollis arrived.

Hollis strolled into Angela's backyard that morning like she owned it. A ferocious, high-haired, low-down jungle cat who led with her laugh, her belly, and her fists. She painted and bit her nails, her knuckles were raw from yesterday's fight, and Hollis always knew just how big of a bitch she needed to be. When you're a Hollis, it better be *big*, and you better be wearing leopard tights. Hollis had exactly two switches: on and *really* on. If she was awake, Hollis was *really* on. *And oh my God, you were, too.* Her laugh—generous, withering, a hurricane laugh—was a horse race, a galloping, gutsy affair that nearly always ended with Hollis doubled over, coughing and blasting her lungs with an inhaler, or a cigarette, or both, because, yes, she *absolutely* smoked and had asthma, what the fuck are you gonna do 'bout it?

Hollis had a Black boyfriend, which in 1980s Fayetteville was, regrettably, still kind of a baseline scandal. Hollis knew it, and she didn't give one fried fuck. For a white girl to be in an interracial relationship, to be so comfortable in her own skin, to have her mother's blessing, it was very rare and powerful to be around. It was *freeing*. She had to mostly keep her boyfriend on the down low, but she was like me in that way, I could already tell: forced by geography and culture to hide in plain sight who we loved. Hollis taught me probably more than anybody how to keep your shit locked down, how to stay alive under fire, how to keep the bullshit onstage—not off—and how to protect the ones you love.

Also, Hollis taught me that no hair ever, anywhere, was ever big enough. Nowhere.

Nobody fucked with Hollis.

Nobody fucked with Hollis's mom, Hattie, either. She was petite, but she packed a punch. Hattie seemed to wake up with the energy of a marathoner, a full face of perfect makeup and a homemade Jimmy Dean sausage biscuit in one hand. She was a hairstylist and a working-class Christian mom, and Hattie's home, family, and job all reflect the beautiful values of Jesus: love one, love all, feed the poor. Hattie worked out of her carport, which became a clubhouse of sorts, for my girlfriends, for Hattie's girlfriends, for the Fayetteville makeup gays in the know, a place to feel safe, trade gossip, do some aerobics, style some hair, and maybe, just maybe, meet a boyfriend. It was the very first gay safe space I ever experienced, and the only one I would ever know in Fayetteville, outside of a community theater lighting booth.

All of a sudden, I had a gang.

I had a clubhouse.

I had *friends*. A band of scrappy princesses, just like me.

I was a part of a *girl gang*.

2.

The Kendallwood All-Girl Gang ran thick and ran wild.

We raised hell, and we did it with the volume turned up *high*.

Renay was always gone, practically living at the B&B, or on the road wherever the cribbage pegs were flying, or out at the lake when the fishing was good. North Carolina has fifty-nine lakes, seventeen rivers, and 3,300 miles of coastline. The fishing is *always* good in North Carolina. Renay followed the Wolfpack during the college basketball season, cribbage during the competition season, and bowling contests all year long.

Renay came home with provisions in a warm drive-thru bag, slept a few hours, rose to pick out her rosy hair, and then went right back out that busted door to one of her three jobs or out onto a lake in Porky's boat, waving goodbye as we hungrily devoured whatever she had thrown on the table as she sailed away again.

We weren't latchkey kids, because none of us ever had a key. We were wolves.

I was frequently left to fend for myself and cook up a can of corn or defrost something frozen and burned, and when Renay was in residence for a meal or a television event, I attended to her like she was a visiting papal dignitary.

I was otherwise with my all-girl gang.

They had become my *real* family, my confessors and sounding board as I began to toy, in the shadow of all their torrid desires, with my own sexual identity and same-sex attractions. It had become difficult if not downright impossible for me to bring up these confusing, burgeoning parts of myself with my part-time mom, who barely had a bunioned toe in the door before she was right back out again. Despite Renay's complete and total acceptance of me, which I knew down deep, and her acceptance of everybody, really, Renay had never once asked me about my feelings. She never inquired into my desires. We never had "the conversation," because we never had to. There was porn and weed and strippers everywhere, so I suppose she rightly thought, *Why bother?*

But I had never met a gay person in our home, and only knew, like most Fayettevillians, the one quiet gay from the bowling alley, Rocky, the friendly neighborhood child molester everybody tolerated because Rocky was *such* a talented florist and cabinet designer. We had no language for gay stuff otherwise, not back then. Gay stuff was hidden behind closed doors. Whispered about. It was a different era in North Carolina, especially, and in that way, the Correns were no different from any other family, even with Renay's well-known deep reserves of radical acceptance, and my hidden-away stack of Dick Dale pulp novels to break the ice.

I turned to my girls.

Renay did not mind the time we spent together. She already knew Sherry Anne, she lived right next door, and Angela was right behind us and over all the time stealing buds from Rabbi and Asshole's weed bags. The girls were hovering over our house at all hours, bossing me and my brothers around, commandeering the television for *General Hospital* or *Knight Rider*. Renay loved domineering, funny, pushy, loud gals. She loved that they fed me, looked out for me, that maybe one or two of them might be getting it on with one or two of her sons. Rabbi, Asshole, and Twin were obviously attracted to and frightened by my Kendall-wood girls. They were strong country women, and they were not in the least intimidated by my stupid brothers. The girls knew my brothers desired them, and they were smart enough to use that to their—and my—advantage. As everybody knows, it's a fine line between death and desire, and in those murky, murderous jungles of my Kendallwood backyard, my girls simply *killed*. It must have pleased and comforted Renay to see me, her youngest and oddest child, this tiny misfit, at last connecting, even if it was with a bunch of redneck bitches who wore too much makeup and short shorts cut too close to the butt.

My girls showed me the world. They pulled back the mildew-stained, plastic shower curtain of Fayetteville and gave me my first, privileged, up-close glimpse of romantic *life*, one seen in the flesh, not in a Judith Krantz novel or riding shotgun down Hay Street. It was all going down in my own backyard. We were a sultry bitch posse focused on two things and two things only: *rock and cock*.

My all-girl gang dated, screwed, and threw over all the guys at Westover and Kendallwood that I could never get within a foot of. Sherry Anne rode with her boyfriend Stanley's biker gang, and so she was the most glamorous thing a Fayetteville woman could ever dare to be: Sherry Anne was Stan the Biker's "old lady."

I *lived* through them.

I no longer had to imagine what real love, real lust, and real hot-tempered desire looked like. I just had to pick up the phone or walk through the wilderness of our backyard, and even though I was scared of being gay, I walked *safely*. That's because I not only lived *through* my all-girl gang, I lived *because of* them. My brothers, all very big, very dumb, and very feared, had done a fine, albeit accidental, job of protecting me. Everybody knew I was the youngest Corren brother, the weakling runt, and everybody knew not to fuck with a Corren. We were *that* family. But we were all separating now: Asshole off stealing eggs and shooting up cars, or vice versa; Rabbi about to get in his first nuclear power plant disaster; Twin with his sports. My brothers were dropping out of high school left and right, forming their own friend groups, leaving each other and me and this house behind. They would all, to a brother, be gone soon. So I was more and more exposed as that crucial part of me, the deepest, most natural part of me, was revealing itself. You cannot bury that sissy shine for long, people, no matter how much flannel or hair gel or Billy Joel you spray over it.

I made an inviting target.

Nobody was monitoring me—or my clothes. It was summer in Fayetteville and I was *done* going down to Miami. There was no school and it was hot as fuck, so naturally I took after my girls and started wearing the tightest, highest, whitest cut-off jean shorts I could find, tucking neon-colored tank tops into them and pulling the whole look together with a pair of purple pastel aerobics shoes I had found in a thrift store on Bragg. I was really coming into my own as a style icon.

Here I was, growing up in a kind of sexual, cultural apartheid state—a small, Southern town with very few gay safe spaces, just three channels on TV, zero internet, and no way to find like-minded souls. I had a Christian hairstylist's garage down the street.

That was it.

When you grow up gay under fire in a state like North Carolina in the 1980s, bottom line is that the simplest, even most innocent expression of desire could get you killed on the spot. There was no way to try out ordinary things like dates or dances or getting pregnant at fifteen. There was no holding hands or having a crush, not for the kinds of boys I was surrounded by, not for the kinds of guys I crushed on. Jocks, bikers, soldiers, closeted Air Force pilots.

Even still, I was lucky.

I had several extra layers of protection, at least. A buffer of brothers, tough bitches, and all their bad-ass brothers, too, all who would ordinarily have piled on me, but instead, they laid off.

My Kendallwood girls did that. They made it safe for me.

The Kendallwood All-Girl Gang loved on each other, made war on each other, doing both like it was our full-time job. Girl battles over curling irons, who could beat up Hollis's brother, who would be the first to fuck Steve Perry, which one of us could get tickets to see Judas Priest, which biker club was hotter, who was more manly, Michael Jackson or Joan Jett. Our fights and our crushes bloomed and collapsed all summer long, allegiances made and lost beneath wilting dogwoods and the molten sun, promises broken at the Cross Creek Mall, friendships mended over literal fences, all of it so hot and passionate and steamy and *female*. Holy Methodist Christ, I still remember those late nights spent in deep Eastover woods, all my girls gathered protectively around me by the glow of Stanley's motorcycle gang headlights, the night air thick with mosquitos and exhaust, the hum of cicada, Iron Maiden, and bongs. Sherry Anne's "old man," who was barely twenty, had long, greasy hair and adorable, boyish stubble. He was *so cute*. Stan's thick mechanic's jeans hung low off his sexy hips, and his gang colors flashed in the dark off his faded leather jacket. How I hungered for just one ride on the back of Stan's hog, arms wrapped around his thin, strong shoulders as the two of us roared down Hay Street at midnight, blasting all the way out to Clinton and back on the Roseboro Highway in the fog.

There were so many boys hanging around so many girls in so many places, and they all just sliced through each other like hot plastic cutlery through fresh Raeford lard. I wanted to get dirty and funky like my girls. I wanted to *get down*. I longed for my own Stan, my own Curtis and Miles, my Jay and my Anthony. I desperately wanted a man *to see me* that summer of 1982.

And then all of a sudden?

I got saw, y'all.

BACKYARD FRUIT

1.

The rules were simple.

Stay out of Renay's bedroom.

Don't steal from her purse.

Secure your Pepsi.

If you fix food, leave food.

Lock up your drugs, don't use the long distance, and for God's sake, under no circumstance, do not, for any reason, *open the laundry room door.*

I get it.

If it walks like a trap house and quacks like a trap house, it's probably a trap house. Nobody ever got arrested or died on Docia, not while we lived there, but it wasn't a church social, either. What it was, was *fun*. Anything could be a cause for celebration. A Dolphins resurgence, a Steelers domination, another Wolfpack playoff. A successful day on Eastover Lake. Doreen back from a nonstop to-and-from-New-Hampshire trip with ten crates of cheap, fresh lobster. Anything went, and anybody, too.

The door was tall, red, and wide open.

Docia was a way station for a steady string of Jewish brawlers, redneck thieves, marriage flip-floppers, gamblers, and dealers. Twin and I might be rousted out of bed by a homeless stripper tiptoeing in off a long shift at the Sassy Lady, or stumble across a heated midnight game of hearts in the living room, or find Butt Check and Renay, those two sleepless cribbage ghouls, slapping cards and insults at each other in the semi-darkened dining room. A small party of Rabbi's friends might be huddled around the TV watching pirated HBO, courtesy of the stolen cable wire that slithered down from the pole, through the trees, and into the house through taped-up windowpanes.

It was a grimy, joyful, everyday noise that never stopped, a home where the front door was never locked, and the cracked doorframe was always filled with exciting new visitors. Renay's life *glittered* to us.

Of course her sons wanted a dollop of what she had, an excess of fun, laughs, and friends in the face of want, or the law, or bosses. I found my glitter in a pack of ferociously tough backyard girls who were grossly underparented, hugely oversexed, and dressed to show some ass for it. My brothers drew around themselves a circle of felons-to-be that Renay begrudgingly admired. She really had a type: canny, up from your bootstraps, street smart, tough, hard enough for the Army, but smart enough to stay out of jail. She housed, fed, consorted, copulated, and cohabitated with a never-ending supply of the shabby jet set of Fayetteville, a veritable who's-who of the *Fayetteville Observer* crime report come to life.

Asshole quit school and was now working part-time at the bowling alley and full-time assembling his Hillbilly Avengers. Rabbi tried going legit after getting his GED at Fayetteville Tech, but had only just barely survived a plummeting tower crane wrench that fell upon him from high above the new nuclear power plant in the sinister-sounding Fuquay-Varina, that exurb of Raleigh where he and so many others had gone in search of nuclear fortune. After touching the face of God, and his own atomic mortality, and after his close brush with Bonnie Doone infamy, and then a lighter brush with an infamously short marriage he absolutely forgot had even happened, we all felt that Rabbi might have finally pushed his celebrated luck to the brink. Rabbi at last confronted, as all young Fayetteville men eventually must, the choice between a life, or a life with the 11th Air Defense Artillery Radar Operation and Patriot Launcher Brigade.

He chose the latter, and that was a wrap on Rabbi Corren in North Carolina.

The rest of us were very busy surviving.

Me and Asshole and Twin spent a lot of time locating food, insinuating ourselves tightly into the bosoms of our own personal protective ecosystems. Twin and I were the only two sons of Renay not yet dropped out, or arrested, or exiled somewhere far-off and exotic, like Chicago. We were thriving in our respective school circles, him with the jocks, me with the dorks and my all-girl gang.

Renay was earning extra cash after B&B closed by riding shotgun with our town's celebrity drug dealer on wheels, D.J. Ledford, heir apparent of the Qwik-with-a-*K* fortune, where Renay also picked up shifts after her celebrated run at the Sunoco gas kiosk came to a felonious end. A hypnotically beautiful dummy with wavy surfer-blond hair, D.J. Ledford operated Fayetteville's one and only drug delivery service, a discreet white panel van that came directly to your door, pizza-boy style, to the delight of his many satisfied customers. My enterprising and cost-conscious mother, always on the hunt for both a bargain and an important alliance, found in D.J. Ledford a friend, a bowling partner, a solid discount on drugs, and, it must be said, an occasional fuckbud. Roaming Fayetteville's new highways and rutted, familiar byways, D.J. on the wheel and Renay in the back, he would roll to a slow stop—but never a full stop—and customers would jump in the back with Renay. Merchandise was thoughtfully scrutinized on the carefully pegboard-lined interior, various popular pills and seductive powders and buds, all tagged and bagged professionally, pinned to the walls, Renay's shapely hands beneath like Janice from *The Price Is Right*, rustling them temptingly as the van bounced the rutted roads to glorious ruin.

D.J.'s van became a fixture to the sweet-toothed set of Fayetteville, treasured for its extravagant curbside delivery service and for always having the freshest product directly off the famed I-95 drug smuggling corridor that bisected Fayetteville like a drunken rhombus. D.J. was a wildly successful, in-demand dealer, lusted after by women and men alike. He was also under constant surveillance by the Fayetteville PD, the FBI, and the SBI, but fortunately for my mother, D.J. was never busted when she was on the clock. He wrote *a lot* of bad checks, though, and that shit catches up with you in the end.

Renay's salary as a co-pilot more than made up for the loss of that Sunoco money. Renay was *providing*, in one of the best ways she knew how: laughing her ass off, high as shit in a drug delivery van. Sure, she got her hands a little dirty, but she did not do all that just for money.

She did it for money *and* because D.J. gave her a discount.

2.

Privacy was completely nonexistent.

I did have my own coffin-sized bedroom, and it even came with a door, so I didn't have to share with Twin, the very first time we had ever enjoyed such luxury. But there was otherwise no place to hide from the overstuffed, 24/7 carnival of Correns on Docia. So many people walked through the door it was honestly impossible to tell sometimes who actually lived on Docia, and who didn't. Frisky, our darling orange tabby, was a mess with all those comings and goings, and had taken to anxiety-defecating on the dining room curtain. Nobody seemed to mind.

I minded.

There was no place for a broody, blue-balled baby gay to turn for quiet contemplation and deeper contemplation of the particularly filthy parts of Great Works of Paper-Wrapped Literature such as *Mister Fancy-Panties* and *Lights Out, Little Hustler*.

I was more than just a horny little baby gay.

I was a creator and a dreamer. Yes, I was a celebrated poet, albeit celebrated only on the sides of buses and in the back pages of the *Fayetteville Observer*. Still, I ached, always ached, to be creating, performing, writing. I knew I needed someplace of my own where I could be free to think like a poet is supposed to think. I craved a place to get away from all the clutter and the cacophony of our never-ending shelter station. I craved a place to have my long-afternoon Flock of Seagulls–induced sexual swoons. A place to jot down my big dreams, to write my stories, to plot revenge on my enemies. I didn't have any enemies yet, but I would. I knew that. Powerful people always attract enemies, eventually. I needed an escape hatch, high above all this transient, nonstop *mess*. As J. Cole, the beige sage of Forest Hills Drive, said, "This shit can go up, it can go down."

I went up.

The roof became my domain.

I used to dream whole worlds up there, up above the laundry room that we could no longer use, because one of us—I never found out who—had busted the washing machine our first week on Docia and flooded a half dozen loads of filthy clothes waiting on the thin gruel of a carpet. Then they left it all just sitting there! Huge, sopping wet,

June-hot heaps of carpet and water and clothes. Those heaps all molded over *within days*, turned a lushly gray-green color. The laundry and the carpet fermented together into a bog after several more days, and we, the seemingly blind occupants of Docia, merely avoided the room, resolutely ignoring the hills of fuzzy penicillin gradually rotting our rags down into a sickening, moldering heap.

We shut that door.

We never went back in there, not once, until the day we left Docia for good—and none of us will ever be the same for what we saw when that hellmouth was finally unsealed. Closing the door on a disaster of our own making, and only confronting it when it absolutely could no longer be ignored? Very on-brand for Team Corren.

Still, even as that door was sealed, the fumes of our decomposing clothes could not so easily be denied. As I sat on the rooftop above, the vapors of our forsaken laundry mingled with the languid summertime aroma of the gardenia tree that hung just above the house. It was fully in bloom, its waxy white flowers evolving their zesty fragrance into a musky, not totally unpleasant mixture of decomposition and dread, with weirdly hopeful undertones of sex and corruption. That's a summer in Fayetteville smell, right there.

Up on the roof, I could unwind, sip a Mello Yello, and practice smoking like Sherry Anne. I could listen to bootleg tapes of Cheech & Chong on Rabbi's portable cassette player and, when Sherry Anne or one of the other girls joined, talk about boys, boys, boys. Biker boys. Jocks. Army boys. Air Force boys. Or the hottest straight man in the whole universe, Rob Halford, lead singer of Judas Priest.

Free of my family below, I began to slowly hatch my plan for escaping Fayetteville. Up there, I dreamed the first contours of the life I wanted to live beyond the 401 bypass. The person I wanted to become was born among fumes of night flowers and rancid wash. It was up there that I realized that to have the courage to leave, I would eventually have to leave her.

Up on that roof is where I had my first taste of imagined life without Renay.

It would be a fight, I knew that.

But what future *isn't* worth fighting for, even one born above the stank of sealed-off failure?

I wasn't just *her son*.

I wasn't just *a poet*.

I was an agent of destiny!

I had a future!

I had a plan!

I had a journal.

And I had binoculars.

3.

It was a hazy, drizzly Sunday morning, June 20, 1982, when I spotted through my bifocals a moving truck on Hearthstone Drive. Next to Angela's house.

I immediately called Angela, but I got her parents, who liked me very much, and frequently reminded me that I was the kind of upstanding boy who could be a *good* influence on their daughter, and teach that girl some manners. They didn't know that Angela had already taught me how to give head using a Polska kielbasa sausage, and how to take a respectable-sized shotgun hit off a homemade beer koozie bong.

The moving van glided into the brick split-level whose backyard bordered our own but felt many miles, and many income brackets, away. It was neatly trimmed, running for about a quarter mile straight down a long hill, ending at the same muddy crick that was the boundary of my own backyard—a bewildering maze of ten-foot-tall weeds, bags of trash, a rusted shed, and—the tumbleweed of the South—a tire swing. The grounds of our backyard cantered uphill, a wild green asylum stopped by our sad brick ranch, seething with its general air of resignation and despair. Their split-level seemed to radiate prosperity and clean teeth and riding lawn mowers.

I stayed on the roof, continued my spying operation deep into the dark gray, new moon night of June 20, observing as boxes, several weight benches, bicycles, two leather chairs, and an electric wet bar were unloaded by a passel of sweaty, friendly movers. In the falling, hazy twilight, I could make out three of them, three strapping, burly young fellows, one a redhead, one a brunet, one with wavy, perfectly parted, light brown hair that fell precisely like the sexy international spy of Port Charles, Robert Scorpio. It was so quiet in the early-summer evening of our woodsy new neighborhood that if you listened closely, you could hear phones popping off all over Kendallwood, ring upon ring, house upon house, as the urgently whispered news of our new neighbors spread like melted butter all over a fresh hot cob of Lumberton Triple-Sweet. Unloading their belongings onto the lawn, as the evening skies darkened, the movers wore progressively less as their lifting got heavier. The night came on muggy, and those boys *glistened*, their clothes now soaked, the waistband of their shorts sprouting sweat stains like exotic flowers. The movers were periodically interrupted by a stern, flinty-faced older woman who I did not respect *at all* for the interruption.

They called her Nancy, and she slapped playfully at their butts, motivating their pace, pushing them to move faster, sweat more.

By the time I climbed down off my roof, my binoculars were fogged with grease, humidity, and a kind of desire I had never before known, stark and plain for all to see, as hungry and eager as the sequestered, aching new moon above.

4.

On the afternoon of June 21, several phone calls were exchanged near simultaneously.

Honey called me, then Tammy called her, then Hollis called Tammy *and* Angela, then Sherry Anne didn't get a call at all, somehow, and so I screamed for her to quickly join me on my roof. By the time the muzzled summer solstice sun sank behind dank clouds and a low, garbled afternoon haze, everybody who mattered in Kendallwood now knew the truth:

Those were *brothers, not the movers.* They were the brothers that were moving *in.*

My new neighbors.

That evening, I was invited to attend a Monday night service with Sherry Anne, as Fayetteville United Methodist doled out a free chicken and pastries potluck afterward, and that is my culinary kryptonite. I attended, so that I might thank God in person for my new neighbors.

5.

By the afternoon of Wednesday, the twenty-third of June, and without the help of the internet, which had not even been invented, we knew their names and their ages.

Kirk was twenty-three. Nico was nineteen. Vin was twenty.

The Rossi brothers.

The Rossis had joined us in Fayetteville from New Jersey, with their mother, my nemesis, Nancy. No father to be seen, but this is Fayetteville, so fuck a dad.

"New Jersey!" Honey reminded me caustically. "It's right near New York City!"

The Promised Land.

"They've probably been there!" Tammy whooped, before sneaking away from us and casually strolling over to the Rossis with some trumped-up, harlot bag of phoney baloney welcome tomatoes and white bread, the Southern slut's calling card. Hollis, Angela, Sherry Anne, and I were forced to watch the whole charade from the roof through my binoculars, and the Rossis were completely taken in by Tammy's ruthless charm. Why shouldn't they have been? Those were some sexy tomatoes, and she had that wide, fake smile.

Sherry Anne, Hollis, Angela, and I wagered that Tammy would undoubtedly become the first of us to bed those brothers, but I had, alas, already double-crossed my fiery Angela and bet against *her*.

Everybody knew Angela was impatient. Angela didn't do *seconds*.

6.

On the evening of June 23, Tammy, flushed and heaving her bosoms excitedly, returned to the fold of our roof conclave and debriefed the All-Girl Gang on developments down on Hearthstone.

She had, as expected, fully unpeeled this Rossi mystery onion, and she brought news that none of us could have, or would have, ever expected to hear in our young lives.

The brothers were here because Kirk, the oldest, had convinced Nancy, their mother, and his brothers Nico and Vin, that there was money to be made Down South in the family business.

They had come to Fayetteville, like hardly any others ever have, to seek their fortunes.

In North Carolina, in the early 1980s, there were many pretenders to the male stripper throne, but there is only one male fantasy revue game in town, the widely respected and much-feared Peter Adonis Male Fantasy Burlesque, out of Charlotte.

Tammy, that stock car harlot, smoke curling out of her nose, that wicked jaw of hers set determinedly, paused for maximum dramatic effect and said:

"INterTAINment. EGGSxotick INterTAINment."

I nearly fell off the roof in a humid pile of wet, clotted desire.

The Rossis were strippers.

My new neighbors were strippers.

Male strippers, who went by the name of U.S. Male or G-Force, depending on what town they were playing, because we were in the Southeast, and there were at least three separate traveling male fantasy revues that called themselves U.S. Male.

Strippers were living on Hearthstone.

Our shocked silence *exploded* as the Kendallwood All-Girl Gang all tried to talk atop one another, unpack this scandalous and magnificent bit of luck that had, quite literally, fallen into our backyards. The girls shifted into high gear, half competitive, half supportive in that reform-school-girl way, where one never knew if a switchblade would be drawn or a hot curling iron rolled across a face. But their X-rated plans for the Rossis faded from my prefrontal cortex, becoming instead a kind of steady, burning buzzing of horny bees that I didn't notice above the sound of all the blood in my body rushing from my head and through my veins, sending a powerful pounding to my downstairs, the likes of which I had never felt before, then *flooding* up into my poor, delicate heart, making it do something I had heretofore never experienced:

My heart was *racing*.

My heart began saying *brothers* and *strippers* and *brothers* and *strippers*, repeated over and over, time and again.

Brothers.

Strippers.

7.

It took only two days before we were betrayed.

On Friday the twenty-fifth of June it was revealed at Hollis's club-house that Tammy had backstabbed us all, her very best friends in the whole world. Tammy had been seen promenading arm-in-arm with Kirk Rossi, spreading her charm all over him at the Cross Creek Mall. *Eating pizza.*

Fucking *bitch.*

Tammy was in very serious trouble.

8.

On Saturday the twenty-sixth of June, I went blind.

I could no longer see my trash-littered backyard nor make out the finer details of Frisky's cat crap, which still clung mysteriously to the stiff patio curtain. Nor did I see Diana's discarded pasties on the dirty bathroom sink, or the kitchen full of dishes and burnt appliances.

I saw none of it.

What I saw instead, for the next, nearly three, uninterrupted hours, was a rehearsal.

Over at the Rossis, on that pristine, manicured backyard lawn stage, the brothers were loudly blasting Loverboy's "Turn Me Loose," which is of course my future wedding song. The Rossis were…working. They were working *hard*. My rival, Nancy, was marching back and forth between her impressively muscled and balletic sons, guiding them gently into one fluid, muscular formation after another, pausing and adjusting. It looked like hard work. They shook their downstairs parts *vigorously* at the imaginary rows of screaming ladies, and they turned and bent over—here I felt my vision swim toward the long fever

I knew would finally consume me—and they bent over and ripped off rigged parachute pants to reveal some fashion shorts. I didn't actually think those could rightly be called "shorts"; they were far too skimpy, too clingy. I had never seen anything like them, made, as they were, out of some *wondrous* fabric that Honey whispered later was called—

"Lycra!"

I spent the next two days bouncing that word on my lips, rolling it across my parched tongue, writing it in cursive in saliva on the roof of my mouth.

Lycra, I would say each night as my head touched the pillow.

Lyyyycraaaaa, I'd sing to the dark of my own, private hell.

Lycra.

It sounded like a promise.

9.

On the evening of Sunday, June 27, I moved a moldering sleeping bag that once belonged to Rabbi and a cooler full of Mello Yello up to the roof. I leashed an extension cord for the phone.

I now lived on my roof.

10.

The following weekend, after a well-attended but thunderstorm-ruined fireworks display over the peeling Eutaw Village Shopping Center parking lot, Honey invited us all to her house for dinner and Monopoly. Because Hollis would be accompanied by her brother Hubbard, a classic school bully who insisted on referring to me as Boofer (no matter how many times I say "please call me Jewboy"), I politely declined Honey's invitation.

Honey said she had invited Kirk and Nico, and so obviously I politely did a 180 and accepted Honey's invitation.

Honey, that lantern-jawed goddess carved out of sexy beef jerky, sat me next to Nico.

Nico was my favorite Rossi.

He was tall and had feathered brown hair, and a little space between his two front teeth that he sometimes spit tiny flecks of tobacco out of, which probably sounds gross to the uninitiated, but that's muskrat right there to the Southern queer. All throughout our dinner of grilled Food Town hot dogs and oven-baked Food Town tater tots, I entertained Nico with a set of my mother's dirtiest jokes. I did not think, or did not think to know, that this was flirting. I was just dazzled by my proximity to one-third of U.S. Male, or G-Force, depending on what city they were playing, and I wanted to take care of Nico forever.

So I made him laugh.

Nico was the only other male who offered to help Honey clear the paper plates, so I began to quietly suspect that Nico, too, might be a little "like me." When Nico later affected to not notice when Honey's mother got a bit too deep into the watered-down Jack Daniel's and made a sloppy pass at his brother, I felt certain Nico was at least sensitive. *Like me.*

Strangest of all that night, a miraculous turning point, was that the jackass Hubbard never said a word to me. Not one Boofer. Nico's smell—Paco Rabanne and Marlboro Lights—*tames even the wildest redneck beast.*

We began playing Monopoly every Wednesday, like a national fucking holiday.

One hundred and ninety-three years after the Storming of the Bastille, on the fourteenth day of July, Nico Rossi's foot brushed lightly against mine beneath the Monopoly table at Honey's house, and *liberté.*

Nico was nineteen and I was thirteen, and so I spent the next five nights living on my roof, in a paralysis of indecision: Amputation? Shellack? *What preserves a stripper-touched foot the best?* I stayed up there, unable to sleep in a pitiful room down below, for fear that I would miss a single, magical moment in the Rossis' backyard. But little did I know that I had lost my rooftop anonymity.

Nico and the brothers Rossi had been told of my secret observation deck.

It was Hollis.

It was always Hollis.

My Hollis. My jungle cat, a big-haired Tessio, the woman I had loved and trusted most of all. *She* had revealed to les frères Rossi that they had a secret admirer across their backyard. I was mortified.

However, after that, whenever Nico thought I was looking over, he'd give a secret wave.

II.

On the twenty-first of July, at our regular strip Monopoly game, Nico removed his shoe and allowed his foot to linger atop my own. Honey's mother fucked one of the Rossis after we watched music videos, possibly her second Rossi. Honey was so deeply ashamed, she poured half the bourbon out of all her mother's bottles and replaced it with iced tea and water. None of us believed bourbon was the issue.

The Rossis, like a fine box of wine, simply could not be resisted.

I felt that gentle, insistent pressure of Nico's foot against my own. I tried to imagine what Young Johnny would do in Lance Lester's erotic masterpiece *Cruising Horny Corners*, so I channeled Young Johnny's adolescent bravery, and I squeaked out super extra casually, in what I thought was a deep baritone, that I would have the house to myself next Saturday because my brothers and their friends were all going to White Lake.

I had made my very first homosexual invitation.

When the pressure on my foot heavily increased, I thought I had been given my answer.

But I could not be sure.

Nothing was sure in 1982.

12.

It was ninety-five degrees by noon on Saturday.

All that morning I did my very best to tidy the place up, to make sure there wasn't anything too awful lying around. I disguised the cloying scent of laundry room rot by burning Renay's dynamic, triple pine-scented, extra-strength candles from her bathroom. I tried not to defile myself, but masturbated at eleven o'clock and two o'clock precisely, because there was nothing else to do and Renay had a brand-new bottle of Clinique just sitting there taunting me. The morning and the afternoon sailed by in a blur of Mid-South Wrestling, repeat visits to the bathroom to mangle at my Jewfro with alternating blasts of hair gel and Victoria Principal Jhirmack spray.

I had no idea where my mother was, and it was just two or three hours before my brothers were due to return from White Trash Lake with the Cusslers. The house was completely empty, as anticipated, but it wouldn't be for long. It never was.

Nico arrived on my doorstep at four o'clock on the dot. His jet-black hair was all feathery and light, shiny with the Wella Balsam and Dep he used to slick it to perfection. He was wearing the cleanest, whitest Izod I had ever seen, tucked into short beige shorts, which made him look like a tennis pro.

Nico seemed nervous.

We both were.

He favored me with his most dazzling, gap-toothed, Jersey smile, which broke the tension.

"Wanna play some cribbage?" I asked him, thinking it would relax us, as it always seemed to do for me and Renay. We played a few boards of cribbage together, and I did not hold back one bit. I knew that I cared for this full-grown backyard male stripper in ways that I did not yet understand, and the way my family showed we cared about strippers, or anybody, really, was to beat the shit out of them at cards.

I trumped Nico two games out of three, giving him the third game by throwing away several good cribs in a row. When he asked to see the rest of the house, I showed him Asshole's garage room, with the garbage-bag-size stash of marijuana that he kept at the foot of his bed, then I nudged him past the sealed-off laundry room. We walked into Renay's bedroom together, like grooms, and sat down on my mother's queen-sized heated waterbed.

I sat across from Nico, surfing waves of nervousness. I was surfing my mother's waterbed with a beautiful male, backyard stripper, and it excited me to no end. I could tell Nico was excited, too. *Visibly* excited.

I had no idea what to say or do, but I did know that I absolutely did *not* want to say or do whatever it is that gay boys do with backyard strippers on heated, queen-sized waterbeds.

I was young, but I wasn't foolish about acts that couldn't be taken back.

"You wanna go up on the roof with me?" I asked Nico, and he nodded, shyly. His eyes were so fucking beautifully lashed and turned down, that wide-gapped smile, little bits of bashful tobacco held back. I was *his*; he must have known it.

"That sounds like fun," he said.

Climbing up the ladder that hung shakily off the back patio door, I paused, midair.

I knew.

I was calling the shots.

13.

Up on the roof, overlooking the overgrown Corren jungle, we sat, side by side, knees barely touching—but touching.

We talked.

He listened.

He *saw* me.

I listened to Nico's dreams. He wanted to be a dancer. He wanted to see more of the world than this. I told him I wanted the same, to be a famous agent, or a writer. Or anyone. Or anything. Else.

Nico plucked a gardenia bloom from the tree that hung low above our roof and he pressed it into my hand. I smiled. I suddenly didn't feel nervous at all, I just liked looking at this man, this stripper, who had traveled from his backyard to my roof. Like I willed him into being through the end of my binoculars.

I was so happy to be up there with Nico. His smell. My flower.

Us.

All of a sudden, like the way it goes in stories, the night was close, all around us, and we had been up there for hours, his hand pressed in mine, the gardenia wilted and syrupy. I had never moved my hand, which had fallen dead asleep hours ago. The sky felt open and perfect. I took the binoculars and I showed Nico the stars with the eyes I used to see him in.

We were two boys about to be men, up on a roof, side by side, passing glasses back and forth, one trying to get close to the other without the other noticing. Nico pretended to spot a falling star, but it was just a plane cutting through the fog on its way to or from Bragg. Our legs touched, our knees too, sometimes our arms. His touch felt closer to me than my own skin.

A promise. The heat. Desire.

It pulled us close, and then closer.

And that was as close as I could go.

I was thirteen.

Each one of those tiny glances of his arm, each laugh that moved him closer, each was a chance I did not take, a move I could not make.

What I was, *where* I was, I knew mattered far more to me than any next move with Nico.

I knew what sex was.

I had seen *Big Bad Mama* and *Crazy Mama* with Renay at the Fox Triple. I read her letters to *Penthouse* Forum. I had read *all* of Dame Jacqueline Jill Collins, OBE. I knew what a downstairs did by now. I knew I was the gay son.

I knew what I wanted.

Here was a real person, in my real life—a warm, beautiful human man with an open, human heart, and he was seconds away from giving me his whole, entire self, if I would allow it.

But I chose me up on that roof.

I chose to stay thirteen.

I still wanted to be this curious, independent, ambitious fellow. I wanted to be proud of the life that I knew I could make. I wanted the decision when, and if, to give *my* gardenia to another man, to be mine and mine alone.

It wasn't mine that night.

This is the way of the world.

This is what a poet looks like, I think.

A glance, a touch, a roof on a hot, foggy night, a boy choosing to stay a boy.

To be a poet is *to choose* to be a poet.

Later, when it was time for Nico to say goodbye, his lips brushed against my ear, and he whispered so soft I could only catch a little of what he said. The touch of his lips made me tremble. I shuddered weakly, and I said, "What did you say? Tell me what you said again."

I could hear his heart.

BUH-BUH-beat.

BUH-BUH-beat.

BUH-BUH-beat.

Nico laughed, and he held me in front of him, his hands straight on my shoulders, like a man does. Like a father. And he said:

"You won't always be…thirteen."

Yes, I will.

BURNING BRIDGES

1.

Detective Midgett nudges a blank yellow pad and a black pen in front of me on his otherwise empty desk, empty except for the remains of a BBQ plate, that is.

A poorly framed print of Erasmus Midgett crouching atop the beached wreckage of *The Priscilla* down on Salvo Beach hangs askew over the desk, but we are otherwise alone in his cramped office, the door to the police station behind him latched, the noise and radio chatter now firmly filtered. Detective Midgett is three times my size, at least, so this dinghy-like room feels airless, itchy, and *hot*. The walls curve up, white and rounded, domed at the top, with two thick, night-darkened bubble windows set high above. The building is an octagon, irregular for a police station, I know, but pretty much everything in Nags Head is irregular in 1984.

Detective Midgett points at his distant ancestor Erasmus, saying softly, with practice, "That man, he knew *right from right*." The curved walls of Nags Head justice seem to exhale in agreement with him. Erasmus is *right* and I am, implicitly, *wrong*.

A rusted silver lamp throws a curiously jaundiced glow over us both, a wan flame illuminating the interior of our vessel, and I try to hide my trembling hands from Detective Midgett. It is hard to meet his exfoliating gaze, but there is nowhere else to turn, except to the quiet, damning eyes of Erasmus Midgett's great-great-great-grandnephew. By marriage.

"You couldn't have done this alone, could you, son? You had to have help, right?" he asks, and not unkindly. "Now look. You tell ol' Midge which of your friends helped you out on this deal, and all this might go away *fast*."

He waits for the answer that I know I must not give. *I cannot.*

The longest coastal winter of my life crests like a frozen wave, right here, tonight.

I am on the wrong side of this shipwreck, and salvation is not on the way from Salvo.

I shall not dime.

It is so hot in here. I am so, so hot, and I know it shows. I know I look so, so guilty.

I am fifteen. I do not know how to *not* look guilty, how not to hide it when I have so much to feel guilty about. I cannot hide my hunger, either.

I smell onion rings. Golden. Crispy. Good ones. "I'm waitin', son," Detective Midgett says again, a touch of Aunt Bee in the voice now, smelling of aftershave, Old Testament, and BBQ plate. "I'll wait all night."

I am not about to dime on my sister.

I am a Corren.

We do *not* dime on each other!

Well, except...okay, there was that *one time* when Renay got busted for the shitload of weed and bongs in the trunk of the Nova, which had rolled downhill on Pamalee and shot across Cain into the woods, revealing her stash to God, and the SBI, one fine Sunday morning after a long night of hearts and Crown Royal. She had left the Nova in neutral. Crash, trunk pop, stash revealed, cops arrive, and Renay confessed.

That it was her *son's* stash, not hers.

So, yes. My mother once dimed on her own son, but just that one time and *only* because he was safely out of state, living in Shithead's driveway in Pine Bluff. Rabbi wasn't in any immediate danger. She knew that. She was protecting us. She's *smart*.

Other than that, we do *not* dime on each other!

We are Correns!

2.

On the first day of April 1957, nineteen-year-old double college drop-out Renay Mandel was no different than the Renay Corren who you've met in these pages: a brilliant, beautiful, fat, horny, fertile, disrespect-ful, disobedient, book-obsessed, gambling redhead who didn't give two caramelized figs for society's expectations. She may have been an out-lier in Eisenhower's America, but Renay was right at home coming of age in booming Miami Beach, that magical, naughty city to which she'd moved with her striving Hungarian parents, Marian and Isidor, after a suffocatingly idyllic childhood in an exurb of Pittsburgh filled with suffocating Hungarians. Miami Beach in the 1950s was gam-bling, development, entertainment, sex, and resorts, and Renay was *in the thick of it*. Miami was *the* perfect place for a girl like Renay to let loose, get laid, get pregnant, and then indifferently raise three chil-dren while she eked out a life on a soldier's paycheck, buzz-sawed her way through jugs of gefilte fish, inhaled trashy thrillers on the beach, and chased bowling balls while her parents stayed home with the kids. Heaven by Havana!

On a warm, overcast evening in April 1957, in a pale green operating suite on the fourth floor of the St. Francis Hospital—an Art Deco *masterpiece* erected upon decades of Floridian lies, exploitation, institutional racism, and trash—the first of Renay's four Miami children, our beloved and only sister Cathy Sue, was born. Shithead was twenty-three, about four years older than Renay, an ambitious Army reservist who hated his parents; had no money; strutted around Miami Beach with fading high school track star, big dick energy; and fucked anything and everything that moved. She was a spoiled, lazy, ham-eating atheist majoring in English, blowjobs, and driving her Orthodox Jewish parents insane. These two horny, idiot Jews had accidentally conceived their first child in a drunken, forgettable rut on a sandy Dade County beach in June. This had compelled a rushed matrimonial scramble down the gilded aisles of Miami's oldest and most deluxe society synagogue, Temple Beth David. The lightly pregnant bride wore a ballerina-length gown of Chantilly lace and tulle, with a flattering, stomach-concealing, waist-length veil of imported French illusion. A mere eight months later, Cathy Sue arrived, "slightly prematurely."

3.

Now a twenty-seven-year-old divorced-and-remarried young mother herself, Cathy Sue was restarting her life for the third time, upon her third island.

From the man-made garbage archipelagos of the Miami of her youth, to the tropical Ryukyu Islands of Southern Japan where she blossomed, to here, these majestic Outer Banks, where she would end her days far too soon on a fragile spit of barrier island sticking up the coast of North Carolina like her own, very busy middle finger.

My sister would spend the entirety of her life facing down seas and plundering their treasures. Cathy Sue was a beautiful, spoiled bitch who didn't yell; she "talked to be heard." She didn't steal; she "took what was already hers." She stormed her way through life, grabbed anything and anyone she wanted, and did it on every single island that she ever lived.

A pirate, through and through.

My God, we desperately loved her.

In 1974, after abandoning high school, and then us, for, disappointingly, Virginia Beach, Cathy Sue more or less lived in two places: her house was in the Tidewater of Virginia with former GI Benny, but her soul and her heart were still back in the Piedmont of Carolina with her family. She came home to us near weekly, and we were always so *starved* for the sight of her. Cathy Sue lit up our lives with her loud, gutsy laugh, her perfect white smile, those freckles, that *gleam* in her one good eye, so wicked, so blue and pure. She was such a confident character, now a teen wife and a teen mother, a self-created and self-mythologized sea beast risen from hot, coastal sands, just like her mother. Her best Fayetteville friend, Brenda, had followed Cathy Sue from Fayetteville to the disappointments of Virginia Beach, and together these two glamorous, homesick hippie moms with perfect smiles and astonishing perms would gather their hair up into teen mom bandannas, stash their weed and their babies, and pile into Brenda's tired old Toyota to make that five-hour drive to and from Fayetteville. Cathy Sue brought us stories from the outside, seashells from the shore, funky music and groovy parties near nightly. Her big, gutsy, room-filling hee-haw of a laugh eventually announced a baby son, too: Little Big Ben, a baby so big he grew out of pants the second you put them on him. Cathy Sue may have moved out, but she never moved on, not from the family she had dominated from her first Miami days. She continued to exert maximum influence over her brothers, all of us eager doofuses who followed her room to room, only ever alive in Cathy Sue's shadow, her former part-time children still deeply bonded to the woman who *really* raised us, changed our dirty diapers, slapped us if we stole her shit. Cathy Sue wielded a kind of maniacal but largely benevolent cult leader control over us, and the same was true for her many, many husbands. Some may call it bullying, some screaming into submission, others the magical power of the pussy, but my sister hacked her way through a gamed patriarchal system and managed to thrive in a world made by and for men, and to amass a small fortune in fudge pots, ex-husbands, and brotherly love. She was always there for us. She never left us behind.

Well, except for Bonus. She did leave him. We all did.

Cathy Sue's family, *her* houses, even in hated Virginia Beach, began to feel more and more like my real home as I grew up. They were clean, had husbands who worked, came home, acted like fathers. There was food on the table.

There *was* a table.

There was an inseverable bond with our only sister, the one-eyed lady pirate of Nags Head Cove. She made all of her brothers feel like *she was home*.

Except Bonus.

4.

By 1984, Cathy Sue and her next-in-line husband, the one who looked like a fatter Dale Earnhardt, held court on the Outer Banks in a resplendently shaggy and shingled house that resembled nothing so much as *an ark*—big and boxy, dry-docked, covered with sweet-smelling cedar inside and out, with a deck tipping out over Nags Head's wide, achingly beautiful sound.

I could stand at Cathy Sue's back door and see the Virginia drivers mow down the wild ponies, or recline on the big front deck and watch the setting sun compete with clouds of purple martins and tourists drowning in the shallow Roanoke Sound. For a starving kid from landlocked Fayetteville, this place was a buffet. A feast for the soul. Twin and Asshole and I could not wait to visit our sister, making the long bus journey out to Nags Head often, drinking in the newness, the smell of hope and sea oats in the air, the freedom from our squalor back home. Our stays overflowed with astonishments: clean beaches, that big house, the plumbing that never smelled.

A nearly six-hour Trailways ride from downtown Fayetteville expelled Twin and me at the Dinosaur Golf on Highway 12. It was like being coughed out of a monster's asshole onto a pristine, magical kingdom constructed of honey-dappled winds and aquamarine waters. Cathy Sue's favorite colors, a pirate's palette of rich turquoise and sparkling gold, glittered from every corner. Nags Head was the still-sleepy and nominally undiscovered cottage country enjoyed primarily by North Carolinians in the know, landlocked Ohioans who were dead inside, and, obviously, teen mothers from Virginia Beach out on parole. It was hard to get to. The Outer Banks wasn't meant for everybody; it was for hardy people who wanted to get far away. It must have been a challenge for my sister to find herself in such a place, an extremely tight and vanishingly small community of natives bound up by traditions and the sea on one side, suspicion and the sound on the other. But Cathy Sue landed herself a good job through her new husband's connections at the 7-Eleven, and her island destiny appeared to be sealed. The Outer Banks, the ocean, the people, the taste of the wild—it all felt like a secret just for us. A place that screamed, *Reinvent yourself here, faggot!* There were even still wild ponies then, who ambled up to the bus and greeted us as we stumbled down the steps, reeking of coppery lavatories that hadn't been slopped out since Williamston.

The Gulf Stream–adjacent waters were crystalline, glinting blue and green. We could see how happy our sister was, waving a fishing rod on a boat, sunbathing in intoxicating light, laughing wildly with Brenda as they cast husbands and beer cans into the Oregon Inlet. In Nags Head, it seemed, at last, a Corren had finally caught a big one. A break.

I was deathly afraid that I would not make it out of Fayetteville.

Like most normal young Fayettevillians with functioning eyesight and a sense of smell, I was a miserable freshman at Westover, a brick box of hormones, stale bread, and defeat erected beneath cruel fluorescent lights designed to break young spirits on the daily. My All-Girl Band were all over on the high school side. Sherry Anne was already graduated and Tammy, Honey, and Angela were soon to be gone. Entering junior high, I had lost my foothold on those tight friendships, and so I retreated inward, turning to the comforts of my mother's books, my library's encyclopedias, and Aaron Spelling's endlessly beautiful imagination. I drifted into competitive dramatics, this thing called "forensics," which is part of the speech and debate world, but really just a subculture for questioning gay teens. I discovered forensics through my classmate Lisa, who had befriended me in home economics due to my high-quality, superior fudge balls. Lisa had the filthiest mouth I had ever heard on a Pentecostal Holiness girl, so I obviously took to her. Sensing my flair for dramatics, she nudged me over to the forensics team and, lo and behold, I got really good. Really fast. I started winning tournaments. For an unparented child who isn't getting enough calories or attention, there is no better feeling than winning trophies. I quickly began racking up county wins, too, beating better-dressed kids from fancier schools like Pine Forest and Terry Sanford. My club sponsors saw a winner and took me on the road, where I began winning statewide, too. I was really getting the knack of acting without moving below the waist, which is what forensics is all about: acting, but not taking a single fucking step while you do it. You are not allowed to move. But I obviously had a knack for above-the-waist histrionics. As a Jewish child of a Jewish mother, I had something other North Carolina kids would never have: a handle on melodrama. I was unstoppable, performing my from-the-waist-only monologue from the book *Max*, by my all-time favorite communist Howard Fast, who pumped out pulpy books about striving Jews as fast as Renay and I could devour them. His Immigrants saga, about the Lavette family, was one of those six-volume masterpieces of shlock that kept Jewish mothers and their gay sons glued together. *Max* is a simple story about a simple Jewish boy trying, and failing, to please his mother, Sarah, who speaks a lot of Yiddish and grows enormously fat as he grows incredibly rich inventing the movie business. She disapproves of him as he sleeps with beautiful stars, then complains endlessly about the mansion he has installed her in, all while his brothers rip him off for millions of dollars.

Then he goes to jail.

I felt this story in my bones.

There I was, hardly fifteen, emoting bitter truths of Hollywood, blowing those fancy forensics people of Charlotte and Raleigh away with my sophisticated rendering of maternal sabotage and my devastatingly naturalistic Bronx affectation.

I was winning.

I was a standout in this glamorous new world, regaling my teammates between matches with stories about my real mother, her bowling alley, my actual criminal brothers, preening in their approval, bubbling in this cauldron of teen intrigue rife with sexual tension. I traveled the length of the state to compete in exotic locales like Hickory or once, even, famed liberal hellhole Chapel Hill, where I saw my very first gay pride march. I had never seen a mass gathering of homosexuals outside of a *Southern Living Magazine* Food Expo at the Cumberland County Memorial Auditorium. I knew about gay people, I knew I probably was one, but I did not know about marching, or equality, or rights. The sight of so many of them made me lightheaded with a kind of Victorian swoon, and I grabbed at the arm of our debate chaperone, Mr. Stanton, softly keening, "Mr. Stanton! Those are gay people! They're marching!" To which Charles Stanton, Westover's portly and beloved English teacher, drolly quipped from behind his neatly trimmed beard, "This is Chapel Hill, Andy. The gays are always marching."

I wasn't a pariah at Westover. Some boys even liked me. You might say I was kind of succeeding. With my mother's early encouragement and my grandmother's dangled connections, I thought acting was my way out of Fayetteville. It was logical that I would become a minor Westover celebrity.

But as you know, fame eventually corrupts and destroys every single thing that it touches.

Actors have a dark side.

"There is a cost to fame," Debbie Allen once wisely and sweatily opined.

Local fame had found me—I had already been written about in our Westover student newspaper, featured twice in the *Fayetteville Observer*—but I was already smart about show business. I knew fame was a prison. I knew fame, seductive as it was, would be my downfall.

I had very recently been beaten up after chorus class by Sharona, a malevolent young woman, very talented in the diaphragm, heavily pregnant, infamous in the halls of Westover for her swollen belly and pet snake. She took an instant dislike to me in chorus, so I should have known better than to make fun of her. Sharona did not appreciate my opining on her somewhat controversial, yet entirely predictable, casting as Rizzo in our spring production of *Grease*. She was visibly seven months pregnant, which I thought spoiled Rizzo's arc. When I announced to chorus that "this is Rydell High, not the maternity ward," it did get a huge laugh, but Sharona was not there for my sexist, high-handed theater criticism. I got my sad little white ass handed to me after school by a pregnant ninth grader. I got stomped, and as Sharona pulverized my tender gay stomach with the metal toe cap of her braided vamp clog from Sears, I quietly resolved to carry with me forever these three, clear takeaways from this beatdown:

1. No woman, anywhere, fears a male Corren.
2. Wearing clogs while pregnant is so brave.
3. Fame, if not used wisely, is used quickly.

I walked around Westover with anxiety and a quiet, gnawing certainty that local fame was a high-calorie, low-nutrition snack that would only keep me imprisoned in Fayetteville. That if I didn't use every trick and advantage that I had, or came my way, this is where I'd stay.

5.

Over the slightly less than eighteen months we lived on Docia, it gradually, inevitably, *descended*.

But what is a descent, when you have slid so many times already?

The Docia House took on the character of the family within and the unruly, sprawling mess of the backyard without. The Correns were not rotten people, but the Correns were in trouble, and by 1983, we were kind of trouble people, I guess you'd say. Rotten poor trouble, at any rate. Our busted roof and our leaking pipes logically led to backed-up sewage and broken doors. Then up crawls the mold, and soon it's just a collective of people passing through and averting their gaze.

Perhaps this mass resignation was the only collective decision we could make as a family. To acknowledge this descent, to *see* what was really happening, would have risked us seeing *each other* for what *we* were, and to see what we had *become*. We were at peace with our filth, and all the guests who came with it. Soon there was no escape from our final guest, the one who came and did not leave.

The smell.

The Docia House stank, and it stank real, real bad.

And Reader? There were fleas.

In the end, the fleas came for their nourishment, rooting deeply into our carpets and feasting deliriously upon passing bare ankles and exposed calves, chasing us room to room until we finally sealed up the back patio entirely with cardboard and duct tape, never to be entered or remarked upon again. It stayed a sealed-off, never-discussed mausoleum like its haunted sister, the laundry room.

In late November 1983 we gathered one final time in the Docia House as a family, for what would be our very first and very last Thanksgiving with all of my brothers and my sister, as well as all of their future ex-wives and ex-husbands, under one roof. It was a frigid and miserable weekend.

Bonus was twenty-five, a Naval reservist in a state with only one Naval Yard: Illinois. He had made a rare and unannounced visit, driving all the way down to Fayetteville and arriving with his first wife, Floridian Emily. Bonus caused quite the stir when he arrived, showing up in a bright red track suit, matching the bright red Christmas sweater of his wife, both looking for all the world like a Christmas tree in a synagogue, filling up our doorway with his tall awkwardness, his estrangements, his dark, bushy mustache, and his overcompensating bonhomie. He could not help himself; he greeted everyone that day—brothers, Cathy Sue, Brenda, Bernie, Butt Check, Doreen—all the same way, with a hale "How the fuck are ya!" and a teeth-rattling back slap that sent the recipient scurrying. Most of us hadn't laid eyes on Bonus since he was released from Duncraig Manor in Southern Pines, and there was this *calcified discomfort* around him, this stranger nobody had seen since he was seventeen and ran off to join the Navy.

Now Bonus was here. There was no ignoring him. He was too tall and too loud.

Renay affected her usual haughty demeanor when confronted with happenings that displeased her, that of offended Hungarian royalty at a banquet, and she only nodded primly at Bonus occasionally, flinching at his backslaps, her rictus hostess smile pasted tight, mildly fearful of what her misplaced son might reveal.

The whole thing clearly pained Bonus. I could see that he just wanted to be a part of this family. Here he was, back among us, back in Fayetteville a married man, *a Navy man*, no less, and he got nothing for it. No respect, no brotherly love, no motherly regard, no hugs.

"If your mother made chopped liver, watch your hands, or I'll bite 'em off!" Bonus bellow-laughed awkwardly, before doffing his red track suit jacket and seating himself and Emily at our fold-out dining table. My mother heaved herself off the paisley sofa, clomped loudly into the kitchen galley to get herself going on her famous chicken liver. Renay's very large sons waited all year long for their mother to rouse herself to make one of the three Jewish things she knew how to cook (stuffed cabbage soup and chicken soup, the other two); today Renay would as expected assemble acres of chopped chicken livers into a thick, mealy pile rising several yards high, a mound that would be fallen upon, spread, and inhaled all this day devoted to eating, farting, cards, and football.

Bonus stayed with us at the Docia House for two uncomfortable, awkward days before he and Emily finally gave up on us and made the long drive back to Chicago. He told me, many years later, that at the time of this visit in 1983, Bonus had been sending Renay two hundred dollars a month, money specifically meant for me, as I was always out of clothes, specialty luxury foods, and hardcover books from Tyler's.

Two hundred dollars a month. Out of his Navy salary. He was twenty-five and married.

Renay never mentioned it.

There would be two more very minor arrests in late 1983—Asshole won't talk about one of them, and Rabbi appears to not recall a thing from 1983 altogether, including his first marriage and the whole nuclear power plant accident thing—but among the seep and the sewage, the fleas and the mold, the lost sons and the sealed rooms, hardly anybody noticed those pesky arrests, anyway.

We all had our eyes on the exit door.

6.

She was twenty-seven, on her second marriage, had her own house, lived in a fairytale sea kingdom, a palace compared to the brothers she had left behind. Cathy Sue was a woman in charge, and this woman knew how to get what she wanted. What Cathy Sue wanted was for her brothers to move to the Outer Banks. So all during those first years of junior high for me and Twin, Cathy Sue pushed and pushed us, pushing on the phone, pushing during visits, pushing this controversial idea: move to her. Push. Push. Push.

I was open to it. All of us were.

I was sad about our life on Docia. I was anxious all the time at school, overperforming from the waist up for any reason, in any class, in constant conflict with my classmates, some of whom weren't even pregnant. Cathy Sue was giving us the chance to come live in paradise.

Twin and I could finish up high school on the Outer Banks. Asshole
could come, too, find a real job, and get his pickled-egg-stealing shit
together. "You can live somewhere clean and safe and normal, for once,"
she enjoined, over and over. All three of us—me, Asshole, and Twin—
we were *so thirsty* for the idea of normal. I was willing, and so were my
brothers, to leap into that ocean of hers, and drink deeply of *normal*.

Asshole went to the Outer Banks, and he never left.

On the bus back to Fayetteville after our last visit, Twin and I
gladly left Asshole behind to start his new coastal life with Cathy Sue.
We were jealous. We didn't want to get on that bus. We didn't want to
go back to that house. Twin finally dared to say aloud the unthinkable.
We needed a mother upgrade, and we needed it *quick*. In a torrent of
confession, Twin said, "We need to get the fuck away from her."

My God.

Things were so bad, my famously taciturn brother spoke eight more
words to me than he had in the entire preceding year.

He saw clearly what we were headed back to.

I saw it, too.

A tornado-torn-apart life awaited. Twin and I were tired of the ran-
sacked house, the constant comings and goings, the power always out,
scrabbling for food. Renay continued to welcome anybody who needed
a bed, a favor, a can of green beans, a laugh. Her best friend Doreen,
between homes, was crashing with us now, along with her little daughter, Faith, and her sister Diana, too. The all-night card games, the stolen cable TV, the utilities that blinked on and off, the dealers and the
strippers, the tide of Docia. Home was just a place. A place where we
stored our clothes, where doors didn't work, where school didn't matter, where the fridge was nearly always empty.

Twin added, in a tidal wave of soliloquy, "She's taking us down!"

"I don't think I can do three more years of this," I bus-confessed to my brother. "Where's she taking us next, *Spring Lake?*" I asked, conjuring the very saddest fate a Fayettevillian could summon, eliciting a silent shudder and rebuke from my brother.

"No, sir," Twin gushed.

Incredibly, we were united.

We worshipped her. She was *our life.* But she was *clearly done* with the *mothering* part of motherhood. We didn't want to go back. Cathy Sue had sold us on the idea of living in the Ark, of starting a new life, instead of living *the old one.* She sold us on being a part of *her* world, not *that* world.

Twin was convinced Renay would never go for it, but something told me my mother would. I surmised that Renay knew that getting rid of us would be a good deal for *her* and for *Cathy Sue*, that my sister might *split* some of Renay's child support in exchange for taking us *off her hands.* It all made a kind of financial and spatial sense. Getting rid of two dependent kids in their final years of high school, while still collecting some of Shithead's child support check? *Where do I sign?*

I know it sounds like I am suggesting my mother sold her two youngest children off to a pirate for a share of her ransom. And I am.

I absolutely am.

After you leave Williamston, the coast of North Carolina, all of the Outer Banks, is done. *The dream is over*, and it's just State Road 64 for miles of corn, tobacco, soybean, until you get back to Fayetteville. It moves pretty slow—it's a state road, after all—and the Trailways won't pick up speed again until after Rocky Mount, when it finally connects to the I-95 corridor and zigs south down that horrendously long last spur, making one final stop in Benson before it all ends on Robeson Street in downtown Fayetteville. It's a long, long way to go on a very, very old bus, where Twin and I felt lucky to be seated up front this time, and not wedged against a toilet box that reeked of ammonia, exhaust, and sweet Trailways road cherries.

We had just passed Williamston, and the smell of cedar that lined every inch and wall of Cathy Sue's Ark was still clinging to my nose.

So what if it was a ruse by Renay to get rid of us. Fine. We were going back to Docia. We were getting our shit. And we *were leaving*.

It was over.

We were getting the fuck away from her.

And so, nearly six years after Shithead divorced Renay, Asshole, Twin, and I all divorced her, too. Maybe *this* was my chance to get away from Fayetteville, the chance that I had been waiting for my whole life. *This* was a sign, a shiny lure dropped directly from God above, and plopped right into the middle of my lake. I had only but *to swim*.

And so I did.

I swam hard.

7.

Detective Midgett shakes his square, flushed head at me.

His eyes, so sad and rueful, are flecked mossy green like the kelp clinging to Cousin Erasmus forever standing atop *The Priscilla*. He won't let me call my sister, and she's the only one who will know what to do. I am paralyzed with fear without Cathy Sue advising me. I know I am guilty as sin—*I was caught in the act*. When word gets out what I've done—and it will, in a town the size of Nags Head—I am *finished* on the Outer Banks. It's all gonna come tumbling down. I will face the hard consequence of a string of terrible decisions. I know that if I don't start naming names, it's gonna get a lot worse. This shit is only going one way: *down*.

Sweat beads my forehead and I swallow nervously, mentally retracing my panicked steps from the Roses Discount Store lobby across the bypass, to Nags Head Police, and upstairs to Detective Midgett's cubby of an office. I try to remember each turn we took, so that I can make a break and run out into the frigid winter night, flee this island, hide from my sister's mistakes.

But I do not run. Even though this is all Cathy Sue's fault—not mine, *hers*—I do not run.

I am a Corren.

We do not *run*.

We descend.

8.

"You will love it here!" she lied.

In June of 1984, the days were long, and the hot dune sands of Jockey's Ridge are warm and glassy enough to slide down with no shirt on, laughing and carefree all the way to the bottom. In June, watching the gold and orange sun set ablaze, ogling all the gorgeous surfers and stupid, sexy fry cooks at the Best Body on the Beach Contest at Miller's Seafood, I would have believed anything that Cathy Sue had told me. "There's so much to do all the time," she lied and lied. "All year long. It'll be the best place you've ever lived!"

Cathy Sue and her second husband and Little Big Ben opened their ark to Asshole, Twin, and me, giving us each a big, empty bedroom that faced pink summer skies billowing like cotton candy. She took us out every night on their boat onto the Roanoke Sound, where we trawled for mussels, flat fish, and clams. We were a family, a souvenir shop postcard *family.*

I unpacked my *TV Guides* and my stolen Lillian Hellman volumes from the county library, and Twin optimistically set up his cleats and his trophies, and together we jumped into that lie of a life on the Outer Banks. *We will be* happy *here*, we lied to ourselves. *We will be* happy *on this small, sparsely populated, off-season fishing community with five hundred fudge shops every quarter mile. We will be* happy *attending the ugly, atrociously underfunded and badly lit high school a bleak ninety-minute bus ride away, located in a seafood shanty called Manteo across a giant, rickety, soon-to-burn bridge. We will be* happy *trying to fit in with the island teens, all from the same five families who have lived on these barrier islands for 350 years and have all known, married, and fucked each other since birth, and who regarded Jews, gays, smart people, and outsiders with suspicion, outright hostility, or, worse: not at all.*

We will be happy *here.*

WE WILL BE HAPPY *HERE.*

9.

We were not happy there.

10.

Winter came.

Pitiless.

A fascinating word, "pitiless." From the Old English *leas*, and the Latin *pietatum*, "pitiless" is one of those perfect words that comes roaring out of history, needs no dressing up, arrives wearing a veil to lower its axe and sever you with a plosive *P* and an exciting *hiss* at the end. Pitiless, condemning you like an incompetent lover in one of the three—*three!!*—hugely popular autobiographies by Miss Hellman that I had stolen from the Cumberland County Library and carted with me on the bus to the Outer Banks, thinking that I would spend every day reclining upon warm sands reading Lillian Hellman by the last pink lights of the Atlantic sun.

The skies turned pitiless.

This winter, the historically shitty winter of 1984–1985, was relentlessly cruel. Dark and wet, we were stalked by salty, iced, haunted death, grim dawn to grimmer dusk. And the wind! The *winds*, plural! Winds that rose from both directions, sea and sound. They nipped and howled and took the sun, rising in November and never leaving. Cathy Sue's Ark, which had seemed so quaint and summer beachy, all cedar and joy, revealed itself to be as flimsy as balsa wood, shrugging its shingles off like a dog shaking off water, rattling with icy death winds that pried at every badly sealed door. Seagulls banged hopelessly against the thin windows to be allowed inside, only to surrender themselves to the frozen winds.

Twin and I would rise in the soupy maritime murk to catch the dreadful ninety-minute bus ride across all of Dare County. This so we could arrive at the drama department–less high school by seven thirty, where I gnawed at my free breakfast grits, which were admittedly very good, only to stay cold and friendless for the next eight hours. I was completely ignored, unless one of the legacy seafucks decided to look my way and mutter an ominous "faggot," or "bitch," which I was starting to look forward to because at least it meant somebody was talking to me other than my English teacher, Seth, who definitely knew I was in love with him, since I desperately followed him to the Manteo Booksellers every day where he moonlit after school to augment his Roanoke Island teacher's salary. I'd stand silently in the bookstore corner spying on him at the register, frustrated in my search for any Lance Lester or Dick Dale gay pulp novels, surrounded by local ghost story lore, boxes of stale, discounted taffy, and the tackiest things ever invented: lighthouse lamps, all casting dim, sallow light upon me, the literary outcast seething in quiet longing, playing out in real life those most dangerous scenes from Miss Lillian Hellman's *The Children's Hour*, except in my case the lesbians were all too real, stout fisherwomen in khaki jorts from Wanchese who drank Four Roses whiskey by the crate, not coy, temperate boarding school spinsters from Maine.

It was always dark, always windy, and there was nothing to do. There was one grocery store nearby, where Twin and Asshole worked part-time; one movie theater with two of its three screens always showing Chuck Norris; approximately fifteen hundred fudge shops; and eleven hundred nautical-themed bars that stayed open *very late*, even when it *ice rained*, which it did often. I spent my time making my way through all three of Lillian Hellman's autobiographies and Cathy Sue's inherited collection of World Book encyclopedias, which I endeavored to read the entirety of, at the pace of one volume per week.

I was dead inside.

I knew I had made a horrible, world-class, historically stupid mistake.

I called home to Fayetteville using long-distance phone cards that I stole from Cathy Sue's 7-Eleven, and I begged my mother once a day to please take me back.

She did not take me back.

"No refunds. No returns." She laughed and laughed.

It rains constantly on the Outer Banks, storms rise and fall off the deadly Gulf Coast with alarming regularity, foundering ships on those shores the way cars crashed daily on the deadly intersection of Pamalee and Cain. Nor'easters, they call them. I had never heard of Nor'easters before my sister fooled me into moving to the Nor'easter-plagued Outer Banks, and soon that's all I heard about, because the next one was always on its way. The power lines on the bypass—brand-new, paid for by the state—sizzled with frozen salt and crusted ice, exploded all winter long, rained tax dollars and sparks down upon unsuspecting motorists far too drunk from two-for-one margaritas at the Jolly Roger to notice.

I was an outcast who hadn't made a single friend by the time Christmas of 1984 rolled around, not even a fellow store clerk at the Roses Discount Store in the Nags Head Mall, where I had taken a job out of sheer boredom. Cathy Sue's Ark shook all day and into the night, and so a retail position was my only refuge. I went to work at the Roses as soon as I stepped off the hated school bus, and I stayed there until closing time, and I was *grateful* for every minute that I was not at that shaking house with its out-of-print encyclopedias and Betamax porn that I could never watch because there was only just the one Betamax in the living room.

11.

Everybody knows those onion rings. They're from the BBQ plate at Sam & Omie's.

Those are damn good onion rings.

I am still stunned at being detained, so I keep my focus on small things. The glint of the ring on his fat left pinkie. The smell of fried onions. The strange paste of his hair glued over his balding pate. Cousin Erasmus Midgett, who everybody called Elmo and once saved ten men in a storm off Salvo.

Think about anything but those dolls.

"Son, you are in trouble," Elmo the hero's great-great-great-great-nephew by marriage says, stating the obvious. "You need to cooperate. You need to tell me just what the hell you was planning on doing with all them dolls."

12.

As far as crimes in Nags Head go, surely this was small stuff.

Stealing dolls. Big whoop.

Nobody got hurt!

It was just a few small, ugly dolls!

Maybe it was more than a couple of ugly dolls, who cares.

Maybe it was *six* dolls, so what.

Maybe it was *eight* dolls. Fine, let's say it was eight dolls!

I stole eight dolls that people were murdering each other in the streets for.

I stole eight Cabbage Patch dolls.

I stole them under the direction of my seasoned crime handler, Cathy Sue.

Cabbage Patch dolls were retailing for forty dollars, but the black market on those stupid foam babies had them fetching hundreds, sometimes even *thousands*, of dollars more—and yes, there *was* a Cabbage Patch dolls black market in 1984—so into my big, unattended Roses employee layaway box they were stuffed, one after another, as per Cathy Sue's instruction to me, her junior crime associate.

My sister *swore* we'd never get caught. Cathy Sue *swore* it was a victimless crime. "Just do what I say, and we'll both get rich!" she barked. "Ain't nobody hurtin' shit!"

I never should have trusted her. I knew my sister took after our mother in *all* ways. Scammer. Grifter. Light-fingered, fast on her feet, whatever you want to call it, Cathy Sue was felonious to the bone. That's just how she was raised: take it, saunter away, don't act guilty, don't get caught. Cathy Sue swiped money, boyfriends, jewels, clothes, jobs, boats, whatever wasn't nailed down. I was kind of a klepto, too, so I was easily enrolled into her schemes. Not much was safe around me, not my grandfather's silver dollars or my grandmother's cigarettes or my mother's stray Quaaludes. So I got my sister; I recognized who and what she was. I did not and do not have a judgment about this, it's just the way we Correns were: *takers*. But we gave, too. Gave love, gave shelter, gave food, money, time, support; we never had to be asked. We also stole from you when you stayed with us. It's just fair.

I gave Cathy Sue those stolen Cabbage Patch dolls and she resold them for hundreds of dollars more on the Virginia Beach black market, where she was *very* well known.

Employee layaway was where we put items aside and paid a small monthly deposit. It's where we underpaid and exploited Roses laborers could pay off our in-store purchases and receive a miserly store discount in return. It was located discreetly off the floor, in the storerooms, and it was completely unsupervised. When I mapped this out to Cathy Sue, she had immediately recognized Roses had a stupid system, one easily exploited. I *began* sneaking into layaway with Cabbage Patch dolls rolled up inside towels, shoving them into my big, empty layaway box, which was about the size of a refrigerator laid on its side.

It could hold *a lot* of Cabbage Patch dolls.

Fine!

Yes!

I took *more* than eight dolls!

I probably stole more than three dozen altogether.

Boosting Cabbage Patch dolls is not a very big crime on the scale of known crimes committed in my immediate family, so stealing a bunch of coveted dolls with names like Sissy Olivette, Augustus Bert, and Valenska Lucille I thought was pretty minor, at least compared to shooting at people with modified rifles, or running illegal casinos, or being prosecuted by the attorney general of New York, like my father's father, "Big" Al Cohen. Now *that* was some crime!

I wanted to be her.

I wanted to be just like my mother, to be brave like her, be fearless like her. I wanted to be like *all of them*, my mother and my sister and my grandmother and Lillian Fucking Hellman. I wanted to survive this pitiless and heartless earth, and do it by any means. I needed to be a *winner*.

By the time I got busted, Twin and I had been living on the Outer Banks for six months, and other than each other, Asshole, our sister, and Little Big Ben, who was now over six feet tall and not even ten years old, we didn't talk to a soul. We weren't *blending in* with the Outer Banks.

Why would the locals want to hang out with me, anyway? What could they possibly see in a haughty, bookish, obviously homosexual fop from liberal, big-city Fayetteville who wore too-tight pants and far, *far* too much turquoise, with hair like a Jewish version of Prince and an impressive, sassy voice? I didn't know the difference between a short track and a super speedway, or that Dale drove the 3 and Million-Dollar Bill the 9. I had *nothing* in common with my island classmates. I was an obvious target for bullying, and they came for me. Twin couldn't help; he was too busy trying to stay alive in the same alien ecosystem of this island high school. By the time Christmas rolled around, nobody at Manteo High knew me by Andy, but they certainly did by Gaybob, Betsy, Little Betsy, Little Bit, Boofer, Homer, Gaybies, GAIDS, Little Betsy Gayby Baby, Pansy, Aunt Pansy, and the absolute worst: Bitch Gaylord.

I was *done* with Manteo.

13.

Detective Midgett taps the yellow pad with two big, nicotine-stained fingers, saying with an impatient look on his shiny red face, "Andy, I need some names."

He wants names?

Here are some names.

My accomplices were Boofer and Bitch Gaylord. My sidekicks were Gaybob, Pansy, GAIDS, and Homer. Gaybies and Little Bit and Aunt Pansy were in on it, too. I didn't work alone. I worked with *a team* of accomplices!

"Roses won't let you go without either an arrest or a list of who was in on this with you. You can call it a night, and we can put this whole mess behind us," Detective Midgett says. It's late. He's hungry, and those Sam & Omie's onion rings were *hours* ago.

14.

Why, of all places, had I chosen *Roses* to work at? I fucking *hated* Roses.

Even then, I knew it was owned by the Popes, a neolithic North Carolina clan hellbent on nuking Durham to ashes. *Why* was I giving them my gay socialist labors?

Because I did *not* love that Kmart rust-red discount store smock look for me.

Why did I steal so many dolls?

I was lonely.

I missed my mother.

All the lesbian fisherwomen from Wanchese were gone.

I was an outcast, nobody wanted me, not even my English teacher, and this was 1984 *when stuff like that was totally okay.*

Then: I had the power.

I had the dolls that *everybody* wanted for Christmas of 1984.

Those stupid, off-white, forty-dollar foam babies with round, lumpy faces, tiny, soft, pudgy arms with close-set eyes, hair made of yarn. Driving people to madness. *Why?* There were actual riots, parents scrambled over and on top of each other like zombies. They would bribe black market pirates like my sister hundreds, even thousands, of dollars for just one of these things made of sponge and pantyhose. People were fistfighting each other in streets for the chance to fake-adopt a fake baby made in a fake orphanage in Georgia. This wasn't just a fad. It was *collective insanity*.

I was drunk on my power.

"The more you bring, the more we sell. The more we sell, the more we make," Cathy Sue urged me on, maniacally clutching a warm mug of Kahlua and coffee close to her thieving, larcenous heart. "We can take a vacation over spring break, maybe take Mom on a cruise!" she lied and lied and lied.

So I stole Candy.

And I stole Turnip.

And I stole Blinks.

I stole Babette Lorraine and Jucy Clementine and Googie Jesse and Esmeralda Doberama, and I stole Darnell, too.

I even stole Darnell.

I stole so many goddamned dolls.

By the time Christmas week rolled around, my simmering contempt for my high school and the *pitiless* Outer Banks itself all coalesced into a cold, festering wound inside of me, an ice hole so deep even the Encyclopedia Britannica's Deadliest Disasters of the Year section—*which I worshipped*—could not melt it. Not even Lillian Hellman's *Pentimento*, the second of her triptych of memoir, that icy cold dagger of lies and sex that landed Jane Fonda her *third* Oscar nomination, could heal me.

By this time, I had padded *two* refrigerator-sized Roses employee layaway boxes with *two dozen* Cabbage Patch dolls.

I was caught with twenty-four dolls.

"What made you think you could get two boxes that size out of the store? Without bein' noticed?" Detective Midgett asks me, laughing, lightly appalled. "Did you really think nobody would say anything when they spilled across the floor?"

They spilled across the floor.

The second box, which I had balanced precariously atop the first in my mastermind plan to slyly secrete them out the door, naturally tipped out of my scarecrow arms and spilled, disgorging its guts in a flood of stolen beige, brown, and yeasty off-white panty-babies that flowed down like an unrolled skein of yarn ahead of me, as if to surrender, or to announce my imminent arrest. A foamy waterfall, a silent cascade of wide-open eyes and button-mouthed puckers screaming quietly. Jelly Bean came first, then Nikki Tikki, and then, horribly, the Cornsilk Kid. The last doll slid gaily and accusingly across Roses' polished, linoleum night floors, stopping in front of the penny loafers of my laconic, hatchet-faced store manager, Anna.

Anna *hated* me.

She delivered me into the hands of Detective Midgett less than five minutes later, who had grumpily interrupted his late lunch from Sam & Omie's to come collect me.

Detective Midgett asks, "You are a Jew, aren't ya?"

Terrified, I nod yes, mentally searching my person for my papers, expecting the worst, because you *better be* expecting the worst after a question like *that*.

Detective Midgett nods, chuckling. "Sort of takes the sting out of getting fired on Christmas, don't it?"

I would walk away free and clear, just another fired, fuckup teenaged store clerk, but only if I named all my accomplices and promised never to return to Roses department store. I pretend to agonize over *that*. Agony dramatics was my forensics debate specialty, after all.

But I *would* confess. I have a list for Detective Midgett.

I begin scribbling furiously on his yellow pad.

My list of co-conspirators is very long. French Revolution tricoteuse bitch sitting and knitting at the guillotine long.

Before I know it, I have over twenty names on it. But it isn't a list of accomplices.

It's an enemies' list.

A list of the children at Manteo High who've tormented me for months.

M., who created "Gaybob" the second I arrived, so absolutely fuck her. D., who every day on the bus to school thumped me on the head and said "Just checking to see if the fruit is ripe." E., who tripped me from behind each and every time he had the chance. N., who told me I would never belong on the Outer Banks and "I should get the first Trailways back to Fayetteville." J., just because he was so damned hot and mean, and hot and mean? That's my sexual kryptonite.

I could fill an entire book of names. It is *easy.*

Burning bridges is *always easy.*

Leaving people behind *is easy. My family has been doing it for years.*

Detective Midgett wants to see a conspiracy. I show him one.

I can hear my mother clearly, calling out to me over the frozen waves. "Fuck 'em," she is saying. "They had it coming," and "Can you get back by February sweeps? *Hollywood Wives* is on. We can have a party."

I stroll out of Nags Head Justice Hut that sleety, wintery island night tasting *freedom* and *sweeps week* and *fried onions.*

I go home and I pack my *TV Guides.*

This experiment is over.

Nags Head is not my home.

I want my people. My bowling alley.

I *want* my mother's tornado, my stained, tired places that I have foolishly fled in search of a false and illusory cedar-lined, taffy-flavored peace that never existed. I am going back home, whatever and whoever that is, *where I belong.*

All I know is that my people aren't island folk surfing waves made of peanut butter fudge.

My people are *Fayetteville*.

I run back.

Back to her.

HOLLYWOOD WIFE

1.

Of course, everybody watched *Hollywood Wives* that February.

You couldn't escape it.

The cover of *TV Guide*, *People* magazine, the *Fayetteville Observer*—all the important press were in a lather. *Entertainment Tonight* had devoted an entire week to hyping it, most likely because Aaron Spelling had given Mary Hart an enormous, splashy cameo in the first episode. The promise of three sizzling February days and nights of Jackie Collins TV wormed itself into mother's and son's souls that winter, and I chased the dream of getting off the Outer Banks and back to Renay in time for the premiere, home for us to be together again on her waterbed, floating on trash, glitter, glitz, and dreams, just like old times. We burned up the phone cards that bitter winter of 1985, plotting our private premiere party when I triumphantly returned to Fayetteville to be by her side, curled up in her legs in front of a toasty fire of crackling bowling pins. Home again.

But where was home?

"I'll figure it out," Renay had said on the phone. "Just get your ass back here and bring me some fudge, would you? Not pistachio. Your sister colors it too green," she commanded.

Before we left for the Outer Banks, and before I returned to Fayetteville, there had been one more house in between, before she moved yet again.

The Devonwood House.

None of us—not me, not my brothers, none of my mother's friends—not one of us have a single memory of the near year that the Correns lived in a darling little green house on a darling little green block up in Devonwood, a tidy neighborhood of darling houses near Westover.

All we remember is that we fled Kendallwood in the middle of the night in early 1984, and then, like some magic spell, my brothers and I were living on the Outer Banks.

It was as if we fled our memory the night we swapped Kendallwood for Devonwood.

It's just *gone*. Devonwood, a whole, entire house, is *gone*.

"I gotta be honest with you. I wasn't thinkin' too much back then," Asshole told me.

"Green house. All's I can 'collect," Twin agreed in his usual hot cascade of gossip.

I lived there for almost an entire year of school.

An entire freshman year.

None of us can remember a damned thing.

What happened in Devonwood?

"She was really bad with money." Butt Check snorted over coffee and biscuits, when I tried to jog his memory of that calamitous time. "It was like she was at war with money, or somethin'."

"She couldn't hold on to a dime if it was stapled to her ass." Twin laughed.

"Things were bad at the end. I got the hell out," Asshole said. "She was *so bad* with money."

"She was *really* bad with money, honey," Doreen affirmed in her New HampSHUH accent. "But she'd give ya the last can of green beans outta the trunk of her CAH, that one. *SAWLT of the earth!*"

"She was a magician. She could make money *disappear*." Bernie roared with laughter.

"Just another place we left," Twin said.

"Why are you even asking?" Asshole glared at me.

Why is he mad at me??

What the hell happened in Devonwood?

Whatever it was: that house was the very last place Renay Corren would ever call her own.

She was evicted in December 1984.

She lost a bunch of furniture, including our old paisley yellow sofa and those mamasan and papasan paintings from Okinawa, and she never had an address of her own in Fayetteville again. She never had a couch again, as far as I know. With the exception of her queen-sized waterbed, which she would also lose in short order, Renay Mandel Corren never again outright owned a single stick of furniture for the next thirty-seven years.

For a big lady, she traveled light, right up until her spirit left her body.

2.

Dame Jacqueline Jill Collins, OBE penned a primal Greek myth that struck a national nerve.

Fifteen million copies. Twenty-eight weeks on the *New York Times* Best Seller List. The paperback that outsold *1984* in the actual *year* 1984, when the actual book entitled *1984* by George Orwell is set. Jackie Collins did *all* that with some leopard-skin pants and a felt-tip pen. *Hollywood Wives* was not just a book. It was a bone fide, coast-to-coast, homosexual brushfire. *Hollywood Wives* finally made it safe to publicly discuss gay stuff like hair-don'ts, fashion, and Andrew Stevens. It even had a wise, sassy drag queen salon proprietor on Sunset Boulevard dispensing devastatingly droll and necessary wisdom, like *The Barefoot Contessa*. It was a story ahead of its time, one that centered couture, gossip, hot sex, tastefully arranged canapes, and forbidden, shirtless twin brothers.

It belonged to women and gays.

It belonged to *us*.

Renay and I fanatically loved *Hollywood Wives*. We had passed the book back and forth, obsessed over every tiny detail and betrayal, speculated over who would be cast as Gina or Montana or the sassy gay salon proprietor. That book was one part holy text, one part sisterhood. Jackie centered her outrageous stories around women we recognized—strong, secure women who had agency, who were vital, educated, cunning and canny, witty and adversarial, thieves and adventurers, getting their money, getting their orgasm, getting somebody else to get them their lunch. Jackie's characters did what Renay did: they traded in jokes and gossip, they fucked and forgot men with impunity, they had bad divorces, and they laughed and laughed it all off, laughed through the worst of it, the best of it, the crumbs, the cream, *all of it. They lived.*

From her earliest days, Renay Mandel Corren demanded one thing from all who entered her field of play: *make her feel. Feed her.* Take her on *a ride.* Make her howl with laughter: the filthier, the more vile the joke, the better. *Hollywood Wives*, with its well-dressed, well-fed, well-fucked women strutting around Hollywood in power heels, *got Renay feeling.* Together we *slid* down under our covers with our flashlights and our Jackie, and we couldn't put her down until it was dawn or we were done feeling.

She would never *be* done.

She just picked that book up and started feeling all over again.

This was the home that awaited me. Not a house.

Not a place full of things that she lost in evictions, or memories that we left behind in a rush to get to the next place that we would lose. Books were our home. Language. *Feeling.* We spoke one language, she and I, written in blood, bullets, and betrayal. *Hollywood Wives*, like all the great stories throughout all time, all the stories she and I shared, told me and Renay who we were at that moment in time, what we *felt* in that moment, about ourselves, about each other. *Hollywood Wives* told me the secret that I most deeply desired, most needed to know, was most afraid of believing:

She was my home.

3.

In January 1985, all the oranges in the state of Florida died, and I returned to Fayetteville.

"You'll regret it," Cathy Sue had glowered as Twin and I boarded the bus, leaving her, Little Big Ben, Asshole, and another husband behind. "You can't keep runnin' back to her every time something goes wrong," she snorted as she raised her to-go mug of Kahlua and coffee in a bitter farewell.

"Watch me," I snapped as the doors shut firmly in her face.

Twin and I settled into our Trailways conveyance for our long ride home. *Farewell, Fudge Island!* I murmured darkly as we bumped over soon-to-burn Bonner Bridge.

"Go fudge yourself," Twin chimed in with the first, and very last, joke that he would ever make in my presence. He had really opened up to me on this adventure. He had also really eaten half of the too-green pistachio fudge we were meant to take home to Renay.

Twin and I practically sailed back to Fayetteville, eager as we were to go back to Westover, back to our friends, back in time for *Hollywood Wives*, and PBS's hotly anticipated counter-programming, James Baldwin's *Go Tell It on the Mountain*. Renay had promised to tape the Baldwin movie for me, and I was *very* excited to see it, as I had, like all questioning gays of that time, stolen my copy of *Go Tell It on the Mountain* from the Cumberland County library thinking it was *Giovanni's Room*, and had thus never finished *Go Tell It on the Mountain* because there was no good gay sex in that one, merely implied masturbation.

Yes, I was headed home.

But did Renay even have a home?

I estimate that Renay Corren had overseen approximately twenty household moves over twenty-nine continuous years of moving, most of them in the last decade, and that after all that jumping off sinking ships, dodging landlords, evacuating weeping brick ranches in the middle of the night, after carting us kids into a new house once approximately every 1.5 years, Renay Corren was out of houses.

We were finally and officially houseless.

That must seem like an awfully fancy and literary way of saying "homeless," but I do not today view my last act in Fayetteville as one of homelessness. After all, I had just left behind a very nice, cedar-shingled home on the island of Nags Head, and even if it was the drafty ark of a one-eyed criminal masterminding a vast, island network of doll theft and Kahlua drinks, I had a home in Nags Head, and I knew that.

But in Fayetteville, it was clear to me, and for all to see: Renay was busted and houseless.

Technically homeless, sure, if you want to be all Baldwin-y about it.

Renay did not. We were "houseless" to Renay, and houselessness had a proven cure.

We were *not* gonna be kicked to Cain Road.

She had two sons gone—Asshole stayed behind on Fudge Island, and Rabbi was living that US Army dream in South Korea—and two sons on a bus heading back to Fayetteville. She needed a place for us all to crash. It had to be cheap, hold a queen-sized waterbed, and stack two teens close to Westover.

"We're bunking with Butt Check," Renay announced, meeting us at the Carolina Trailways, where I was so happy to escape the cherry ammonia of the bus and to see Fayetteville again, I bent over and tidily, gratefully vomited upon a revitalized and de-hookered Hay Street. *I was back, baby!*

"We *are*?" Twin said, thrilled. This was good news. Butt Check was not only our brother-in-B&B-arms, but he was also working at the Cumberland County Memorial Auditorium, so that meant free or discounted tickets to Mid-South and Jim Crockett Wrestling. *A very big deal.*

"Back to Scotty Hills, boys," Renay said, a touch defiantly, wiring the back door of the Nova shut with a coat hanger, grimly determined to fashion this next house into a home.

Going back to Scotty Hills was quite a step down.

We were going right back to the starting line, not even a quarter of a mile from where it all began, our old house on Pamalee Drive. Before the divorce.

Pamalee was seven houses and a lifetime ago. Our last real home.

We were going back to live in the shadow of our old family.

It seems that, after her two youngest sons were sold...I mean, shipped off, to her pirate daughter, Renay had been lightly evicted from the green-shingled house in Devonwood by the owner—or rather, *the owner's ghost*. The owner had died shortly after we decamped for Nags Head, and his kids wanted to sell it quick—but Renay had nowhere to go, so she wouldn't budge, then a long game of ghost landlord chicken ensued with his squatter tenant, until my squatter mother and her big waterbed were evicted.

Penniless, burdened by encroaching diabetes and bowling bunions, hounded by bad checks and an allergy to any financial planning whatsoever, Renay turned her abundant charms upon her mentee, part-time son, and best friend, Butt Check. Yes, he was a mere twenty-two, more than half her age, but in Fayetteville that's Socrates-level wise, just the way my mother liked her local scoundrels. Butt Check was smart enough to stay out of Fayetteville jail, keep a job, and keep an eye on his younger sister. Renay was pushing fifty, busted, and had two teenage sons incoming from Fudge Island, and she needed rooms *fast*. Ever since Butt Check's dad passed away unexpectedly at the age of thirty-eight, he didn't know what he was missing. But Renay Corren made *sure* he knew. Butt Check was missing *family*.

And so: *enter her family*.

Renay Corren and sons moved into Butt Check and his sister Lizzie's big, empty—wait for it—brick ranch at the Dickensian-sounding Oglethorpe Court.

This would be Renay's final house in Fayetteville, North Carolina.

It wasn't hers, but it was a place where we could all pretend to be at home together.

Was she trapped in her own history, as the tremendously gay French philosopher James Baldwin might have asked? Or was it that Renay's own history was trapped too deeply inside of her to ever excavate, to lead us anywhere but back beneath the shadow of our last real home? I know there was a lady with desires for a home buried down there somewhere beneath all those lies, bounced checks, evictions, and Pringles. But I was raised by a woman who simply refused to allow that version of herself to be reeled up into the light. She liked the lower depths. She liked moving. She liked gambling. She liked not knowing if she was gonna win or lose or be kicked to the curb. She was like one of them ancient catfish that just circles and circles Glenville Lake until it steals your nightcrawlers, then heads on back downtown for the cooler, darker waters below.

It physically hurt to drive by that Pamalee house, to see a whole other family just living and playing and existing in our old home, while we were banished blocks away, living in its shadow. Renay never surmounted her history. She never had to. Even with no good options, she always managed to play a kind of winning hand. This was her move. Cards down. She landed us. Even if it wasn't a home, this was a place where we could play at family.

That was plenty enough for her.

We never knew what or who would stroll through our family's doors on Oglethorpe Court.

Yes, there were professional wrestlers.

4.

Oglethorpe Court.

A single-story treasure that appeared in that late-era, wild brick craze of 1974, when Fayetteville's last setting rays of optimism finally slid to their death on the slippery banks of the Cape Fear, murdered by a collective Cumberland shrug of architectural indifference.

I found myself living in the very last house I would ever occupy in Fayetteville.

It was not my home, nor was it hers. It was barely Butt Check's. But it is where I lived until the end.

It belonged to the people of Fayetteville.

Oglethorpe was populated by a never-ending stream of transients, roommates, visitors, jocks, soldiers, and high schoolers, all of us disconnected, overlapping, either untethered from families or schooling, scattered like cracked pepper medley by Fayetteville divorces, remarriages, the Army, or jail. Everybody who crashed on Oglethorpe was pursuing their ambitious and all-hours Fayetteville schedules that never quite aligned, were frequently shady, and except for holy Sundays (wrestling, racing, laundry, or football) were conducted off-site.

We rarely saw Renay.

I tried to be away from the house as much as possible, made plenty sure I had my plans and my school and my rehearsals organized on the daily. When I was back at Oglethorpe, it was generally a tumultuous environment—hard to study or read in, filled with Twin's high school buddies in their horny, brawling, teenaged prime, who came back from their games and partied *hard* into the night, cops coming by to break things up, what have you. There were always two or three of my mother's and Butt Check's B&B tribe flowing in their wake, too, the usual gamblers and the card sharks, Mucket, Porky, Bonzo, the sidekicks who rolled up after the lanes closed and slapped at cards all night, into the dawn, cigarettes and joints, a haze of Pepsi and Crown Royal in the air.

There were guest stars, too.

I might wake up or go to sleep to the sound of one or the other half of those hugely popular Mid-South Wrestling champs, the tag-team sensation known as Rock 'n' Roll Express. There was World Class Championship Wrestling, Jim Crockett and his National Wrestling Alliance, and the World Wrestling Federation, and they all came to Fayetteville then, all to fight, all the time, where they were loudly worshipped as the redneck opera stars that they *absolutely* were. Thanks to Butt Check, Twin and I went to all the matches. We were wrestling *freaks*, born and raised. Every show at the Memorial was a sell-out, a screaming, clomping, stomping, *thrilling* hair-pulling mess of *fun*.

Rock 'n' Roll Express came around the house lots, fighting as they were not only for belts but for the hand of Lizzie, Butt Check's gorgeous, green-eyed, petite firecracker doe of a little sister, who was either eighteen or close enough to eighteen that nothing statutory was going on. Close to eighteen is basically a forty-year-old grandmother in Fayetteville years, anyway. Lizzie was *always* being pursued by one of those sweaty, baby-faced beasts, and a melodramatic opera frequently played itself out on Oglethorpe, as the Express made their pitch for Lizzie's tiny, perfect hand, then body-slammed each other in the living room, or on our patchy front lawn.

Thurman lived with us, too.

He worked the late shift at the Pizza Hut on Bragg Boulevard and nightly decompressed by rinsing his rust-and-beige smock off in the kitchen sink, sitting with me afterward to munch his way through one of his many cans of cold corn, his favorite late-night snack. As the late hour progressed, Thurman gently segued from canned corn to spooning up softly folded squares of Wonder bread, which he pressed deep into a coffee mug that he had filled with maple syrup, and microwaved on high for two minutes.

Thurman had an eclectic palate.

Thurman would amble home in the wee hours, tomato-stained and weary, poke his head into my doorless bedroom, give an all-clear signal that he had some good leftovers with him, and I would groggily rise in the dark to have some laid-back therapy as I dipped fat cold crusts into room-temperature tomato sauce and unwound with my midnight pizza therapist. Together we bemoaned the fallen state of civilization, and the atrocious table manners of white people. Thurman would recount his adventures with the starving classes of Scotty Hills, and

I would unpack my own troubles, cold crust by cold crust. I picked Thurman's brain on how or whether to ever exact revenge on a pregnant ninth grader who beat the living shit out of me, or whether to simply let things go. Thurman was the first person to help me understand what it meant to be a fatherless boy adrift, and that, like him, like Butt Check, "We had to be fathers to ourselves." Thurman knew that I was a gay, and he never judged, whispering only encouragements at my opening-night jitters while he rinsed off his uniform carefully in the sink with dish detergent.

"People who don't tip ain't good people, ain't bad people. They *sad* people," Thurman once said. And "Know why they ain't make pizza a square? Everybody equal on a circle."

A midnight kitchen philosopher, with a big heart and a cold can of corn. I loved Thurman intensely.

Granting a gay sixteen-year-old a house filled with jocks, wrestlers, and free pizza was God's final Fayetteville gift to me.

Twin and I swam back to the comforting, familiar, stale smells of Westover, and we kept our heads down as we barreled our way through sports, academics, drama, ROTC, parading through the next two years largely unmolested. With Asshole back on the Outer Banks beginning his extremely slow, still-a-work-in-progress crawl toward respectability, and with Rabbi far, far away in the Army, and Bonus—well, I could not tell you where Bonus was in 1985—I had two short years to figure out where I was going after graduation.

I went *hard*.

I joined every club that would have me. I returned to my position as a witty companion for all the smartest, funniest, nerdy drama girls, my few remaining All-Girl Gang members like Hollis, but also newer friends, Delaney, Victoria, and Ristin, all women, all flamboyant, all *on*, all the time. I was their fop-at-large, their escort for rent, their safe boy with a wardrobe of rags that screamed to all the parents: *No sexual threat here, ma'am.* I leaned into my identity as big-time thespian, starring in one smash Neil Simon production after the other. I solidified my position as King Drama Nerd and prized teacher's pet. I became a vice president of the state Thespian Society, which was merely honorary, and I remained extravagantly bitter that I had lost the presidency to a girl from Boone who had campaigned with bespoke sweethearts candy with her name printed upon them. You. Can't. Beat. Free. Candy. I joined the French Club. I joined the Literary Club, and then I seized the typing editor position of the Zephyr, Westover's yearbook.

I clung to Miss Mattie at the Zephyr, Miss Laura at the Thespians, Mr. Stanton in English, all the adults who had somehow naturally understood that this uptight, driven, neurotic little starveling needed compassion, understanding, free food, and lots and lots of books. They knew I was going *somewhere*, and they were determined to help get me there.

There was no question that Renay expected me to get going.

So I was going.

It was never even discussed, but I would be leaving Fayetteville, and leaving her.

My life became that of an ambitious young Fayetteville actor, devoted to high school acting and the Fayetteville Little Theatre, an *amazing* bit of luck in downtown run by Olga B. Thorp, a saintly, civic-minded, wealthy Italian woman from South Carolina who gave me not just a shot, but increasingly demanding roles in her productions. I took everything Olga B. gave me, and Olga B. took my heart and soul, my time and complete focus, in return. I gave it all gladly. I took on more and more responsibility at the Fayetteville Little Theatre, which required nothing so much as an absolute commitment to being totally Olga's, and totally gay.

5.

Hollywood Wives was a *smash.*

Number one for the night, a 22 rating, a 33 share. One in three television sets tuned into the same glossy drama. *Nothing could touch it.* It was high class, high camp start to finish. From Andrew Stevens to Angie Dickinson, it was a feathered romp written in fur and diamonds. The world was hooked.

We were hooked.

We were reunited.

Me, a queen-sized, heated waterbed, Stefanie Powers, and *her.*

Renay and Ann, together again.

"You can be your own woman, Montana, or you can be *married,*" Renay giggled, ensconced deeply within her rust-orange corduroy television-watching husband, and shaking the waterbed with her laughs, the water warm, heated up high to offset the damp and chilly Fayetteville night.

Together again.

"Neil is her writing *partner,* Renay. They are writing *a movie* together. She will *never* leave him!" I crowed from my usual position at her feet, exhibiting an unnatural, even eerie, understanding of the power of a greenlit movie script over all other earthly arrangement.

"I don't know why they call this shit *Hollywood Wives.* It should be called *Hollywood Ex-Wives.* It's not about *marriage,*" Renay said. "It's about *freedom* from marriage. Freedom from your *parents' marriage.*" She belly laughed, lazily plucking another errant fine vellus from her already denuded eyebrow.

"You can have a life, a *real* life, Montana," she murmured. "Or you can be married."

I floated with Renay like this for three nights, rocking gently on her warm waterbed waves to the glow of the TV, startled periodically out of our story by her outbursts of derision and joy with each revelation and shocking twist, as I painted her toenails and buffed her feet like old times. She expertly dissected the rookie mistakes of those glamorous women, married ladies she and I pitied but also really wanted to protect. *We'd* never lower *ourselves* to be with losers like them, but we would be there for them, when they inevitably fell. We loved a good mop-up. When it came to men, Renay Corren knew the score, and knew when to bail. She had even cut ties with her boyfriend Dan Marino, grimly stitching her broken AFC heart to the Steelers after the spectacular collapse of the Dolphins' defense, and Marino getting sacked all those times. Yinz for life, Steelers Nation to her very last breath.

If you had asked me then, I would have said that night that Renay Corren was the wisest, toughest, smartest woman in the entire world. That is not what I believed. That is what I knew.

Yet mothers and daughters, am I right?

We inevitably pull away. We cannot help but seek out our own way, thinking that we can be free of those that made us in their image all too well.

"Ross doesn't love you, Elaine," Renay admonished. "He loves what you can *do* for him."

"Come on, Mom, you'd marry again to live in a house that nice. To live in Bel-Air with a real housekeeper," I said.

"Nah. There is no 'me' in 'team,' Ann," she said.

"There actually is a 'me' in 'team,' Renay," I dared to correct.

"Well, there's no 'Renay' in 'team,' not that kind of team, not ever again." She shuddered in distaste at Elaine's slavish devotion to her cheating dummy husband, Ross.

I spent fewer and fewer of my remaining Fayetteville hours in the company of my influential advisor Renay, and more and more at the knees of the women who held the keys to my future: my drama teacher, Miss Laura; my yearbook advisor, Miss Mattie; and Olga B. Thorp, my beloved taskmaster at the Fayetteville Little Theatre. They gave me the daily drops of courage and encouragement that I needed to dare to believe that I could dream, and *get going* on that dream. That I could do what those people on the TV could do. I knew instinctively, on a level that I would not fully drag into the sunlight until spending a fortune on therapy many, many years into the future, that this leaving, this pursuit of mine: it would make Renay happy, too.

I did what it took, I asked for help, for guidance from women who were not encumbered by the same type of complications as my own family was. I figured out before I even left Fayetteville behind that Renay Corren probably wouldn't be my agent much longer. I'd be hers.

By the time *Hollywood Wives* was the number one show in America, Renay's time as my mentor and advisor, and mine as her mentee and client, was a nearly complete phase, and our roles had begun to completely reverse, the way the North Equatorial Current in the Indian Ocean does every November, moving for months in the opposite direction against the impending monsoon.

There was simply no more that Renay could do for me in Fayetteville.

So Renay, in essence, became *my* Hollywood wife.

One from whom I was both desperate to be—and desperately afraid of being—completely and utterly untethered.

6.

By 1987, Renay Corren and I were merely roommates.

Sometimes we crossed paths or ate bagels together at the B&B, but otherwise Renay had her life, and I had mine. She came to all my shows. She bought me an old wreck of a car so I could drive myself to and from rehearsals. She even made it to my graduation. She showed up for the big stuff. But she was *busy*.

Renay was by this time a nationally ranked cribbage player: some say eleventh in the nation, some say thirteenth; some say my mother is completely full of shit. She was, all the same, *busy*. If not at the lanes, she was on the road a lot with the Wolfpack, or playing cards in Hickory, or bowling tournaments everywhere. I was left in charge of the house. That probably sounds like I was a housekeeper, because I was. I kept our house. I began taking on all the responsibilities of the home front, for shopping and cleaning, for keeping track of her travel to tournaments, her spending, making sure she had clean clothes for her trips, packing for her, running her baths, keeping freshly baked goods on hand.

By the time 1987 rolled up, Renay Corren was no longer just my mother.

She was my client.

I had become Sue Mengers, albeit on a budget, and Renay was the one who wore the muumuus. She was my number one client, and I was incredibly proud to represent her.

She would stay my number one client until the day she died.

7.

Shortly after I turned eighteen years old, I left Fayetteville forever.

We all left.

On our own or married, under the power of the Army's sail or a sister's wind, we left.

Twin, much to the derision and scorn of his family, went south to the United States Marines, down to Camp Lejeune for his brief and notorious run at Semper Fi. I left for a low-budget acting academy in the western part of the state on a full scholarship from the school, and a five-hundred-dollar scholarship from the brilliant lady who played Flo in the TV series *Alice*.

That's right, motherfuckers, Flo paid for my freshman-year pizza.

Notably, at the wheel of the fancy gold car driving me away from Fayetteville for the very last time in August 1987, off to the college adventure and destiny that surely awaited me, was not Renay Mandel Corren.

I was driven away by Fayetteville Little Theatre's very own Olga B. Thorp, my great friend, my part-time mother, my Italian South Carolinian mentor.

Renay couldn't get the day off from work.

"Andy—"

AY-YUN-DEE is what it sounded like when Olga said my name. Her astonishingly rich, honey-throated, Carolina purr greeted me as I loaded up her fine-smelling car.

"Andy, do you have everything? Did your momma pack your sheets and your towels?"

In fact, as you all must certainly know, Renay had done no such a thing.

I had two of Shithead's old Vietnam trunks stuffed with all my clothes, a tiny microwave oven from the Best, two paper grocery bags overflowing with boxes of Little Debbie snack cakes from the Food Town, a bunch of soft fruit, two new exotic and mandatory dance belts I had *no idea* how to wear, several of Stephen King's and Jackie Collins's books that I could not and would not ever live without, a pair of still-shining unworn character shoes, and a used desk lamp Renay stole from Howard at the B&B.

I had packed nothing else.

"Andy, darlin'." Olga *tsk*ed. "A man needs clean sheets to wake up on, on his first morning at college."

"I'll buy some there, Bo," I said, using the name she was affectionately known by, to one and all.

"God gave us gifts, Andy," Olga said solemnly as she made up my dorm bed later that day, spreading out a set of crisp, classic Polo Ralph Lauren sheets in Jonquil Blue she had purchased along the way in a soaring, pink Thalhimers department store in fancy Durham. The fitted sheet had wide, proud blue stripes, the flat a jaunty blue oceanic scallop that galloped magnanimously across the waves stitched atop.

"Lord knows, Andy, He gave me mine. Some I wish He hadn't. Other times, I am so glad He did," she said, resting and tucking those billowing sheets on my otherwise bare thin metal cot of a bed.

They looked so beautiful to me.

They looked like *home*.

"Thank you for bringing me home, Bo. Thank you for *everything*," I whispered into her brown, fine-smelling coif.

"Oh, I just gave you some sheets." She laughed. "Try and keep 'em clean, is all I ask."

8.

Renay took one look at Cathy Sue's cedar bedrooms in Nags Head, and she moved right on in.

I only went back to Fayetteville one more time.

After Renay bailed, there were no more Correns left in Fayetteville, so why go back?

None of us ever did.

We never stopped into the B&B to look up Mucket and Howard, or Mona, Wanda, and Porky. We never went over to see Doreen and

Faith, to settle Steelers scores, pay off bad checks at the B&B front desk, like D.J. Ledford finally did when he got out of federal prison with his dad.

We never fished Eastover again, or Glenville Lake, or the bottom of a pickled egg jar at Bev's Place, or a pin out of a jammed-up pin-setter.

We never sat around reminiscing about the good old days.

We didn't remember many.

Maybe we didn't think hard enough.

Besides, I wasn't in the remembering business. Not anymore.

I was in the business of forgetting.

I was in *show business*!

FOUR DAYS IN EL PASO

1.

Prologue: New York City, December 2021

I think my brother just told me that the Pittsburgh Steelers killed our mother.

"Is it the blood clots?" I ask.

"It ain't the blood clots," Asshole reports in his flat, clipped drawl.

"Is it the 'unknown mass'?" I ask.

They recently found an "unknown mass" on Renay's liver, but it has, heretofore, stubbornly remained "unknown."

"No. It's not the liver mass. It's not the kidneys or the sepsis or the diabetes this time," he says, pausing, taking a deep breath. "We was just watching football. Steelers. Normal day. Looking at pictures."

Okay. So it isn't the "unknown mass" or the kidney disease, or the sepsis, the diabetes, the hypotension, the second bout with breast cancer, or the second mastectomy. It isn't even the Omicron wave crashing over me, her, the whole fucking world in December 2021 that has taken my mother out of the game and benched her back at the hospital once more.

This time it's the Steelers.

I knew it would be the Steelers that broke her in the end.

"How is she? Can she talk?"

"Intubated. Sedated. No," Asshole grimly reports.

The Steelers won four straight: Broncos, Seahawks, Browns, and Bears. Yes, they tied it up with the Lions on their own home turf, Heinz Field, which was admittedly an *incredibly embarrassing spectacle*, but hardly life-ending stuff. Maybe it was losing to the Chargers? It's possible. That *is* pretty humiliating, just ask the Dolphins. If I had to guess, I'd say that's the most likely culprit. It was simply unbearable in the end for Renay Mandel Corren to see her beloved Steelers fall before the lowly Chargers. She is Steelers for life. They go, she goes.

"Steelers went to third place in the AFC North. She must've figured that," Asshole says sadly. "You need to come home," he barks. "It's past time."

I was overdressed in too much worsted wool for this warm night out in Gay Brooklyn to see a gay drag Christmas concert in a bombed-out old opera house. I had a jaunty Christmas scarf and a poncy Christmas hat on. I looked desperate. Sweaty and ridiculous. Which is how I felt, cradling the phone to my sweaty ear. My friends had jokingly said "Plague festive," so I, typically, overdelivered.

"You need to get your festive ass home. *Quick*," Asshole grunted grimly.

Renay was dying. No two ways about it.

"I can't stay here forever. I got a job to do," he said, irritated.

His voice reels me back fifty years and eight hundred miles south to the sewers beneath Pamalee Drive, to the green pecan–carpeted, piney yards of our childhood, to the noisy old pin-setters of B&B Lanes. Asshole always knew how to get those villainous machines to cough up a chipped pin, to get that lane rolling again *quick for Renay*. Asshole is rough and direct, unvarnished as a new wall. He is always sturdy and grim, but particularly so tonight, as he relays the grim and grimmer news.

He's also the only one of Renay's sons still talking to me.

"Just looking at pictures," he mumbled again, pained.

I look up into the muggy Brooklyn night, standing only miles from where my nana Minna Katz fell out of the night sky over New Jersey. I seek her strength now. I seek her memory, her fire, her endurance in the face of plagen. The blessing of suffering.

"It's long past time for you to get on down here," Asshole says again.

I know it. He knows I know it.

She's dying for real this time.

I honestly didn't know if I could even afford a ticket.

I was broke.

I was a fifty-two-year-old show business flop, a parody of midlife floppitude.

Out of shape, childless, single, exiled from my own body, living on government loans, chugging gin and borrowed time. After a decent, decade-long run at Hollywood, nearly everybody I had once represented as a talent manager had fired me. I went from having three clients starring on Broadway, actors in films, actors on hugely successful long-running TV shows—a lively boutique management concern with business hopping on both coasts and on three continents—to not even being able to get a call returned from an unrepresented seventeen-year-old kid in his first Off-Off-Broadway musical.

I was expired. A carton of spoiled showbiz milk. I think I even smelled.

I had already lost my apartment before my business went up in flames during the pandemic, and I was clawing onto any purchase to stay relevant, stay in New York. Stay alive. My very identity, that show business creature that Renay had fashioned out of nothing except a 1975 Sue Mengers interview with Mike Wallace and a very, *very* close reading of *Hollywood Wives*—Ann the caretaker, Ann the manager, Ann the Hollywood kid—it was all falling apart.

And now she was, too.

"She ain't waking up," Asshole says in that Coastal High-Tider accent of his.

Asshole, who had fled Fayetteville for the Outer Banks back when me and Twin did in 1984, had never left. Like, never actually left. As far as I know, the first time he even got on a plane as a full-grown adult was two years ago, when I brought Asshole and Twin down to El Paso for our one and only, *hugely terrifically bad* Texas Thanksgiving. It ended with us at a steakhouse, everyone furious at each other, and Twin not speaking to me for the last two years because I yelled at him about his stupid jackpot phone game.

Not a word between us since.

Asshole has stayed put on the Outer Banks for thirty-seven years, thirty-two years with the same wife, living in the same house he built with his own hands, working for the same boss installing the same deluxe swimming ponds, one after another, at vacation wedding houses and bankers' mansions. All the while growing a long beard, becoming a grizzled biker, fishing and grilling and living the same, perfect, predictably breezy and blood-red sunset redneck life.

In that same thirty-seven years, I have been fired by a half dozen entertainment companies and innumerable ambitious actors. I have moved house twenty-three times—including three different times each to New York and Los Angeles—started and failed at three different careers, been dumped by every limited-engagement boyfriend who dared to win a prize from a scary Jewish clown, and had been politely but firmly rejected by six or seven prestigious writing programs.

As I stand outside that chic, bombed-out Brooklyn opera house, talking to Asshole and steaming in my too-warm suit on a too-warm night in too-expensive Brooklyn, it occurs to me once again that most of the people that I am related to have no idea what I do for money. Or for love. Or even where I live. They have all given up on me. Given up trying to keep up with me, understand me, *know me.*

I have outrun them all.

But you can't outrun yourself.

I comforted myself, sometimes, by thinking at least I didn't live in *El Paso*, or that I was doing better than Twin down in *Virginia*. Two rough divorces, double alimony—lost all his money, got a big ass, then had a couple of heart attack scares, a life he maybe feels he didn't get quite right, and now he's got some kind of gut cancer we definitely can't tell Renay about, since hearing the news would surely kill her. Twin is a middle-aged, tobacco-dipping redneck with gout, diabetes, a shit heart, and rotting intestines. His best friend, who is also *my* best friend, is dying.

Renay is not leaving behind a super happy bunch.

"I made my peace, Andrew. Gotta git back to Shirley. Been nearly a month," Asshole says.

Asshole's wife, Shirley, is from up near Dismal Swamp, and that Dismal Swamp dialect of hers has rubbed off on Asshole like skunk on a dumpster. We talk multiple times a day, since Rabbi, too, has stopped speaking to me. Asshole is my only source for reliable information in El Paso. Now he's bailing.

Asshole had been at Renay's side since she was discharged from her most recent rehab stay at Patriot, where she had endured the worst of the pandemic, and remarkably well, I might add. She never got Covid, because they kept that place on *lockdown*. We felt lucky that Renay had fallen the year before, smashed up her wrist, fucked up her hip, and ruptured…*something*. We never figured out what, exactly. It got her from the hospital to rehab right as they locked it all down. Renay's life didn't change all *that* much—she was used to being alone, used to texting, FaceTime-ing, calling people at all hours, playing computer cribbage with her scattered boyfriends across the country.

After almost a year at Patriot, she got out, but it was at the cost of her one remaining breast, as a spiteful, late-life recurrence of cancer reared its ugly head. She didn't mind. She bore it all—the diagnosis, the surgery, the recovery—with tremendous dignity. Just another surgery, another mastectomy for Renay. She wanted to get home, she didn't care what it cost: *Just do it quickly. Take the tit. Take me home!*

And that's where she was, at home with Rabbi and his second wife, Lourdes, the wife he clearly remembers this time. Home in El Paso alongside visiting Outer Banks dignitary Asshole, recovering and happy to be reunited with her Roku after such a long pandemic separation.

Renay was watching the Steelers go down to the Chargers, was agitated after Roethlisberger got the ball back in the fourth. Renay knew full well that the Steelers had bungled the AFC North. She went quiet and fell into her last, irreversible coma.

The ambulance was summoned, as it had been so many times in these roller-coaster years of Renay's decline, and Asshole, Rabbi, and Lourdes accompanied Renay to Providence, where she was sedated, intubated, and marooned peacefully on a fentanyl cushion in a hallway-facing ICU, on a back-ass section of the hospital, with a single window looking out onto an alley.

That's where she's been for the last three weeks.

"She ain't going home," Asshole spits. "She ain't walking ever again, tell you that. I doubt she'll be able to talk. Sepsis is real bad. Something on the liver. She ain't getting up. It's over."

Ridiculous. Nothing can kill Renay, not even Roethlisberger's final season.

"She made you power of attorney. You're on."

I'm on?

This was surprising.

This was the first time anybody—including her, of course—had so much as mentioned that I was power of attorney. I didn't have the first fucking clue what that meant, and, like all this worsted wool on a warm December night, it made me *quite angry*. But I had no children. No responsibilities and no business to tie me down. It makes sense to have me be the designated adult.

Yet still I shall be aggrieved.

"What does that mean!" I sputtered weakly into the fetid Brooklyn night air. "She never said word one to me about this!"

You are my retirement plan, Ann.

Okay. So maybe she *had* mentioned word one or two about this over the decades.

Fuck a plan. You're the plan, Ann.

"It means you need to come home," Asshole said.

That's a funny word to me, "home," after thirty-six moves over fifty-two years.

Doesn't quite stick the landing the way it used to, does it?

"Bonus is on his way," he said.

That one really shocked me. Bonus had only made that drive a couple times in Renay's fifteen years in El Paso.

This meant things were *bad*.

"You need to get a plane," Asshole said.

Then, after just the tiniest pause, Asshole adds with grim urgency, "And don't dilly-dally."

Don't dilly-dally.

I angrily yanked the gray-and-white checked suit jacket over my head and balled it up, disgusted, wondering what in the pretentious

Brooklyn hell I had been thinking wearing *worsted wool* to a Brooklyn Christmas drag concert, when it was over fifty degrees out and my Jewish mother was *dying*.

Don't dilly-dally, he says.

That's what he said when Cathy Sue was dying.

2.

What can I say? Cathy Sue is dead.

She's been dead for fifteen years.

After thirty-four years, one of us was bound to be.

My money was on Rabbi, if I'm being honest.

He smokes, he doesn't exercise, he only watches CNN, things fall on him *all the time*.

But no.

It was her. I wish it didn't have to be.

Wishes are ashes in history's inferno.

My sister Cathy Sue is dead.

Cathy Sue died on a sweltering hot, late July day in 2006. She was forty-nine years old.

Cathy Sue's liver finally quit on her in a Richmond hospital, where she had been taken after she'd become critical, no longer a story for the struggling Outer Banks doctors to tell, but for big-city doctors in big-city Richmond to try, and fail, to tell. After lingering on life support for one last desperate week, struggling in the shadow of a gigantic Confederate general's monument soaring sixty feet in the air atop an onyx replica of General Lee's Traveller, my sister rode off into the blazing hot, Richmond eternity.

It was awful.

We had fought.

We hadn't spoken much in the embittered previous year. My pirate confidante and I had allowed an estrangement, a shadow to grow wide and resentful atop an ugly falling-out over *nothing at all*, some meaningless argument over politics, not even worth mentioning except that because of it, *because of a single disagreement*, Cathy Sue and I had decided to be complete bitches to each other for a whole year. Her last year. A quick and sudden decline, with no warning or farewell at the end. No reconciliation or mutual forgiveness or cinematic deathbed scene. I missed my only sister's last year on this earth because I am a stupid, stubborn twat.

"Don't dilly-dally," Asshole had told me back then, urging me to quickly find a way back to Richmond, because Cathy Sue wasn't pulling through this time and they weren't sure how much longer she would hold on. The family was gathering. I was all the way out in LA, where I had been for the last five years, cosplaying as Sue Mengers, failing horribly, but living otherwise as far as I could from my history, my geography, my blood. I was doing what I could for Renay from afar, sending money from time to time, calling and listening to her, enduring my separateness, living only for me or, much better, for all the pretty actors who would eventually fire me.

I took four planes; I flew through the middle of that terrible night on a dark journey that took me through one dimly lit cavernous glass airport underground after another, one shuttle and people mover after the next, first to Phoenix, then Denver, then Dallas and Atlanta, before I was finally ushered into a panel van and driven directly to my sister's hospital, where I walked into her room with just seconds to spare.

Asshole was there with his Dismal Swamp wife Shirley. Twin. Renay. Rabbi. Cathy Sue's very tall, now very gay, son, Big Gay Sam. Her third husband. Maybe her fourth. Everybody wrapped in blue hospital gowns and blue hospital masks, a full room, overflowing with crying bent-over, blue paper ghosts. My family. A clock counting down. I may have missed her last year but I was here now for Cathy Sue's very last minute.

I took my sister's swollen, jaundiced hand. I had to steer my blood-shot eyes away from her discolored skin, looking instead at my mother's weeping, blue-shrouded face, which hovered over Cathy Sue's bed. It was the longest, saddest minute that I have ever known. It was a year. It was a lifetime.

Not sixty seconds after I walked into her room, Cathy Sue was dead.

"She's gone," the nurse said.

"She's gone," the nurse said again, confirming just how truly gone Cathy Sue was by fruitlessly pressing a cold stethoscope to my sister's unmoving chest, nodding once quietly to herself as if she were learning her lines, then coughing awkwardly and looking somberly all around the room, meeting each masked gaze and shaking her head, as the long, red siren of a stilled heart monitor screamed out into the empty air.

"She's gone," she said again.

When the wails and open-mouthed cries of all her brothers and her mother and son and several husbands subsided, we couldn't get out of Cathy Sue's Richmond hospital room fast enough, and directly over to the Golden Corral. We were starving, and our Cathy Sue was *not* in there anymore. She was waiting for us by the salad bar. Cathy Sue was in a far more real, far more accessible place for the likes of this crew.

She was in the past.

"Hey, where's Bonus?" I whispered to my mother as we filed out, one scratchy blue paper ghost after another, away from Cathy Sue's ICU, and toward the steak-and-gin wake. It had been decided that Golden Corral was what Cathy Sue would have wanted.

"Where's Bonus, Mom?" I asked her again.

"Oh, shit, somebody needs to call him," she says, aggravated, digging deep into her giant brown purse for a phone.

"Oh," I said, stunned.

We forgot to call my oldest brother and tell him his sister died.

"Cathy loved a Golden Corral," Renay says, eyes wide, shuffling forward, her hands in her big brown leather bag.

3.

It was an astonishing bit of good luck that the last of Cathy Sue's husbands—her third, or maybe it was her fourth; we all lost track—was not only a *really* nice guy and a Methodist, but Paul was a nice Methodist preacher's kid.

His parents, the Reverend and the Mrs. Reverend of Richmond, opened their home, their church, their family crypt, and their funeral potatoes to this broken, swamped collective of assorted Jewish nuts who could barely tie their own shoelaces, or look each other in the eye, let alone muster the solemnity required to bury a beloved sister.

Needless to say, we did not acquit ourselves with Christian valor in those terrible, dark days in Richmond. We were ugly to each other and to ourselves and to God. We were all exhausted and had no practice in the arts of dying. Renay was a trembling, hypoglycemic wreck, the look of the battlefield etched in her eye. We were shocked and angry. Angry at Cathy Sue for dying. At each other for letting this happen. At the Methodist Lord, the Vengeful Jewish God, the menopausal Mother of Nature, anybody. We were angry at the sun. We were all so *angry*.

She was only forty-nine years old.

It was so hot on the day that we buried Cathy Sue, the last Monday of July 2006, that everybody—myself included—unironically resorted to beachwear. It was a jorts, T-shirts, shorts, tank tops, and ball caps affair. It was a struggle just to breathe. I am not proud of wearing jorts to my sister's funeral, but it was a sticky ninety-eight degrees with 85 percent humidity. So fuck it. Jorts-and-tank-top sendoff for her.

Bonus wore a suit.

He had been reached finally, but only too late.

Now he was here in a silver-gray jacket.

He had dressed and rushed out from his home in rural Texas to make his own series of calamity connections to Richmond, but Bonus sadly found out that his only sister had died while he was still deep beneath the bowels of the Atlanta airport. Who could blame Bonus for being frightened of what lay ahead? Not only was his sister, who was just *one year* older than him, suddenly and tragically dead, but he hadn't even been in the same room with any of us in nearly a decade.

The last time we all laid eyes on each other, about ten years earlier in Miami, was for the ninetieth birthday celebration of our beloved grandfather Joseph Katz. We were summoned to Florida and we all came from the corners we had scattered to, me, Twin, Asshole, Rabbi, Cathy Sue, Renay, and, to the surprise of all, Bonus. After our respective escapes from Fayetteville, and Bonus from his institutions, none of us were in regular touch with each other, just with our sister. Cathy Sue acted as a kind of authoritarian switchboard, passing along orders like a camp commandant, requests for money for our mother or a brother, resentments, updates, threats, illnesses, recoveries, births. Those calls from Cathy Sue were long, extravagant affairs, as she idly ticked through her enemies' list: *who pissed her off today; which brother or frenemy was on the outs; who shall remain nameless or unforgiven; did Brenda really say that shit? give Rabbi a call, somebody got stabbed again at Players; no, don't send Renay money for tires, she's lying, she doesn't need new tires.*

Cathy Sue kept this whole family connected. Except Bonus. She barely tried with Bonus. There was something between them, a river of bad blood that flowed all the way back to childhood, to Miami in 1958. Whatever it was, it never got sorted. So it was a great surprise when Bonus joined the Correns for Papa Joe Katz's big ninetieth birthday bash in Florida in 1997.

He ate Wolfie's bagels with us, posed in the same cowboy hats that Rabbi had brought up from El Paso, laughed at my jokes, hugged his uncomfortable, wary mother, avoided his glaring sister. Bonus seemed *joyful*; he *glowed*. He celebrated Joe Katz with us, toasting the war hero, showering him with love, and hooting at his many accomplishments.

Joe Katz's wife and greatest love, our one and only Minna Klatskin Cohen Katz, had gone to Jewish heaven—a cemetery in Coral Gables— just two years previous, in 1995. Joe Katz still grieved her deeply—we all did—but a loss to Alzheimer's dementia, as anybody who has ever borne such an agonizing burden knows, is a long, long series of losses. Joe Katz was now a single, horny old rascal with still-decent vision behind those chunky, socialist bifocals, one good dancing knee, and the sexiest thing an old man in Florida can have: a long, fat Buick with a legal driver's license. Widower-on-wheels Joe Katz was *enormously* popular with the ladies of South Florida, and Joe Katz was gonna make what time he had left on this earth *count*.

The only other time we had all seen Bonus before Joe Katz's fabulous ninetieth had been thirteen years before, at our cold and disastrous Thanksgiving weekend in Fayetteville, when his arrival had been another kind of surprise, with the same long silences that trailed him room to room. Over the past twenty-two years, my oldest brother and I had seen each other only twice, and only then with three uneasy brothers and a couple of suspicious Jewish women standing between us.

Now Cathy Sue was dead. Bonus made it to Richmond the day before her funeral in 2006, and, like us, was graciously received into the Lladró-figurine-filled sitting room inside the lovely home of Reverend and Mrs. Reverend. This was the first house of anybody I was even vaguely related to that was not a brick ranch, and certainly the first that came with a sitting room *filled* with Lladró clowns and Lladró ballerinas, Lladró geishas with baskets of Lladró puppies, so I of course thought the Reverend and Mrs. Reverend must be quite wealthy. Their house was two stories high, brick and stately, perhaps not a colonial, but then again: *perhaps it was*. It was lovely, a perfect place to host a dead sister's sudden and hot summertime wake, ceramic clowns notwithstanding.

Renay kept a respectful distance from Bonus most of that day, far too deep in her own trenches of pain to reach across their decades of estrangement and touch her now oldest living child's hurt heart. She had only wanted to live in the past that day. She spoke only of past hurts. Past meals. Stunts and capers, decades ago, when Cathy Sue had ruled and laughed and walked away unscathed, alongside her. Her partner in crime. The past was where Cathy Sue lived now, and so Renay would, too.

Bonus wept loudly and effusively as Cathy Sue was eulogized in that dark Richmond crypt. My Navy brother looked lost, but a sailor in distress always knows how to navigate through a summer storm. Bonus carried his sister's coffin with confidence and dignity.

He may have arrived too late to see her out, but still he came, and he carried, and he buried.

Then he left without another word.

That would be the last time I would see or hear from my brother Bonus for the next fifteen years. When we met again, our mother's dying body would lay between us.

4.

In the fall of 1988, Renay Corren left Fayetteville for the very last time. She had spent two decades in this quirky, pollen-choked Piedmont hideaway where she most felt at home. One by one, each of her children had fled to set up their own homes on distant shores, exotic locales, or, barring imagination or money, *Virginia Beach*. We left behind our fantastical, ferociously funny, flatulent mother, this woman that Renay was so proud to have located, saved, and nurtured.

Twin and I were the last to depart, he, in a shocking twist for an Army family, for the Marines down in Camp Lejeune, and I for another type of barely closeted, fetishized militancy, an acting academy where I had been mercifully scholarshipped. We left for good in the summer of 1987, without a ride from our mother, a check, or a stick of furniture. Renay wasn't much of a hugger, either, not with us at any rate. The year before I graduated, she did manage one grand and loving gesture for me—and for herself of course—when she pawned Shithead's wedding ring at last and split the cash from that Miami diamond between herself and my brand-used, rusted-out orange VW Rabbit. I was the first Corren child to be bought a car.

And the very last, too.

Still, we got good wishes from Renay as Twin and I headed out to make our way in the world, and a stern warning from the floating lady on the taped-up waterbed that she wouldn't be there for much longer, "So don't come looking for me if things go wrong."

No deposits. No returns.

She had done hers.

Renay Corren had kept us alive and out of jail. Long enough, at least, to get the hell out of Fayetteville and find out what was waiting for us on the other side of the 401 bypass.

Turns out it's just a lot of hogs, tobacco, and soybean fields.

Renay lasted one more year in Fayetteville, living with Butt Check on Oglethorpe, banging around in all those empty rooms without us. No more wrestlers came around, but Renay made do with her all-night card tournaments, hanging out with Doreen and Bernie, all her friends at the B&B, and following Porky and Howard all over the state and Southeast as they trailed after the Wolfpack and Coach V in search of one more try at number 14. She still made the occasional foray out into Fayetteville's dark alleys, standing in the back of D.J. Ledford's still very popular delivery van, but her financial burdens had lessened considerably with all those sons out the door.

She was freer than she had ever been in her entire fifty-one years.

No husband. No kids. No house. As she had once fruitlessly coached Montana Gray in *Hollywood Wives,* "You can have your freedom, or you can have a husband." Renay strictly came down on the side of freedom. I heard she had a regular side piece way out in Spring Lake during this time, a guy named Bill, but I never met him. There was another fella, too, a Jamaican dude down in Florida named Gary that Renay supposedly hooked up with whenever she was summoned down to Miami to assist one of our extended Florida tribe into the grave.

She was a fifty-one-year-old woman with bad feet, diabetes, a hilariously bad grip on money, no house, no credit, and no prospects. She loved fishing, dick, Pepsi, offal, and cards. She needed *people,* and she needed them *all the time.*

Renay headed out to the Outer Banks.

She moved in with Cathy Sue and Cathy Sue's second husband, as well as Cathy Sue's oldest son, Little Big Ben, who was by now over seven foot tall, and her new baby son, the delightfully redheaded Big Gay Sam. Renay glued herself to her new couch and her new redheaded gay baby grandson like a dirtbag bubbe to a thirty-two-ounce Manischewitz-and-Pepsi, and she did eventually consent to take a paying job, leaning behind the desk at the brand-new beach bowling center in Nags Head. But the Outer Banks can be quite grim in the winter, you might have heard, and she was without her usual crew, so it was quite the after-hours comedown for our revered Lady of the Lanes, who was used to staying up all night dealing cards and stealing hearts.

Maybe the old bowling alley magic was gone, or maybe Renay's spirit just wasn't in it. She didn't quite take over that beach bowling alley like she used to, the same way superagent Sue Mengers didn't quite turn the William Morris Agency around when they seduced her back to run the motion picture talent department in 1988. Renay was tired. Everybody she was related to in Florida was like the once-mighty William Morris Agency itself: ancient, Jewish, near death. During those years, Renay gently helped the elder Jews of our tribe die with dignity, and then just as gently helped auction off any of their good furniture so she could drain a minor executress fee before that gravestone was unveiled. After every single Hakamat HaMatzeveh, you could find Renay dancing down that fancy meat aisle of her cherished North Miami Publix, inheritance cash burning a hole in her fuck-it pants. That woman *loved* a Publix.

Renay spent every cent she inherited during this death's door decade on cruises, King Crab buffets, Seminole casinos, and regular trips to Vegas with Cathy Sue, Paul, and Big Gay Sam to catch up with Bernie Alphabet, to raise hell on and off the Strip, to play bingo all night long, and feed those one-armed bandits all day. She was *lightning* at the blackjack tables, too. She made a bundle during this decade. Then she gave it all back.

From 1988 until 1999, when sixty-two-year-old Renay Corren officially retired in order to be closer to her paltry Social Security check, she would couch surf between the home of her dyspeptic, depressed, shingles-plagued mother Marian the Hungarian, now a nonagenarian, dozing on a yellow fold-out couch in North Miami, or head back up to North Carolina, where she crashed with Cathy Sue, on a fold-out in their living room, holding court on the cordless phone, wielding the TV remote like a scepter, instructing Big Gay Sam on the finer arts of hard-R pay cable, the best early-bird buffets in Nags Head, and how to approach the vital task of properly shellacking Gran Renay's toes.

Though she was only fifty-one when she departed Fayetteville and would live another thirty-three years, Renay Corren would never again live in, own, rent, or oversee any home in her own name, anywhere, in any state. She was done with all of that. Her plan was us.

Fuck a plan, Ann. You're the plan.

After the last of the Miami elders passed, Renay lived on the Outer Banks full-time with Cathy Sue; her last husband, the Good Methodist Paul; and Big Gay Sam. Renay lived contentedly and itinerantly like this for eighteen years. It was her happily ever after.

Happily, that is, until Cathy Sue fucked it all up by dying on the hottest day of 2006.

After we buried Cathy Sue in July 2006, Renay thought hard and long about what her next move would be, and how best to stretch out all those inheritance checks she had tucked away in her mattress for just this eventuality.

Ha! I'm just kidding.

She was broke.

She gave it back to her casino overlords, donated it to Danish cruise operators, to Seminole Indians, handing it over, dollar by dollar, over two decades of nonstop, continuous fun. She had a *very fun* time not being a mother, a homeowner, an employee, or a wife. She didn't get much in return for all this fun, some all-you-can-eat buffet coupons, the vivid memory of being urinated on by one of those gay German tigers in Vegas, several interior cabins, no view. But it was enough for Renay.

When Cathy Sue died in 2006, Renay had no real choice. She could come to LA and live with me, I guess, on the couch in my peeling, second-story dingbat on a poorly lit side street of Mid-City whose closest contact to actual Hollywood glamour was that Chunk from *The Goonies* had once lived across the street from me. Or she could relocate to El Paso, Texas, to live with Rabbi and his second wife, Lourdes, and, yes, it must be said, their vibrantly gay, Mexican Jewish son, Adam. Rabbi was by then a disreputable billiards hall operator who'd built a weekend club that featured the most stabbings per square foot of any pool hall in Northeast El Paso.

Because my mother was sensible and loved nothing better than a split-level brick ranch converted garage bedroom that came with a Roku and another young, gay grandson she could mold, she wisely chose Northeast El Paso. She lived out her last fourteen years of life in a place I always jokingly referred to as "Plus-Sized Fayetteville," which it was, right down to the bikers, the combat boots, the bloody mops, the no Jewish delis, and the bar stabbings-du-jour.

In 2007, Renay moved for good to Plus-Sized Fayetteville, Texas, where, most strangely and most hilariously, she would live in the same house—Rabbi and Lourdes's house—for the last and longest, most uninterrupted period of her entire, strange, miraculous, itinerant, and slow-moving death and life.

Don't dilly-dally, Asshole said.

And so I wouldn't.

I didn't.

5.

El Paso, Texas,
Wednesday, December 8, 2021

The stillness of a West Texas ICU.

It is no stillness at all. All around me is war. Warring brothers on my texts and in my ear. Warring lights. Warring nurses. Clashing color concepts. *Teal and tan.*

"I hate hospitals," I mutter to Asshole on the phone, moving quickly, hunched and masked, haunted by pandemic paranoia and acres of fluorescent light panels bathing wall after wall in its autopsy glare.

This light makes me look old and tired is what I thought.

I ascend slowly in the interminable cargo elevator to the fourth floor, wedged into the back of the packed car, whispering into my phone, pressed against the back wall as strapped stretchers of Covid war dead rolled on or off, on their way in or on their way out, each followed by teams of weary, masked nurses holding bunched tubes of fluids.

"I cannot believe you left me here alone with Rabbi," I steam.

"Eh, he's harmless once you get to know him," Asshole says.

"I despise hospitals," I whisper.

"We all hate hospitals, Andrew," he says grimly. And it's true.

"You there yet?" Twin texts.

"Yes," I type. "In an elevator brimming with Covid," in response to which he sends a vomit emoji. "Hope things are great with you and sorry again about the cancer," I reply.

Families are made of such stuff.

We all hate hospitals for different reasons. I hate them for the lighting and the decor. Asshole hates them because Asshole never gets sick; he has a mythic constitution. It must have been hell for him to all but live in this madhouse of disease and despair for nearly an entire pandemic wave, hardly leaving our mother's side as she succumbed to her overlapping syndromes of collapse, having to bear up against Rabbi's repeated waves of assault on logic, reason, and sanity. Asshole has every right to flee El Paso and get back home to Miss Dismal Swamp 1982. He knows that I'm here. He knows that means he's here, too.

Especially since I am the one who has the power to turn things off.

In my official capacity as Renay's death conductor, I am still getting acquainted with what "medical power of attorney" means and how to advocate for my mother's health. I am frankly just now understanding the basic situation, the totality of her collapse, all the syndromes, machines, doctors, medicines. It is like drinking from an open fire hydrant spewing medical charts.

I steady myself before one of the sprawling, black-and-white, Ansel Adams–ish prints that gallop along each of the fourth-floor hallways, grizzled cowboys and rearing steeds in the setting sun, all those noble Texas cactuses stretching out their arms, centering themselves around the ICU campfire, signifying that all is *not* well on *this* Western front.

"She won't know you're there. She didn't with me," he warns. "You might want to believe that she hears you or sees you, like Rabbi does. But she can't. She's too far under. She hasn't made a sound. She's gone." Asshole spits that out in that grim, flat High-Tider way of his. I can hear him nudging his thick glasses back up the bridge of his nose, then I'm there, and there's nothing to do but shove open the noiseless pneumatic doors of Renay's last home.

I see her. Felled. Floating. Falling.

I really don't want to. My eyes don't want this poetry.

It can't be this.

Yes it can, I hear her say. *Oh, but it can.* She laughs.

I stand before Renay at last, on the fourth floor of the unlovely side of Providence, bare brown, scrub-dotted Franklin Mountains looming up behind us, El Paso's Cinnabon-flavored and stucco-covered airport to the east. I can hear a family weeping softly in some nearby ICU corner, coughing and grieving behind glass like a diorama of pain. Televisions hum softly everywhere, room to room, soaps and TV judges and jingles playing in symphony with beeps, alarms, quiet summons, all the silent wars that all these families, and ours, arrived with.

"She still sleepin?" Twin demands, and I give the thumbs-up emoji, an absolute weak-ass reply.

"You up?" I ask her, squeezing a hand.

I stare down on Renay's sleeping, sedated face where two wide, white plastic bandages on either of her cheeks hold in the ventilator tube, giving her a kind of clownish, devilishly familiar, wicked Renay Corren smile.

Oh, I'm up. Up to something, alright. She smirks.

The tube passes by her horribly chapped lips, disappearing into the dark interiors of her gaping throat, wending and snaking its way into her lungs, granting her air, and life. A blond nurse in a black smock, with a full-blue tattoo sleeve crawling up her left arm, passes behind, on her rounds.

When did they start wearing black? I wonder.

Maybe it's navy, Renay says. *Ever think of that, smart guy?*

You're the smart one, Renay. I'm the catty one.

Meow, meow, she says, laughing.

The nurse nods. Another is right behind. I lean over my mother and say, "We're gonna get you out of here, Renay," stroking her newly white, luxuriously snowy deathbed hair.

You bet your bippy you are, she says.

Her room is wrought entirely out of bubbling plastic tubes, piles of discarded latex gloves, four tall sentries at the head of the bed, giving Renay her medicine, her liquids, her breath. Loyal. Dependable. A bladder bag with a purple nipple drops lacteal white globules one by one like a leaky bag of milk, rolling fat cream drops down into the hoses that run into her bruised and bandaged arms, both limply at her side.

Another pump squirts Levophed.

Another sodium chloride.

Another norepinephrine.

Another fentanyl.

It just goes on and on, bags squirting into bags, then more bags rustle and wheeze above her head, some flat and crushed, half-empty balloons bouncing around like cannonball jellyfish on a stormy Kitty Hawk afternoon.

Pieces of neon tape with big black letters, A or D or C, are slapped on each of the IV poles as they trace their way back into my mother's arms, each parsimoniously dispensing small squirts of hydration and titration, vasoconstriction and nonadrenogenic hemodynamic support.

She's deep under.

"We're gonna get you out of here," I say again into my mother's ear, because it's the only thing I can think of to say.

Ann! Come closer, I hear her urge. *I need to tell you something important.*

She can't fool me. I know this old fart trick.

Come closer! she roughly barks, and I lean in and stroke her brow, her snowy white hair, marvel at all the red that has fled Renay's crown. I lean in further to hear what she will say.

You see? Renay whispers. *This is how you die!*

I can hear my mother cackling as she says it, too. She knows, and I know that she knows that *I know* who said those words. Coco Chanel's last words. That Nazi.

And now she's got that devious, misbehaving schoolgirl look she's always got in the corner of her eye. *She died at the Ritz. Buried in Switzerland*, my mother says, impressed.

She was horrible, Mom, and an antisemite of the first order. She literally fucked Nazi generals. Do not quote Coco Chanel on your deathbed, Jewish woman!

You always have the best gossip, Ann. My mother sighs happily. *Bury me in Switzerland?*

This is what she made me for. To laugh at death alongside her.

She will depart at the stroke of my signature, a thing relegated to the past, living where her long-dead daughter still laughs and lives, still stirs at her metallic pots of Calico fudge, and bosses a bunch of husbands around.

Renay will *gladly* become a memory by the curl of my sloppy, cursive crest of an *A*, and the flick of an eye of the trough, the rising face and the falling crash of the wave of my *Y*, if it means she gets to live with Cathy Sue again.

TDY.

It means goodbye, she says, that vestigial Army wife part of her laughing softly.

I am here to sign my name.

But first you have to get the pen out of Rabbi's hand, she mutters darkly.

The impending death of his one and only friend, his roommate of fifteen years, has launched my brother Rabbi into the exosphere of crazy. Rabbi is simply not a rational actor these days. He has become a believer in miracles, a denier of objective truth, a hater of medical reality. He doesn't want his mommy to die. My balding, sixty-one-year-old brother is hunched on the opposite side of Renay's bed, grasping her hand, staring down intently, his wide, guileless eyes blinking constantly behind round Rite Aid spectacles, willing Renay's still, upturned face to respond to him.

Rabbi has an idea. Rabbi knows what can cure Renay.

"Mother, your favorite son is here," Rabbi implores without looking at me, holding her still elegantly manicured fingers, squeezing one peach nail softly, urging her to squeeze his nicotine-stained fingers back. "Mother? Little Andy is here," Rabbi says in that twangy, doofus Texas Jew way of his.

"Hola, Mamacita," Rabbi says. "Andy came to see you all the way from Los Angeles, Mamacita," he continues in his tinny, semi-Spanglish argot. "We are going to get you up for him, and then home for the Steelers tomorrow, Mother," he continues. "Gonna get you up, back home, and I promise you the Steelers gonna *win*, then they will get a wildcard, and go to the Super Bowl, but *only* if you watch, Mother. So you gotta get up. You gotta help them beat the Vikings. And then the Titans, the Chiefs, the Browns, and the Ravens, okay? Mother? Hola!"

I hold my tongue and inhale deeply, reminding myself that everybody grieves in their own way. Rabbi's way of grieving is by alienating all of his brothers, then retreating into the belief that Renay will rise up, cast off her many miles of tubes, head home, and sit in her favorite swivel chair to watch the Steelers, and that the Steelers will defeat the Vikings, even though everybody knows Kirk Cousins *is throwing literal fire.*

In Roethlisberger we trust.

I shake my head sadly. I am used to these non sequitur, semi-incoherent displays by now, but both Asshhole and I have long been over our older brother's antics. It just isn't helping things in these trying hours. We need one of those sturdy Maglite flashlights that cops use to cut through the fog, not Rabbi's funhouse lighthouse carnival of madness adding more confusion to a dying mother's last days.

"All the way from California, Mamacita. Isn't that nice?" Rabbi says.

I roll my eyes to the heavens. I ask for patience and surrender, and a bigger talent for forgiveness than I currently possess.

I haven't lived in Los Angeles for more than three and a half years.

That Rabbi knows this, that he has seen me deplane right here in El Paso more than half a dozen times in the last three years directly from a New York City airport, does not matter. His mind is a sieve. Burned.

Beaten. Drowned twice over. Rabbi doesn't hold on to *facts*. He sorts the present condition for how it makes him *feel*, how it *benefits* him, or raises his prospects for *survival*.

In his mind, I will always live in Los Angeles. That is what works best for him.

I glance up at Judge Jerry yelling on the TV. Renay's afternoon lounge music. Didn't matter where she was, if you reached her between three and five o'clock on any weekday afternoon, somebody was getting yelled at by Judge Jerry. Today, Tenaja is bickering with her mother Kim about a piece-of-shit car Kim's boyfriend totaled on the Brooklyn-Queens Expressway. I think it's very brave of Tenaja to sue her mother Kim, and Kim's boyfriend, on national TV, a fairly dramatic escalation for any family, and one, somehow, my own has never descended to.

Not yet, I hear my mother roar. *There's still time!*

I dip the thick yellow and blue sponge wand into a capful of room-temperature Pepsi, and dab it onto Renay's parched lips, then run it over her dry, sandpapery tongue like a mop.

Did your mother have any children that lived? she asks, aggravated.

Not gonna lie, Renay, I say. *We're all out of macadamia*, I offer apologetically.

Damn, she mutters.

There is nary a reminder of the lascivious, loud, grand, greedy, gleeful life that she had led without pause for more than eighty-four years. Not a shred of the old Renay remained before me, not even a single, dyed strand of her bright red hair to cling to.

She is very nearly in the past.

Except those hands.

Her nails. Renay's swans. They look *amazing*. Her nails have simply glided on, cool as can be, over the hellfire below. *Her nails are immaculate*.

I knew all this would be hard.

I knew it would make me feel sadder and uglier and older than I had ever felt before.

I knew all of this.

But the drive from the airport, the awful desert art crawling along the walls, the terrible, pitiless lighting in every room, the broken brothers, the older mother, it just smacks me, all at once. Rabbi hasn't brought over a picture or a candle, not a nice blanket or one of her stuffed pigs, not so much as a cozy lamp or a familiar sound, unless you count Judge Jerry railing on Tenaja.

Which I do, I absolutely do! Renay nods emphatically, rooting for Tenaja.

"Are we living, or what?" Rabbi asks Renay.

"This ain't living," I say. "Wake her up and ask her if this is living. If this is the life she's been dreaming about."

Hey, I'm breathing over here, dipshit. Judge Jerry is on, and I've got Pepsi on my lips. I'm good, she says defiantly.

You won't be good for long, I say. *Not without a full team of doctors and some skilled nurses to clean your pipes, turn you over every few hours like a prime rib at Lawry's. You can't even afford that Pepsi, woman. Overtime is over.*

Do you remember the Miracle That Died? Chargers-Dolphins Orange Bowl? she asks.

Remember it? Renay has talked about that game her entire life. We watched it on NBC the day after New Year's in 1982. We woke up cold as shit and started burning bowling pins for heat like mad, feeding them into that greedy, frozen fireplace. That game was our heat. It kept us warm.

Best overtime in history, she says. *Winslow had a pinched nerve. He was dehydrated, had cramps, had fucking stitches on his lower lip!*

That man was destroyed. They had to carry him off the field at the end, remember?

How could I forget, Renay?

They say he lost fifteen pounds during that one game.

Bullshit. No way that's true! I said.

But it sounds true! she says.

I regard her cheeks, still rosy and plump, secretly smiling up at me as she says, *Gonna need a little help getting off this field, Ann.*

It has taken two long, dark pandemic years, all of my money, Rabbi's patience, Asshole's money, Twin's health, all of the life force we had remaining, all cobbled together ineptly between us from afar, just to get her here. We've kept her at home in El Paso with Rabbi and Lourdes, who both worked tirelessly to keep her comfortable as she descended further into immobility and decay. We scraped enough together to get meals delivered, pay all her bills, keep her room cleaned, hire Lydia the Shower Lady to keep her clean twice a week, get her a bunch of visiting nurses, all of whom, weirdly, were also named Lydia. Lots of Lydias in El Paso. It has been a nightmare of comas, blood, and near-death midnight ambulance rides for Rabbi, Lourdes, Adam, and the Lydias, a sad and frustrating and scary long-distance spectacle for the rest of us. Renay and her swans, meanwhile, simply sailed blithely above it all, getting manicures at Elva's garage when she was able to walk, popping Oxys and pot gummies back at home when she couldn't, plopping deeply into her favorite chair, blasting *Dr. Pimple Popper* and ordering Chinese, contributing only her laughter and a middle finger, and her continuing, inevitable decline.

Rabbi blames me.

He blames me for Mother's decline, he blames me for the stress fractures in his marriage that keeping Renay at home has caused. He blames me for not being closer to El Paso, for living in Los Angeles, *which I haven't even lived in for three years*. He blames me for not taking her, even though he spoke up first to take her when we all gathered in the Reverend and Mrs. Reverend's kitchen, the day Cathy Sue was buried, to conclave on what to do next with Renay. He blames me for showing up to make sure she's dying with dignity, and not betting on her magically rising and walking out, carrying Roethlisberger and the Steelers lineup off the bench and into Minnefuckingsota.

He blames me for all of it.

Rabbi and I haven't spoken for three months. Our last conversation, he told me to go die.

We have been talking to each other *solely* through Asshole and Twin, which is complicated, since Asshole is a stoic wall constructed entirely out of human assholes, and Twin hates me, too, ever since the Worst El Paso Thanksgiving in History two years ago.

I swore to myself I would not show up in El Paso and struggle with Rabbi. I'd be civil and generous and patient with him, with all my brothers. We'd do everything *together*. We'd decide things *together*. I told myself it didn't matter anymore what had happened two Thanksgivings or twenty Thanksgivings ago. It didn't matter what Rabbi had said, or what he believed. None of it mattered anymore. Renay was dying. It was time to be purposeful, dignified, and orderly. This is what she deserves. This is what she wants.

This is what I made you for! I hear her maniacally giggle through the fentanyl- and Joy-foam-filled bathtub of her imagination.

With a terrific inhalation of breath, I stand over my mother's quiet, wrecked body, and I vibrate with the certainty that she has chosen correctly, that there is at last a grownup in the room with her who knows exactly what to do. Who has *anticipated*. It is *I* who will be the one who calms the troubled waters ahead, who rides the wave with her to the very end.

And so it is with that selfsame dignity that I violently scream "Fuck you, assclown!" to my brother Rabbi, then I lean over Renay's bed, smooth her snowy hair one more time, kiss her forehead, and whisper *We're gonna get you out of here* yet again.

I march virtuously past Rabbi, screaming at the bare walls and the pitiless fluorescent panels and the alley adjacent window to Providence. "You couldn't have at least brought her a blanket from home?" I screech in my usual, dignified hospital manner. "A picture?" I yelp. "Something that smells nice? Where is her fucking Sassique Body Powder? *She needs her Tea Rose.* Do I have to do *everything?*" I roar to the shocked, pallid face of my brother, hitting that highest sissy octave he and my other brothers recognize and respect so well. I shout in my upper falsetto registers to be sure that every nurse and every doctor in all of El Paso know that I am here, that *I* am in charge, and then, before dramatically stomping out of my mother's badly lit, poorly decorated death chamber, I attempt to slam the room doors upon leaving, as one with a useless BFA does when making a dramatic stage exit, but all of the doors in this ICU are pneumatic, so they don't slam, they just close real, real slow. *Real slow.*

Tremendous work, Ann, acting school was a solid investment, Renay snickers.

From the other side of my mother's ICU door, I watch Rabbi watch me through the glass window as the door closes slowly in our exhausted faces, and when it does, I turn and properly storm off, stage left.

I will buy her the most beautiful Goddamned death I can afford on my Visa balance. Some pillows, perhaps. Some light. They say your hearing is the last sense to go, so a speaker, for sure. Some music for Renay. A few candles. A nice deathbed lamp.

She'd like that.

We'll go to a Target, she and I. We *love* a Target.

You can buy anything at a Target, I hear her sigh from above. *Anything!*

6.

El Paso, Texas
Thursday, December 9, 2021

I rose before dawn, the room spinning, naked and hungover in a king-sized bed on the fourteenth floor of my semi-chic downtown El Paso hotel.

I have been going to El Paso since Rabbi first posted up here after mustering out of the Army way back in the nineties, more frequently since Renay moved here. I have watched this dusty brown cowtown grow up and out, enlarging and *dramatically* improving its personality and its bridges over the ensuing decades. I have spent more time in El Paso than *any* of Rabbi's other brothers, and I have grown quite fond of it, too.

Still nothing, and I mean *nothing*, surprises me more than how unbelievably dicked down I get in this cowtown, no matter how late I arrive, where I am staying, or who happens to be dying. It doesn't matter how shitty I feel about my looks, my body, my car, or my bank account—all the things that keep me congenitally *un*-laid in other, bigger, liberal towns. I am a sex magnet in these regional hubs. I can't explain it. Lubbock. Albany. Richmond. This border town. I am an 8.

I am an Albany 8.

Unfortunately, back in New York City where I live, or that freeway that calls itself a town, LA, I am barely a 3. If I'm lucky, then *maybe* if you use a strong filter, I can pass as a solid 4. Those places can be devastating to the practicing, middle-aged, urban homosexual. *Devastating.* Not for the faint of heart.

So let's hear it for the Albany 8 who woke up in El Paso with a naked, sleeve-tatted soldier lightly snoring next to him in a hotel bed. *Mateo? Cameron?* I'm just gonna call him Mateo and hope for the best. Mateo told me last night over bespoke tacos that he's deploying to the Middle East soon as a highly paid PMC, where he will work for the next two years interdicting Captagon all up and down a famed, druggy corridor of Dubai or Abu Dhabi. It might've been Qatar. I don't know. I was sad, drunk, and horny. Our evening was a potent and sudden Southwestern mix of ass, grief, desperation, and aguachile.

Doesn't get much more Renay Corren than *that*.

I was awake, but in no hurry to return to Renay's bedside. The lifelessness that I knew awaited me there, the lack of recognition, the bare decor—it all flattened me back into my big, messy bed. It would be like pulling off the Blue Ridge Parkway and walking into an abandoned coal mine. Leaving a planetarium to stare up at a cloudy, starless night.

So I suggested to Mateo that we instead repair to the shower, which he agreed to sleepily and amenably, and we proceeded to have some fairly basic but cinematic and soapy El Paso morning shower sex. Shower sex with a soldier. *Pure rejuvenation.*

That is some El Paso 8 shit, right there.

We ate breakfast together downstairs, or Mateo did, and I watched him eat farewell chilaquiles while I drank a gallon of good Texas coffee and picked at the monstrous, pistachio-crusted French toast that, if finished, would ensure my permanent banishment to the El Paso 4 Hall of Fame. Halfway between eight o'clock and nine, outside in the still-deserted downtown El Paso streets, I discreetly bro-hugged my departing lover, pecked his stubbly cheek, and sincerely wished him well.

TDY, soldier.

TDY always means goodbye.

I slowly made my way over the hill and up those looming Mordorbrown Franklin mountains to Providence, sitting absurdly low in the dusty driver's seat of my brother Rabbi's loaner, his ridiculous side piece of a car, a menacing orange Camaro. "Inferno Orange," the dealer called it. My Inferno Orange 2013 LS1 Chevy Camaro, an absurdity of Texas masculinity, makes loud explosions of speed on even a modest turn. *I worship every single detail of this car.* I am, deep down, just like my brother, a simple son of Fayetteville, predictably basic about hard bodies and muscle cars.

I *loved* how Rabbi's Camaro made me *feel*.

Rabbi has had one or another model of Camaro since the early 1980s, some he bought, some he built himself. He was a Camaro man, through and through, and it's one of my favorite parts of his many-splendored, schizophrenic personality. You can *really* tear ass down those Texas freeways in a Chevy Camaro, too. You can *fly*. This was the car that Rabbi drove when he wasn't on the road making deliveries in his monstrously oversized King Ranch pickup. Rabbi had been a truck driver since 2016, when the US Army Command at Fort Bliss and the violent gangs of Northeast El Paso both conspired in a series of high-profile stabbings, murders, and shut-downs to at last close the door of Rabbi's infamous billiards hall for the very final time. Rabbi was much, much happier as a truck driver, even though it's hard work, his boss hates Democrats, and the days are long. But it was simpler and less dangerous than running a stabby pool hall, and Rabbi liked the long drives, as he basically had the emotional intelligence of a recently resuscitated five-year-old on a go-kart track. Truck driver pay was decent, too, and his long-suffering wife, Lourdes, didn't have to see or talk to him for weeks at a time. Everybody wins.

My Inferno Orange chariot was packed with piles of bags from my Target run, the one down on Gateway I hit last night before sex and tacos. I had nearly five hundred dollars' worth of deathbed decor ready to unload. I was ready to dress my mother's room, to make it look and smell and sound *full of life*.

An antechamber fit for a queen.

Then I was going to sit with her end-of-life care doctors and nurses, listen to her team, go over all the options that we didn't have, none of which would fix, extend, improve, or miraculously amend the life that was so clearly ending before our eyes. After that, I would affix my signature to the thickly folded stack of papers that sat in the front seat of my Inferno Orange chariot, like two tickets for passage over the River Styx.

The papers that would, in effect, kill Renay.

I really needed last night with Mateo. I needed all the vibrancy I could find, taste, touch, or smell. I needed that shower sex. I needed every bit of life I could hold on to, to do what I knew I had to do, which was the very opposite of life itself.

I pass over the gullies and brown alleys of the El Paso streets all named after blasted states—Missouri, Wyoming, Montana, Nevada—crawling north on Mesa with a car packed *with life*, and I see the hospital loom up before me. Long and tan and teal, sitting high up on a hill, Renay inside that thing somewhere, waiting for us. Waiting to die.

Waiting for her sons.

Bonus and his wife, Lady—who I've also never met—left for El Paso late last night, Rabbi told me yesterday, and they've been driving straight through to get here. They will arrive any minute from Vernon, Texas.

I will never know if his name was Mateo or not.

Just as I will never know where Vernon, Texas, is, either.

7.

It is just after ten o'clock in the morning.

Energized by Camaro and cock, I have completed re-dressing my mother's entire suite, changing the lighting, adding soft music, comfortable bedding, even some art. It looks like an entirely new room. It looks like *fancy people* die here. Rabbi was at the hospital when I arrived, but glowered at me and my Target bags as he left, heading back downstairs for a smoke by the ER entrance, where he positioned himself every five minutes to exhale another cloud from the long line of Marlboro 72s he inhaled. My brothers view everything that I do as either gay, communist, or clownish, so redecorating Renay's room actually tracks.

Bonus and his wife are due at the hospital any minute.

Bonus and Lady married in April 2003 in Vernon, Texas, which means Bonus has been married to the same fine Baptist woman for eighteen years, and I have never once laid eyes on her. I have not spent one second with him since our sister's scorching-hot funeral.

I had removed several rods of that hideous, gaseous fluorescent hospital lighting that I hate with the white-hot passion of Mercury's fifty-nine days in the sun, pincering them out from the ceiling by hand, then secreting them inside a closet filled with old IV poles and folded-up hospital trays. It immediately lowered the garish temperature of the hospital room and gave Renay's bed a much-needed break from all the merciless, vitality-reducing, flattening light. It considerably darkened the whole room, however, so I added a pert ginger-jar lamp that threw an excellent amount of moody, deathbed languor all about her. Now she was giving low budget Barbara Cartland. Renay was wrapped like a burrito in a thick, rose-tinted quilt, and I fluffed her up even more by setting a rose shag pillow just beneath her head. A rose crown, restored. I have arranged all around her bed several dozen Target-branded rose- and tea-rose-scented candles, none of which, of course, the nurses will allow me to light because they are all joyless Texas plague witches with no sense of fun or feel for death decor. *Fire hazard*, one of them, Bonnie, the blond lady with the blue sleeve tattoo, grunted with obvious disgust as I tried to light the first of Renay's candles with a matchbook I had snatched from the hotel, snarling at me, *Don't even try it. This is a Mexican town; everybody tries that shit here. Just don't!*

I did arrange a few more of those tall Spanish Catholic veladoras candles, saints for protection just to be safe, in case Renay stumbled across Our Catholic Lord while she was dying out here in an El Paso desert. These, too, stay unlit, alongside their agnostic sisters and some framed pictures. At my request, Rabbi has carried up several photographs from Renay's converted garage bedroom, one of which was a gilded, fancy-framed 1958 studio portrait of Cathy Sue dressed as a spoilt Florida princess, strangling a stuffed brown-and-white rabbit who's looking back up at her in shock, a portrait which sat in a place of honor on every dresser Renay ever used for the past sixty-three years. She loved that picture of my bitch of a sister murdering a little rabbit. I cannot explain it, or the cruelty in Cathy Sue's downturned eyes as she ends that cottontail's life. A mother's love is so mysterious. I have set it on a rolling tray at the foot of Renay's bed, surrounded it with offerings of Pepsi and candles and Reese's King Size Big Cup Peanut Brittle, also from Target. It lends the whole wonderfully lit tableau a kind of soft pink Jewish-Mexican ofrenda, a Day of the Dead joie de vivre, but with bold accents of Judaism and Texas Target bargain bin. It all just feels *so right*. I know that if she weren't in a deep coma, Renay would approve of every single detail, except, perhaps, for how much I have spent on candles.

Nobody needs to be putting two hundred dollars' worth of Target candles on their Wells Visa. *Nobody.*

She laughs, waves at all the Catholic saints. *Better safe than sorry,* she says, mocking me with her freshly plucked eyebrows. *Forewarned is for boobs, as they say.*

That's not what they say, Renay, I tell her. *Mexicans are amazing about death and dying. They honor their dead through the lives of their living,* I say a touch defensively.

I really did love Mexican Valium, she says. *I wish I could come back as a Mexican pharmacist.*

I know, Renay, I say. *Maybe next life.*

I have also bought a portable Bluetooth speaker, and it's currently playing soothing tones from Renay's favorite soundtrack, which is of course Spotify's "Casino & Gambling Sound Effects" playlist. This is what she will listen to until she dies. The music of Vegas lends Renay's now-groovy ICU a kind of lively, pulsating roar that drowns out the dreary hospital grind on the other side of the glass, making me feel like we're in a *pretty decent,* mid-sized, off-Strip casino, like Binion's or the Gold Dust, maybe hit the buffet later at the Palace with Bernie and Butt Check, then back to the bandits with Doreen and Cathy Sue. They all loved those dumps off the Strip. The house was always just a *wee bit* more generous, Renay used to say. Bernie once won a new car while playing the slots over there, and she never got over *that.*

I proudly showed it all off to Twin on our video call, momentarily forgetting that neither of us likes each other very much and pride isn't in our love language.

"What are you doing?" Twin asks. "What is all this?" he drawls, throwing a caustic, suspicious glare at the lamp, the low lights, the pillow, the music. He trains his icy-blue, furious eyes on me like the pinprick of a blue laser sight on my forehead. Twin pulls one small Styrofoam cup up closer to his lips, angrily spits out his chew, resumes glaring at the camera, offended, waiting for an answer.

"What do you think is actually happening?" he demands.

"I'm making things nice," I say, a pit in my stomach. "Making things nice *for her.*"

My brother Twin and I have grown far, far apart over the years. We are no longer twins in any way, shape, or form: We are at this point barely even brothers. I don't recognize the man who so rarely lights up my phone camera, and Twin clearly doesn't know the one he sees in his. It is as though we've stumbled across one another on an alien planet, or a Sonoran desert.

"I'm hanging out with an unconscious lady who looks a lot like our mother," I say, trying, and failing, to joke my way out of his haughty demeanor.

"Another funny joke from the big-city comedian," Twin says, staring me down.

"I'm here to advocate for her because it's what she asked me to come here and do." *ME, not YOU, fuckwit,* is what I want to say, but say instead: "So I'm doing that, okay?" I try to sound tough, but end up sounding exactly like the Renay simp that I am and always have been.

Twin shakes his head, grunts in disgust, says, "Yeah, *fast* work, *buddy.*"

"This is my fifteenth or twentieth time in El Paso, Twin. How many times have you gotten on a plane and come here? Once?" I jab. Twin has famously only flown twice.

"Some of us have *real jobs,*" Twin says, and I cannot argue with this.

I never have.

I work in show business. You can call show business a lot of things, but "real" isn't one of them.

Twin seems like he's in a more than the usual bad mood and has a lot more he wants to say. I just can't tell if it's to me or her, so I keep holding up the phone to show him our sleeping mother, wrapped in her rose quilt and plastic tubes.

Twin has pretty much been in a bad mood with me for the last couple of decades. But we've been holding back whatever it was that we *really* wanted to say to each other, and just endured whatever time we had to spend in one another's company. So I usually try not to stir shit up with Twin. I stand down; I hold back my witty retorts. I choose silence as a refuge whenever I want to ask why he's treating his body, which used to be his pride and joy, like a nuclear waste dump, just a junkyard for sadness, a repository for his failure to live up to whatever it was somebody once said was his "potential."

We've been in a kind of cold war for years, Twin distrusting me, misunderstanding me, lacking interest in my life. A great, stony silence just grew and grew between us. I am not here to bridge it or fight with Twin.

I am *hers*.

I walk to Renay's side, take her warm hand into mine, stand over her, watch her dreaming eyes dance back and forth, skipping beneath paper-thin lids. I spread a palm gently on her forehead, and I leave it there. A benediction from Twin, to me, to her.

"Twin says hey, Renay," I say.

I bend over and kiss her forehead, smooth her snowy white hair again, then stand straight, a silent sentry, like one of her IV rods, and I can hear my brother start to cry on the phone.

Twin watches Renay, listens along with me as her chest pumps full, then falls, falls then rises, then it's full again. She's a metronome, she's our mother, not a body hooked to a machine that's wheezing and beeping and chirping.

"What is that sound?" Twin asks, annoyed.

"Vegas," I say. "Although it could be Reno, too. It's a smaller house for sure."

Twin sighs as the waves of slots, craps, roulette, blackjack, and Vegas casino floor chatter emanate cheerfully from the Target Bluetooth by Renay's bed.

"You go down there," he says quietly, gritting his teeth, his bottom lip swollen with fresh-packed dip, "with your hard heart and your big-city ways, and you wanna...what? *Rush us?*" Big, fat, country-boy tears spill down his trembling cheeks. "Rush into *killing your own mother?*" he asks. "You are *dark*, Andy. This is some *dark city shit* you're about," he says, spitting into his cup, hardly looking at me.

And then my heavy, historically silent, chew-dipping brother Twin begins to weep.

He heaves *gigantic*, wracking, tormented sobs, his body shaking, the phone camera bouncing up and down, ceiling to floor, convulsing along with him. The great, cracking sobs of a sliding subaerial glacier, calving into a fjord.

I have not heard any brother of mine cry since Cathy Sue's funeral fifteen years ago.

I don't much remember Twin that day, I'm sad to report. I was incredibly hot, shamefully wearing jorts, glued to my Valium bars and gin, stuck at Renay's side all through those awful hours in Richmond, literally dragging this weeping wreckage of a mother across the threshold of Cathy Sue's crypt, then the Reverend's colonial mansion, then, yes, a Golden Corral for steaks and a salad bar and more gin.

The last time I can recall Twin crying before that was when those insidious vespula wasps of Fayetteville swarmed up from their lair and swallowed us in a cloud of relentless and vicious stings one sorry summer afternoon deep in the woods off Pamalee Drive. How we *both* screamed and cried, all the way to the hospital. Renay screamed, too, when she was told she had to drive all the way back from a bowling tournament in Hickory that same day. She was *pissed* at the two of us for fucking up that weekend trip.

That was four and a half decades ago.

Twin roughly balls his fists to his eyes, barks at me, tears still falling.

"Do you have somewhere important to be, Mister Cold Heart, Mister Big City? Is that why you rushed down there to make it all pretty, so you can feel good enough about yourself to pull the plug and get on back home?" he demands.

"She asked me to!" I shout, never taking my eyes off our sleeping mother. "I am here *for her*, not *you*," I say, and regret saying it instantly, because I know that isn't true. I know it isn't.

"Well, just you remember you're unplugging her from me, too," he says, spitting chew into his cup. "Every day of my entire life, we talked, me and her. About everything. About nothing. Every single day. Never missed one day. Sometimes we just watched TV together, didn't talk at all. We were there for each other. Always there. So how about maybe you don't fucking *rush*, Mister Cold Heart," he says as tobacco juice and tears run a hot marathon down his chin.

Now my tears come, too, and this time without the assistance of a disturbed yellowjackets' nest between us. This time the sting of tears hurt far, far worse. A hurt so much worse than bees.

Despite the impression I may have given, dear Reader, I am a very, very sad man right now.

I know it seems otherwise. I get it. I am a clown. I make jokes. I fuck super-hot tatted soldiers in El Paso hotels after bespoke tacos, then I eat pistachio-crusted French toast and speed down highways in borrowed Camaros. I shop. I *decorate*. It must look like a pretty fun party. I must seem quite *happy-go-fucking-lucky* about all this death.

I am wrecked to my very DNA.

I have not leaked so much as a single tear since Asshole called me, since I fled that cursed Brooklyn Opera House. I haven't cried. I haven't allowed myself.

I am in charge.

She named me.

She did it decades ago, casually (*You're my plan, Ann*), and then months ago by fiat. It is *my* name that will set her free, and I have to take that seriously. *I have to manage.* The manager needs to remain clear-headed. I knew that shedding even just a single tear would be all that it took to unzip my manager guts right there on the floor of that mountainside hospital, and spill 'em out all over the brown hills of El Paso.

I knew that if I let go—*even for just one second*—I would not be able to find my way back.

I would not be able to let *her* go.

Twin and I are frozen, and then I hear a quick, sharp knock on the ICU window and turn.

"Oh my Lord up high, is that my little brother! Is that my baby brother!"

Lady and Bonus have arrived.

Lady waves gaily at me from the ICU window, where she and Bonus stand out in the hall, tourists on the gangway of a very sad cruise.

Twin gives a last, surly look, hears that his oldest brother is here, raises the traditional Corren family single-fingered salute, then hangs up.

Bonus looms in the doorway, smiling tightly at me, ducking his head beneath the top of the frame—*he is so goddamned tall*—nodding politely at the passing doctors and ICU nurses who never stop rolling in or out of our room. He nods at me.

I sheepishly wave.

"Hey," he says.

"Hey," I say back.

"I am *so* happy to finally meet you!" Lady says, mercifully grabbing me into a *strong* hug.

Lady doesn't *shout*-shout, but she's not *not* shout-shouting, either, in the way Texas ladies are born to speak. Her voice is just *room sized*.

She's tiny, almost half Bonus's size, maybe five foot four with boots on, with short, mannishly neat and unfussy brown hair, and she's encased in a thick, snug cardigan. Lady's wide eyes and her warm heart are the captain of this team, you can just tell. Those eyes are roving, loving, forgiving, *seeing, swimming* with the love, exhaustion, compassion, and anticipation of getting to this bedside in time. She immediately paddles over to Renay's bed, takes my mother's right hand to her own heart, and whispers encouragingly, praying with her.

"Lord Jesus is in the house, Renay, His protective hand is upon you. Be you not afraid, my darling," Lady says, giving powerful and convincing testimony.

I believe her.

I love Lady so instantly, right down to her Baptist boots. I didn't realize it until the very moment she arrived and began praying, but I needed Lady desperately.

I needed a sister. Jesus Christ sent me a Lady.

"This is my wife of nearly twenty years, the love of my life. Lady," Bonus says rather formally, his eyes unblinking. *Message received.*

"I am *so glad* to finally meet you," she whispers, still clutching Renay's hand in her own, then reflexively reaching down to straighten the Target quilt, fussing and caretaking like the lifelong family practice nurse from Vernon, Texas, that she was.

Lady and my mother had spent the last decade first getting to know one another, and then falling in love with one another, building a bridge of sorts, a way over that vast, frozen chasm that had long soared between Renay and Bonus. They had somehow achieved a kind of tenuous rapprochement these last years, even a kind of love, all thanks to the sturdy ministrations of this tiny, determined, loving Baptist woman from Vernon. Renay and Bonus, in the painful decade and a half since Cathy Sue had died, had carved out a little bit of peace. It was all because of Lady.

My mother loved Lady.

"Your mother *never* stopped talking about you, Andy," she says, and when she says my name, it is a three-syllable, Texas picnic, *AH-YUN-DEE*, which I love so much. "And your brother was always *so proud* of you, Andy." Lady beams as Bonus sort of nods, sort of grimaces, goes over to one of the matching vinyl chairs, yanks it forward on the vinyl floor with a long, vinyl squeal, then folds his denim coat over it and sets his Mountain Dew and Navy ball cap down. He faces his mother from the foot of the bed.

"Hi, Mom," Bonus bellows in his full-trucker voice, all bass and barely contained rage, a caged roar, really. "I made it," he says, nodding. "I'm here for you, Mom. I am right here. I made it, Mom," he says again as Lady pats his hand, too, and then the quilt, and then Renay's other hand, and then her heart, as she praises His name the whole time. She holds us, and the whole world, as her husband quietly folds himself into a quick series of sharp, tall man sobs.

"I made it, Mom," he says between choked breaths. "I made it this time."

"I love you, baby doll. You are my strongest man. She is *so glad* you made it here, baby," Lady whispers to Bonus.

This is Lady's third marriage, and the second for Bonus, and it's quite obvious for all to see that these two perfect people *are insanely in love.* The way Lady looks at Bonus. The *strength* and *light* he seems to instantly receive from her, from her eyes directly to his soul. The *power* that flows between them.

I have never known anything like this look that passes between my misplaced Jewish brother and his petite Baptist wife.

Where did he learn how to do that?

Not from me! Renay snarks, then winks.

"We drove straight through the night after Bonus got off from work," Lady tells me as she smooths and strokes Renay's milky-white hair, as she massages Renay's supple hand, speaks in that low, lilting North Texas country nurse cadence. "He only had to stop once, at a park off the interstate, just to sleep for a little bit. But he was so determined, Andy, and God was so with us, I wasn't worried *one bit* about us getting here, *nothing* could stop your brother," she says. "He's a strong man, your brother, but his heart is *so tender* when it comes to your mother, the history between them. I'm so glad we're here. Now come here," Lady says, "and give your sister a *real* hug."

I thought we *had*, but am *enveloped* in a longer, fine-smelling hug by Lady.

Lord, it feels so good, too.

Bonus smiles at the both of us. He's in head-to-toe rumpled denim—denim shirt, denim dungarees—and he's so tall his graying head nearly scrapes the ceiling of this ICU. His bristly mustache is thicker than ever, but it's flecked now with salt and pepper, and his icy-blue eyes icier, even, than Twin's, crinkle at the corners seeing his wife and littlest brother all mushed together.

Bonus puts out a hand to shake. "Hello, little brother. It's really good to see you," he says gruffly. "I made it on time, this time," he nods, pulling me closer, one arm on my elbow.

"You sure did," I say, and I let Bonus pull me in for a hug that goes a little sideways, then zigs a little awkward, but sails through the goalposts in the end zone for three points. So it counts.

I'm pretty sure it's our first.

"Jesus is good. She squeezed my hand," Lady exclaims in her not-shout, standing at Renay's bedside.

Her smile *beaming*, Lady nods down at my peaceful, sleeping mother. Lady gives Renay's hand a long, warm, confident squeeze back, presses it against her blue cardigan-warmed heart.

"She knows we're here together," she says. "Renay knows her boys are here."

We are all here.

"Her biggest and her littlest. I know that makes her *so* happy," Lady said.

For the first and last time ever, we had to do something together. Something right here. Something for her.

We had to agree to extubate our mother, which would likely send her floating away forever.

I knew what she wanted.

What I wanted was to have unanimity with us all. For once.

It took days to get us all together, all on the same page, all in agreement for her in these last days and nights of struggle. We tussled mightily over what would happen next, roaring at each other back and forth, cursing each other, will we or won't we, should we or shouldn't we, screaming at each other over phones, over texts, over her bed, rushing down hospital halls pounding on walls, slamming down phones, hitting the emergency room exit for cigarettes and deep sobs, hurling accusations like poisoned stars at each other, all while grabbing multiple consultations with Renay's end-of-life care team, grabbing desperately at Rabbi's theories to prop her up for another day. There were bitter and hurtful conflagrations sparking between us all, brushfires that fell and bloomed, collapsed and exploded under the weight of their own insubstantiality, or importance, or desperation. First me and Twin, then Bonus against Rabbi, then all of us against each other, praying or crying about what to do, pissed off at each other for not knowing more about it, wishing somebody would tell us what to do, reduced to staring at those thick, folded sheaths of unsigned medical directives that we all knew, to a brother, must be signed. Fighting and fighting against the truth, against each other until we stopped fighting, finally. Then we stopped crying, too. We took a deep breath together—our very first deep breath as brothers ever—and we, all five of us, began *listening to each other.* Then to the doctors, and to the nurses, and finally: *to her.*

We were there for each other.

"Renay Corren is about living," Bonus said. "Living is what matters most to Mom."

"I want more than anything for her to know that she is loved and at peace, and that we're here for her. *With* her," I said quietly.

"I know one thing. Our mother don't do baby food," Asshole said darkly.

"Steelers lost to the Vikings. Fucking Kirk Cousins. *He did this,*" Rabbi said, trembling with an ancient Jewish vengeance that frankly terrified everybody. Would he really not sign off on letting Renay go because the Vikings demolished the Steelers?

But he came around.

Twin, too, finally.

"She had a damned good run. Living on tubes ain't what she wants, or deserves," he said. "Do it. Just do it," he cried.

And so we signed.

8.

Unbelievably, it is still Thursday, December 9, 2021, in El Paso, Texas

We are an exhausted group, Bonus and Rabbi in windbreakers and ball caps, crowded next to each other into a tiny nurses' break room, gathered around a speakerphone so Twin and Asshole can be here too, joined for a consultation with our death doula, Dr. Agustín.

He is very sexy.

It's utilitarian in here, just a bare changing room, badly lit and lined with scratched metal lockers, walls papered with vibrant fentanyl overdose posters. Lady is seated next to me. We are all wrung out. When a parent lies dying, first there are the fears, then the rush of facts, then the endless horror of facing them, and then, finally, comes the fatigue of acceptance. We look like what we are: a deathbed vigil on sticks.

All the same, Lady and I are *misbehaving*, kicking each other under the shaky table, laughing and staring. Because Dr. Agustín is *so* fucking hot.

Dr. Agustín, to be sure, is a highly credentialed physician, a graduate of the prestigious Universidad Autónoma de Guadalajara. He was born right here in El Paso, and he has made quite a name for himself, assisting dying El Pasoans, giving them the classy end-of-life care and dignity that they deserve. Dr. Agustín is *very* in demand the December of Omicron 2021.

Dr. Agustín is our death doula, and today he will be helping me and my brothers understand how Renay is going to pass away. *Unfortunately, our death doula is sexy as shit.* It's incredibly distracting. Renay would have sat up and died all over again if she laid eyes on this guy. She'd have been tickled pink to have this Latin movie star costarring with her in her final picture.

Dr. Agustín *is* movie-star handsome—tall, lean frame; chiseled chin—and he had that relaxed, penetrating way of looking at you the way that movie stars do, like he is *way more interested* in you than you are in him. Dr. Agustín wears dress loafers and a casually coordinated ensemble of sandy browns mixed with ruddy bricks. His bedside demeanor is so calming, reassuring, and caring—it is the stuff of soap opera legend. He makes you want to check yourself into the hospital with a fake gunshot wound, just to hang out. Even sitting, Dr. Agustín is tall. Not quite NBA tall, but super fit with broad shoulders and the bearing—it must be said—of an angel heralding a new dawn. He has two angelic, perfect deep dimples on his cheeks, and a casually but expertly groomed beard. He smells so nice, too, like an old-fashioned Sunday Texas dad smell: leather, cologne, and creosote. God. So fucking *hot*. *Why??*

Lady and I cannot stop staring at Dr. Agustín, casting longing, uncomfortable looks at his warm, chocolatey eyes, then turning away and giggling real quick and low to each other if he caught us. Death and dying should not be like high school, I agree, but there we are, the cheerleader and the clown, cutting up in the cafeteria.

I think Renay would have approved.

"This is what will happen when we extubate tomorrow," our sexy death doula advises, all of us staring back at him, each windbreaker at full mast, Lady kicking me lightly under the table each time I stare too hard. "Why extubate? There is not much more we can do for your mother here in the ICU," he says gently, meeting the gaze of each of us. "Your mother's body is shutting down. At eighty-four years of age, after three weeks of mechanical ventilation, and with no signs of improvement, with such a long and profound history of ailment, this is, I am afraid, where modern medicine ends and hard decisions, and personal faith, begin. Keeping your mother in a living state after extubation would require a transfer to a skilled facility with 24/7 nursing and dialysis, as well as a PICC line for nutrition and a tracheostomy for breathing. Assuming she recovers from the procedure, she will have a difficult-to-impossible time speaking or eating normally. So. You would be keeping her body alive. But your mother, this vibrant, colorful woman who you all knew and loved and cherished for eighty-four years, would vanish with those procedures. Should we proceed to extubation without those life-extended procedures, you will, it is my considered opinion, be following your mother's stated medical directive, as well as give your mother a gift. She will reunite with her free soul. Sometimes that happens quickly, sometimes in a day or so, but upon extubation she will rest trouble-free and beautifully, and have a completely painless and comfortable transition home to her Lord, should her body not support further respiration. I do not see that it can, or will, not unassisted. So. My solemn promise and duty as her doctor is to care for your mother, but importantly, as a son and as a Catholic man, too, to ease and end your mother's suffering. End-of-life care is my highest calling. Your mother has already begun her journey home. It is clear to me. It is only for the body to join now. And then her journey will be complete."

You can hear the windbreaker sails deflate. We're all crying now.

Lady and I finally grow solemn.

A roomful of stunned faces turn to Dr. Agustín, then we look at one another, speechless for once.

Bonus says, "I think we know what she would want. I don't think it's a question."

Then Rabbi lets out a long, weary heave, as though he had been holding it in for a decade. He says quietly, "Mother wants to go home."

We slowly nod at one another in recognition.

"And that's where she's gonna go, Rabbi," I say. "Home. I promise."

"It's the right thing to do," Asshole says.

There is no fight left in this room.

We finally did it.

For the first time in history, there is no fight among any of Renay's sons. Just tears.

Just love.

An irrefutable truth spoken aloud. We all know it's time. We have seen what we have seen, and nothing is going to change our mother's condition. Nothing will ever convince me that her options after this ICU could be called "living."

We trust Dr. Agustín.

Well, some of us trust him, and some of us trust him *deeply*, if you know what I mean. I have always loved and respected a man who can deliver bad news and still smell so *good*. Sexiest thing on earth.

"You will be doing the right thing," Dr. Agustín continues. "You would be doing what I would, were I faced with the same choice. It is what any good son would do," he says, looking at me, and then, perhaps seeing more than he wished in my eyes, looking away with a nod to Bonus and Rabbi, sons in deflated windbreakers and ball caps, looking at them in a way that commended their courage and closeness at this difficult time.

"You are a good family," Dr. Agustín says.

9.

We had agreed to let the old girl float away.

And so we signed.

We trusted our doctors, we listened to our nurses, we opened our hearts.

We asked the inevitable question: "What would Renay want?"

The answer was obvious to all.

Order some fucking takeout, some Pepsi, and get on with it.

Renay Corren was packing up again.

Just like the old days.

Except this time we had a Bonus brother.

We had Bonus and his big Texas gravitas, and his Lady's quiet, dignified faith to help her pack. We had each other.

We had one more day with her.

We were her sons, still.

Here we were, Renay's nearly intact family. Reunited.

Naturally, I ordered up a mess of Panda Express to the hospital.

We stood, Bonus and Rabbi and Lady and I, letting Asshole and Twin call or video in, all of us talking and eating, sometimes even laughing, gravitating back and forth between big containers of fast-casual Chinese and our mother's bed, sometimes to hold the camera up for her to hear a son, sometimes out to the hall to cry. We began cracking jokes, letting some tension out of the room as Renay's ICU filled with the robust smells of spicy orange chicken—her favorite—and black pepper Angus—her second favorite. Bonus and Rabbi circled each other warily, eyeing one another possessively over their mother's bed as they forked mouthfuls of Chinese and Mountain Dew into grateful, tired mouths. As we all shared one last dinner with our Renay.

I looked down at her as she slept, wondering if she could still hear us all in here with her, all her little fuckups together, laughing and eating and loudly razzing each other. I wondered if she was dreaming she was back home on Pamalee Drive, standing out front in a house dress waiting for that Charles Chips van to putter up our hill and for those big beige barrels of fresh chips to come tumbling off. I wondered if she was hearing us out here, and if she was aggravated at being ignored, and was hollering for all of us to get down from those trees and off that damned roof, and to clean up our shit and get inside for frozen dinners and fine-quality chips after.

I wondered if she was standing there now, and if she saw us, all of us, all the little servants of her shabby court, and I wondered if it made her happy to have us home.

I hoped it did.

10.

El Paso, Texas
Friday, December 10, 2021

She woke up.

Dr. Agustín said it might happen, and it sure as shit did.

On Friday morning, after nearly three weeks of complete unresponsiveness in a deep, assisted sleep, *Renay Corren woke up.*

Lady and I were there when Mrs. Lazarus arose.

Rabbi and Bonus and I had taken turns the night before, holding vigil, telling each other, and her, stories from our times together and apart, wiping her brow, laughing together, all of us talking and staying upright until nearly dawn. But the Chinese takeout and the long days of struggling against one another had taken its toll. One by one, we slipped out into the dark of night, back to find a couch or a mattress at Rabbi's to sleep fitfully upon. I returned to my hotel around four o'clock in the morning, alone this time, unaccompanied by soldier or sailor, just another lonely El Paso 8 weighed down by heavy thoughts and heavier fried rice. It was a restless night alone in a big, empty bed. I tossed and turned, dreaming of dangerous roads in Qatar, bad cribbage hands, and stock car races, until, after just a few hours of restless rest, I gave up, threw my covers off, and headed right back to the hospital. I had been gone less than three hours.

It was just me and Lady this Friday morning, Lady sweet and warm as an apple pie straight from the oven. *The bedside manner of this indefatigable woman.* I wanted to stick a straw in her and drink deeply of her sunshine, of whatever it was that made Lady so unbelievably kind, loving, and full of tender, tireless grace. It's probably Jesus, isn't it?

It's Jesus, Renay says with an arched eyebrow.

Whatever it is, I don't think you're allowed to drink Jesus with a straw, but I am no expert on the blood of Christ.

Speaking of Jesus, on Friday morning the tenth day of December, after three weeks of coma, intubation, and assisted breathing, Renay Mandel Corren sprang suddenly and quite unexpectedly back to life in the ICU. Wide awake, she saw me.

She saw me for the very first time since I had arrived two days ago.

Renay *saw*.

"Darling, I think your mother is awake," Lady said, her voice trembling. "Darling, she is looking right at me. I think Renay is here. Lord Jesus on High, I do believe Renay is *right here in the room*," Lady said, laughing and rejoicing. "She's here, she's here!"

There she was. Blinking. Smiling. *Seeing me.*

Dr. Agustín was right. Despite the impression I may have lent that I spent our entire changing room consultation daydreaming about running away to El Paso to marry my mother's sexy death doula, I *had* listened to Dr. Agustín yesterday.

"You may be pleasantly surprised by a short return to consciousness," he had gently advised. "She may even be able to see and communicate with you. I hope she does. It is a beautiful gift. One of God's most generous." He's right. It is one of life's incredible mysteries, what happens at the end. People wake up sometimes, all their senses come alive, maybe even senses we don't know about. *She was here.* In the room. *With us.*

On her very last full day on this earth, Renay Mandel Corren was awake and conscious.

There you are, you old rascal, I thought. "Hey, Mommy. It is so good to see you. I am right here," I said.

Her eyes rounded, filled with a kind of wonder, then water, then she smiled wide at me.

It's good to see you, Ann.

"Look at that smile!" Lady said, beaming right back down. "Look at the way she loves you, Andy. Oh my Lord. We just love you so much, Renay Corren, all of your sons are here, and they are gonna be so happy to see you," she said, clutching Renay's hand. Renay looked up at her beneficent daughter-in-law, this human angel from Vernon, Texas, who she simply adored, and she just smiled ever wider with those eyes that saw clearly. *That saw into us.*

"It's so nice to see you smile again, Mommy," I said.

"Praise His name," Lady whispered, smoothing Renay's brow. "Bless Him."

"You just about ready to get out of here, woman?" I whispered to my mother, softly stroking her hair off her forehead, trying and failing not to cry. "We gotta get you a manicure and a color set, Renay. Can't do that in here," I said.

Renay Corren, my mother and co-pilot for fifty-two years—one year for every card in the deck—all eighty-four and a half years of her, riddled as she was with tumors, sepsis, failing kidneys, blood clots, anemia, diabetes, possibly pneumonia, for sure something *real bad* in the liver, she just laughed up at me, lunged for my hand *hard*, gave it a solid, long tug. Still looking up at me with those two shining, all-seeing card shark eyes of hers, she nodded *vigorously* and *affirmatively*.

Deal me out, Ann.

I nodded. I got it. I heard.

"Loud and clear, Renay," I said. "Loud and clear. TDY, soldier."

TDY. It means goodbye, she chirped.

"The choice needs to be yours, Renay. Everybody over here thinks I'm killing you for the inheritance." Here she practically guffawed. "They think I'm rushing you down to hell. So it's up to you, old girl. They take that vent off, you breathe on your own, or you don't, but it's off, and you can rest. Or you can be on a trach breathing tube, and a pick line feeding tu—" But Renay didn't even let me finish.

She grabbed my hand *hard*, pressed her sharp peach nails *deep* into my palm, then shook her head violently back and forth, then forth and back. Her eyes wider and rounder than ever, nearly *angry*.

No. No fucking way, Ann. Let's do this thing. Let's roll.

"You sure, Mommy? You ready for a long sleep?" I asked, silencing my sobs with a bite on my lip.

Renay stared back up at me, her eyes clear as the middle of a Texas summer day, smiling, just a single tear rolling slowly down her shiny, plump cheek. Skin so soft. Rosy. Beaming.

Nobody, and I mean nobody, has ever been more ready, Ann.

"Okay, Mommy," I whispered. "I love you to bits. Always have. Always will."

Not always, Renay joked with a wink. *But I forgive you, son*, she said.

Me? You forgive me? What a bitch move, I thought.

"I forgive you, too," I said, laughing. "In case you need to hear that, okay? I really do. Sort of."

Good enough for me, she said, the two of us now laughing.

Here she was.

Here lay before me the woman who made me out of lies. For better or worse, she *did* make me.

Those days, it seemed a lot more of the worse than the better. Yet there I stood. Unbowed.

Maybe charting a course from Fayetteville to here based on the *Hollywood Wives* and Sue Mengers playbook wasn't such a hot idea, and maybe zigzagging back and forth across the country, moving every eighteen months like a woman with five kids to feed, wasn't exactly a strategy for success in love. Maybe freedom, the kind of freedom she taught me to cherish and fight for and protect at all costs, can lead a man to some pretty lonely places, too.

But there I stood. The rest of me. The best I've got. The best of her.

"Here I am," I said to her, kissing her cheek. "And here I will stay, I promise you. Here I will stay."

I am hers, completely.

She *made* me.

Oh, but she made me so smart and tough!

So I was grateful.

I kissed my mother's forehead, long, hard, and slow. I wanted her to *feel* it, so I pressed harder and harder. I wanted it to never end. I wanted to leave a mark on her, like she did on me. I stood up, and I dried my eyes.

I am the manager. So I will manage.

"Get everybody over here," I said to Lady. "I'll call Asshole. Get Bonus and Rabbi, wake 'em all up, tell them to head over. Tell them I said *not to dilly-dally*—you be sure and say exactly that."

Don't dilly-dally.

11.

Before we unplugged her that night, we threw Renay a farewell party.

Everybody came.

Her boys, of course. Her sons. Her gay grandsons. All her twinklies, her fuckups. We were all there. We invited Doreen. Big Gay Sam. Bernie came, obviously, and Butt Check, too, half son to his half mother; he wouldn't miss it. There were others. I lost track. I was producing, *managing*, organizing Zooms and FaceTimes and Google videos and text chats and phone calls and nurses and doctors, getting it all set up and going, bringing the computer closer to Renay so she could see, and they could see, that this was really happening. I was adjusting lights, sounds, hopes, all the way to the end.

Make 'em laugh, Ann!

We brought them all into the room. There was Doreen, still blond and still New Hampshire as hell, even after forty years in Fayetteville. She showed up first. Doreen always showed up first.

"I was just a girl. Twenty-three and single, a new mom. Brand-new to Fayetteville. On my way to my first day at friggin' Burger King in my shitty car, wearing my shitty brown polyester, when my shitty Chevy ran out of gas on Bragg. Right near the Sunoco that would change my whole life. You gave me a tank, Renay, then you hauled me right over to that B&B, and you got me *a job*. Where I met my husband. Where we raised our kids. Where I built a whole life. Because *you*. Now my *grandkids* run around there. *Because you took a stranger off the street*, Rosie. I owe you a couple of lives, honey. First I gotta do a little better in this one. Be more like Renay. Be *louder. Be strong, and not afraid.* I will pay you back *so hard*. I'll pay you in crates of lobster right from New Hampshire, I promise," Doreen Noyes DeJaynes, weeping into the camera, says in her still very thick, legendarily stubborn New Hampshire accent.

Renay tries to tell her, using all her strength to move her lips around that vent, "I love you," an effort that is seen, received, and returned.

"Well, Renay. You were my best friend," Butt Check says, struggling to get through his words. "And my part-time mom. Hell, my roommate for life. My cruise partner. Best friend I ever had. We was friends through the best times of my whole life, Renay. Long story short, I got the opportunity today to say 'I love you' one more time. I think I'll say it twice, 'cuz I'm a cheater and a wiseass. But you know that. You always knew that. I love you, Rose. I love you, Renay," he says, then signs off with a bushy-mustache kiss and a dance of those notorious Butt Check of Fayetteville brows.

Bernie came, too, all the way from that glittering city that Renay loved so much she gave it all her money. Bernie Alphabet from Las Vegas, Nevada, comes on. "Rosie, God loves you infinitely—but I think I love you more," he says, smiling and crying in his suburban Las Vegas home. "He certainly blessed me the day I met you at that PBA tourney. Remember? I ripped my pants. I think you gave me a pair of your ex-husband's to wear. I loved you on the spot. We had a bond like no one else, Renay. Joined like Siamese twins. I don't know what it was. You saw something in me I didn't even see. We weren't this or that thing, we just *were*. Two halves. *Us*. *A whole lot of fun*. You were my wingman, the best I could ever ask. You just...you had my back, Renay. Now I've got yours. God's got you, Renay, I know this much. Whether you like it or not, I'm praying for you, but I know the Big Guy's got ya. We may be separated for now, but we'll never be apart for long, Rosie. You are my first, and my best, and my greatest friend. I will never have to say goodbye. *I will see you again*. I know this. Have a beautiful sleep, Rosie. Rest in peace and comfort." Bernie's beautiful blue eyes sparkled like free diamonds in the fountains of the Bellagio as he said goodbye.

Big Gay Sam asked his beloved Gran, "Who am I gonna call to talk about junk TV now, Gran?" and it is a question that the whole room, including Renay, ponders, before everybody, including Renay, points to me. I don't even like *Dr. Pimple Popper*!

"You know, Gran," Sam continues, "when Mom died, you gave me extra time. You kept her alive for me. You told me stories. I wish we had one more cruise, one more story, one more buffet. Thank you for teaching me to gamble, to cook, to never fear eating alone in public, to try new foods, to live without fear or shame. Thank you for the adventures of a lifetime, Gran," Sam says, crying. We're all crying. That redheaded gay redneck kid breaks our fucking heart.

My mother's eyes simply *shined*. She heard the praise. She heard her daughter's name. She saw us all around her. She gripped my hand so tight, swaying and laughing. She said it loud with those eyes, and that smile.

This is what I made you for, Ann. For life!

To live!

To live every day like it's your last. L'chaim, you know?

לחיים!

12.

At five o'clock in the evening on Friday, December 10, we stepped quietly out of Renay's ICU so that the gentle nurses of Providence—saints, every single one of them—could carefully extubate Renay from the ventilation tube she had been attached to, and had so deeply hated, for nearly a month.

She was free at last.

She would never rise again.

13.

All that night, and into the next morning, we watched.

We watched her heart.

We listened to her breath.

She slept.

We told stories.

We kept vigil.

I read to her, whole passages from the latest Nicholas Sparks, *The Wish.*

Oh goody, Krantz in pants, Renay cackled when I cracked open that new-smelling book.

She always called Sparks "Krantz in pants," which made us both laugh.

14.

El Paso, Texas
Saturday, December 11, 2021

What I did, I did for love.

I did what I felt was *necessary.*

In the end, I had to hurt Lady.

I am not proud of it. Sometimes dying is ugly, and beautiful people get hurt because of that ugliness.

Lady is still not speaking to me, and Renay's been dead for an hour.

By eleven thirty that Saturday morning, Renay was disconnected from all of the machines that had tethered her to El Paso, all but a quiet monitor for her failing heart, which labors mightily through the ever smaller peaks, and ever deeper valleys.

She is no longer getting enough oxygen. It is nearly over.

Her end is in the room with us, and soon the woman called Renay Mandel Corren will no longer be. The answer to so many, many months and years of pain, loss, and illness is right there in the room; we can all feel it. Twin is shellacked with grief on his camera phone, pasty white and staring bleakly off to the side, wishing, no doubt, he was anywhere else, or back on the phone with her, shooting the shit about nothing at all. Asshole stays completely silent, stoic and hiccupping with tears. I think he is even praying. I know I can hear Shirley praying. Two wounded hearts, reeled from far away into this grim room, this painful task that he, her shepherd for so long, must see to the inevitable and terrible finish. Rabbi whispers softly. He's wearing a yarmulke and holding a white leather-bound prayer book, and he's pacing intermittently, throwing anxious glances between his mother's muted heart monitor and the more muted ESPN above her bed, which is rattling off NBA scores and power drink commercials. Bonus sits in a deep chair, pulled close to her bed, his tall self now collapsed over hers, his full head of bushy, white-and-black hair bobbing up and down like a fishing lure on a lake made entirely of dying mother.

I am the one at the foot of the bed, managing.

I am adjusting the Bluetooth speaker, so it plays Sinatra just right, "My Way," her favorite, so Renay can hear it on the way out. I am spraying rose- and tea rose-scented oil from Target all up and down the pink quilted blanket, giving my mother the rose red carpet treatment she expects and deserves for this, her very last dramatic exit.

A good death, Ann. Good work, son.

Lady, my supremely kind, surprisingly hilarious, and Baptist-as-hell sister-in-law, Mrs. Lady Bonus, is on Renay's left side, close to the window, which beams hazy El Paso morning light into our Target ginger-jar-lamp-shadowed room. She's doing what comes naturally to a fine, upstanding Baptist woman from Vernon, Texas, in times like these, times of trial and mercy and surrender, doing what she's called to do. I am down at the foot of the bed, lightly massaging my mother's feet for the last time.

"Renay, you take His hand!" Lady preaches. "You take it! That's Jesus' beautiful hand, Renay Corren, and if He is holding that hand out to you, you take His precious hand, my darling, you go on and take it!" Lady cries out, bidding for the marked-down soul of my bargain-bin Jewish mother, my wickedly scabrous, profanely funny, atheist mom, this irreligious, indiscriminate inhaler of porn, trash, sacred cows, and shellfish. Lady wants her to take the glowing, outstretched hand of Jesus Christ?

Jesus Christ, Lady, I can hear Renay saying.

Now at last I cry.

I am weeping lustily and forcefully, gales of grief and tears, but also I am choking back peals of swallowed laughter, garbled sobs mixed with hysteria as I imagine my mother, every grand rabbi's mortal ham-eating nemesis, taking Jesus Christ's lovely hand, imagining what Renay would think of all of this, of Lady, who Renay just *loved*, praying over her dying body. And what would she think of Rabbi, spitting a few bars of the Prayer for the Dead, rocking back and forth, davening old-school Jewish style, spontaneously invoking the Mourner's Kaddish. It's something I have only heard spoken aloud in this family once before, and that was over the body of a dead dog named Licorice Katz, back in 1978. The Hebrew incantations merge with the weeping of Bonus, my gigantic mystery brother, with his big, broken heart and lifetime of bad breaks, now folded up in an agony of surrender and release, covering his mother's body. Twin and Asshole are crying, too, and we are all united, joined as one, *brothers, a family at last*, in this unbelievably messy, calamitous, mournful, and, *now suddenly, utterly hysterically funny*, last breath in the life of Renay Mandel Corren.

She is passing.

She is going away while Frank Sinatra warbles in a corner, her broken sons naked in their pain before her in the soft, rose-colored light of a Target lamp and the flickering glow of the NBA recaps sparking glitter down upon us all, and I sprayed *and I sprayed and I sprayed* the smell of roses for Rosie to follow out and into the next world.

It was all, all of it, so *perfect* and *holy* and so perfectly, perfectly *Renay*.

Except for the Jesus part.

"You just take His hand and you let Him bring you on home, darling! You take Jesus' hand, Renay! He loves you so much! *He loves you!* Take it! Do not be afraid! Take it! *TAKE IT!*" Lady *seizes* Renay's hand in a fierce grip, enthusiastically clutching it to her breast, praying *hard* alongside her husband, who is crying over his fading mother's final breaths, letting her go at long last, letting his separation from Renay and this family go along with her, finally, *at last. This* time *he* is the one letting *her* go, and it means so damned much to Bonus. You can feel it.

My mother's breath begins to seize and hiccup, her mouth gaping, her breath ragged as that lure and line sink to the bottom of that shallow, flat lake. I know there is not a single moment to spare, and so *I leap* from the foot of the bed, and I *vault* to my mother's side, and I *yank* Renay's right hand, as though I am about to conduct a tug-of-war with the vicar of Christ himself, right here in this room, and I shriek wildly at my generous, lovable, absolutely indispensable sister-in-law, screaming in a blind, raging fury as I raise my mother's limp hand up and say, "She is *not* taking *Jesus'* hand, Lady! If she's taking anybody's *fucking hand*, it's Sammy Davis Junior's!" I bawl, using all of that expensive New York therapy and quality low-budget Southeastern regional actor training to bring the room to a complete standstill.

We have silence.

We have Sinatra.

We have the Mourner's Kaddish.

Renay sips her final breath, her struggle ending as the last chords of "My Way" and the last phrases of Rabbi's keening Mourner's Kaddish—Yitbarach v'yishtabach, v'yitpa'ar v'yitromam—entwined in an odd and fitting, irreligious challah bread of a funeral hymn for my odd and irreligious, always famished mother to feast upon at her funeral buffet.

She dies *beautifully*.

She dies *noisily*.

She dies surrounded by *her* people, and by pretty things purchased on credit.

She dies *her way*.

I am confident that the very last words Renay Mandel Corren heard on this earth were her gay son screaming *"Sammy Davis Junior!"* and her fuckwit son whispering "o-meyn" in Hebrew.

Amen. אמן.

15.

El Paso, Texas
Saturday afternoon, December 11, 2021

Renay died an hour ago.

Naturally, we are all gathered downstairs in the hospital parking lot, sitting in trucks figuring out which steakhouse is our next move. None of us planned a wake or a funeral. Nobody has ever planned for shit in this family, except for Bonus.

I'm in the passenger seat of Rabbi's King Ranch. He's tail in, facing the hospital. Bonus rolls his enormous cherry-red Silverado over, Lady in the front, and he noses his truck in so his driver's side window is directly across from Rabbi's driver's side window.

Lady, all bundled up in her cardigan, won't look at me, not so much as a turn of the neck.

Still kind of mad, I think, *about the whole "hand of Jesus" thing.*

Who can blame her? Renay's soul would've been a damned good catch back in Vernon.

Sorry, suckers! Sammy 1, Jesus 0.

Bonus sticks his head out of the window of his Silverado, and he's straining so hard to be heard over Rabbi's King Ranch V-8, his neck turning the same reddish-purple color of Minna Katz's prized red onions. With no preamble, no warning, Bonus has decided that right this minute, an hour after the death of his mother, *right now in this hospital parking lot*, he will have his say.

And so, he is heard.

"You will *never* have the right to tell me what I am, or what I am not," he says to Rabbi, jabbing his finger at him. "I am a *brother*. I am a *son*. I am a *part* of this family," he says, and this time he's looking right at me.

Because he's right.

He *was* apart from this family, and it was none of his doing. It shouldn't have happened. It was his parents' fault, not his. It was our fault, Cathy Sue's, mine. It was this whole confused, unprepared, emotionally illiterate collective of dingbats, all these frightened, sullen men chasing shadows we had *nothing* to do with unleashing.

We made sure Bonus stayed apart.

We did that.

Bonus and Rabbi are the very last two people on this earth who knew the whole Renay, the one who was a mother, a wife, a woman soldiering through the lows and lows of military life. They are the only two people I know who knew my sister Cathy Sue as a young, foolish woman making young, foolish mistakes. They are the last two people left on this earth who have any muscle memory remaining of a woman named Renay Mandel Corren, who knew her before she lost a breast, a body, her feet, her future, all the pieces of herself that she willingly and defiantly sacrificed to stay alive, to keep her sons alive, to keep us close.

"She *wanted* me here," Bonus says between clenched teeth. "And I am in her life *forever*. I was *proud* to be a part of her life to the very end. I forgave her *for everything*, and you know what? *She* forgave *me*. I have wasted forty years asking myself *What did I do to you, to deserve this hatred*? I never found an answer. Because there never was one," Bonus says, now weeping freely in his Silverado.

I love that he cries easily, like I do. I love that *somebody else* in this family cries in pickup trucks, like I do. I have cried alone in so many pickup trucks, y'all.

If you were to ask any of my brothers why they hated Bonus, or why they couldn't deal with Bonus, or why things were so fucked-up with Bonus, none of them would be able to give you a straight answer. Not one. It was just…legacy. Decades of calcified ghost residue. A half century of shit. That's really hard to scrape off.

"I have *loved* you. I have *forgiven* you. This whole thing has messed me up, man! I had to *fix* myself. And I only managed to do it with the love and generosity of my amazing, beautiful wife, *who my mother loved so much*," he cries. "You never had a right to leave me out of this family," Bonus says between tears, then bends his head to cry again.

He cries so hard, hanging out that Chevy Silverado window.

We all do.

Eventually he stops crying, and then we do, too, and then we are just a bunch of rednecks with bloodshot eyes, sitting in a couple of pickup trucks, grizzled and hungry.

"So we going to Borderland for steaks, or what?" Rabbi asks innocently.

"That place is *fantastic*," Asshole says from the speakerphone.

"Were you listening this whole time?" I ask.

"Every word. Every delicious word," he says.

"Didn't we go to Borderland for Thanksgiving?" I hear Twin ask. *I think we did!*

"Mother loved it. She loved the ribeye, and the view," Rabbi says as he ditches a 72 out the window, then immediately fires up another. "And the fried pickles," he says.

"Do they have gin?" I ask the sky, my face pressed so far against the glass of the King Ranch that I've left an oily, impressionistic smear of my whole soul upon it. "Do they have lots and lots of gin?" I beg.

"Gin was your father's drink, you know," Bonus says from the Silverado, his eyes twinkling and wolfish.

"Get out of here!" I shout over to him, grabbing for one of Rabbi's 72s. "No fucking way!" I say, appalled, lighting my very first cigarette in more than three years and heaving myself back up high into the bucket seat. *No way do I drink Shithead's drink.*

"Hand to God. Your father's drink. You're him," Bonus says, giggling. "You're on."

"No way," I say, sliding down the sweaty, enormous bucket seat. "No fucking way."

16.

It was close to one o'clock in the afternoon on Saturday the eleventh of December 2021 when two behemothic pickup trucks in Southwest El Paso—one an inky-black King Ranch, the other a shiny, cherry-red Silverado—rolled slowly out of the Providence Sierra campus parking lot, one inching behind the other, winding down Mesa to catch Route 54 back up to Northeast El Paso.

They were headed to Borderland Steaks, on Alabama.

It's great.

Terrific sunset views over the Patriot Freeway.

EPILOGUE

Fayetteville, North Carolina
May 7, 2022

On a muggy Saturday afternoon, 147 days after Renay died in El Paso, Texas, Big Gay Sam and I are spray-painting ten bowling pins we've pirated from B&B Lanes.

We're coating them in a thick, bright, phosphorescent pink, spraying them gaily in the backyard of a lovely two-story brick cottage I have rented for myself and my brothers, and for Sam and his boyfriend, Gordie.

It is our first time staying in the still *very* ritzy Haymount neighborhood of Fayetteville.

I spent the last of my savings on Renay's obituary, her bowling alley memorial, this cottage, hell, even this spray paint from Lowe's. Sam is an assistant manager at a Greenville Food Lion; his boyfriend a sharp and goofy Republican military man. They have helped me tremendously in reorienting myself to what queer even means anymore in this New Queer South I left behind long, long ago, and I am so grateful they are here today to help us celebrate Renay.

Together we are organizing her memorial at B&B on my first homecoming to Fayetteville in thirty-four years. Since I left her. *Since I left my home.*

Butt Check is bringing over four dozen glazed from the Krispy Kreme on Bragg. Sam and Gordie bought Pepsi-themed ankle socks at the Food Lion. I got pink roses from the florist at Eutaw Village, right across from where that Sunoco kiosk, and Renay, used to stand sentry. Asshole will throw the final ball, Renay's very last frame, at the end of the memorial. Doreen is too scared to read anything publicly, so her daughter Faith will read us a poem. Twin came down from Virginia, God bless him. Faith from Raleigh, Asshole from the Outer Banks. Doreen never left, except for occasional lobster runs to and from New Hampshire. Her son Andrew now runs the pro shop that Porky, his dad—who Renay introduced Doreen to—once ran with a resin-coated fist. It's like Porky and Renay never left this place.

It's like I never belonged anywhere else.

Once, long ago, we escaped, she and I, from Fayetteville's stifling summer, just the two of us on a quick road trip in the Nova, busted out of Fayetteville's stupefying languor for a day. We drove out to White Lake, that luminous jewel in the tiara of the celestial Bladen Lake Group, because it's cheap and close by. She told me tales of how racist it all used to be when she first moved to Fayetteville in 1966, how White Lake was for the whites and Jones Lake was for the Blacks, and how she longed to dip a toe in the *much more fun-looking* Jones Lake. How she wanted to fish the mother lake most of all, Waccamaw, but was saving that trip for another time. I always dreamed of going there with her, swimming to the center of Waccamaw and waving to her on that shore, where she would be fishing and gobbling biscuits like a boss.

At the end of Renay's memorial, Asshole stands on cue to roll the final ball of Renay's final frame of her final bowling game ever, down a center lane darkened especially for her. The entire bowling alley grows hushed, and B&B Lanes, eternally busy on a Saturday afternoon, pauses to hold its collective breath. Asshole practiced earlier in the day, but my brother is rusty as hell, and nervous, too, no longer the ice-cold, bloodless champion of Fayetteville he once was.

He throws, and he leaves seven pins standing. It is awful.

Then he gutters.

The whole house groans, I along with it, thinking of my poor besainted mother, how Renay's last frame at B&B, her last frame *anywhere*, is such a sad, embarrassing mess, and at the hands of one of her own sons, no less. *Typical.*

I look up, imploring somebody, begging *anybody* to please come over to our lane and roll this nice dead lady a strike. That's when a sweet kid practicing one lane over, a junior at Westover—my high school, of course—named Dykashie "Kash" Harris strolls over.

Kash just happens to be North Carolina's state champion bowler, but I don't know that. He smiles that confident, cocky smile of all pros everywhere, and he raises his ball at those ten *beaming* pink pins winking back at him, and that kid, some other proud Westover mother's son, well, he just lets go and...rolls a perfect strike.

All of Renay's pink pins *dance away.* Then the whole bowling alley *roars.*

And so Renay Mandel Corren departs us at last, precisely the way she would've wanted: with a little bit of luck, a second chance for her sons, drowning in applause at B&B Lanes, and nudged along by the money and kindness of sons, strangers, and fans.

After the memorial, I'm gonna take her to Waccamaw Lake.

Hell, maybe I'll even fish.

Hook it through the lips, son!

Not a chance, Renay.

We're using bloodworms next time.

We'll be broke, so we'll be fishing with bloodworms.

We'll be broke.

But we'll be *together.*

ACKNOWLEDGMENTS

To the legions of friends and believers who kept me alive for the more than half a century it took to excrete this damnable Greek-thing: *thank you*. That I undertook a book, that this memoir exists at all, is thanks *solely* to the genial and tireless compassion of the brilliant Colin Dickerman. Thank you, too, to Ian Dorset, Albert Tang, Lori Paximadis, and all the respectable people at Grand Central Publishing who allowed me into their nice building. The bonkers Latvian illustrator Robert Rūrāns did the heavenly cover art and he *completely* understood the assignment. To Asheville book marm Carrie Frye: this Oxford comma, and this book, is for you. I have been blessed by the faith and grits of Jennifer Gates of Aevitas Creative Management, who is the agent and book mommy I always dreamed of having. Thank you, too, to woman of business Michelle Foti at Platinum. To my friends who listened to me read bad drafts, cry, then eat ice cream crying, bless your hearths: Kirsten & Buddy Ames; Eric & Henry Souliere; Hillary, Bob & Dory; Maura, John & Walter; Josh & Bula; Pam & Roger; Cheryl & Arron; Patrick & Troian; Tom & Tab; Steve Vaught; Sarah Thyre for the love and the realest MFA; and Sarah Weinman for a truly life-altering retweet. I benefited tremendously from the egalitarian generosity of

Alexander Chee, Melissa Febos, and Jami Attenberg, and was imbued daily by poets Stephen King, Jermaine J. Cole, James Baldwin, Mary Kerr, Megan Jovon Ruth Pete, Michael Herr, Loren Eiseley, Kim Stanley Robinson, Judith Krantz, and obviously Dame Jacqueline Jill Collins, OBE. Thank you for talking, Faith Belcher, Elizabeth Thalhimer Smartt, Sam Trammel, Jackie Wein. Thank you especially to my four idiot brothers who, notwithstanding what you have read, I have always loved and always needed. I respect Lourdes, Shirley, and Laura Corren much more, however. Thank you from the bottom of my heart to Renay's indispensibles Bernie Iwascyzn, Doreen DeJaynes, Don Buchek, Nancy Baum Schenk, and everybody at the fabulous B&B Lanes: *you* were Renay's perfect 300. Big ups to my therapist Sam, who never seems bored. A tremendous thank-you to the fine doctors, nurses, and Lydias in El Paso who cared for Renay at home, at Patriot, and at Providence. You are the best people with the biggest hearts in all of Texas. Lastly and predictably, I could never have undertaken such a twisted and maternal betrayal without my shaggy son, my best friend, my all-weather fur companion, Hudson D. Dog. *He* wrote *me*. Then: I dared to write a book!

ABOUT THE AUTHOR

Andy Corren was born and raised on the wrong side of Fayetteville, North Carolina. He barely graduated Westover, got fired from every job in show business, and has no MFA. Andy and his son, Hudson D. Dog, live in Greene County, New York, and Harlem, USA.